ONE UP on WALL STREET

How to Use

What You Already Know

to Make Money

in the Market

PETER LYNCH
with John Rothchild

A Fireside Book
Published by Simon & Schuster
New York   London   Toronto   Sydney   Singapore

SIMON & SCHUSTER PAPERBACKS
Rockefeller Center
1230 Avenue of the Americas
New York, NY 10020

For information about special discounts for bulk purchases,
please contact Simon & Schuster Special Sales:
1-800-456-6798 or business@simonandschuster.com.

Designed by Elina Nudelman

Manufactured in the United States of America

50   49

Library of Congress Catalog Card number 00025839

ISBN-13: 978-0-671-66013-8
ISBN-10:   0-671-66103-5
ISBN-13: 978-0-7432-0040-0 (Pbk)
ISBN-10:   0-7432-0040-3 (Pbk)

To Carolyn, my wife and best friend for over twenty years, whose support and sacrifices have been critically important to me.

To my children, Mary, Annie, and Beth, whose love for each other and their parents has meant so very much.

To my colleagues at Fidelity Investments, whose extra efforts have made Magellan's performance possible but who have received none of the favorable publicity.

To one million shareholders in Magellan, who have entrusted their savings to me and who have sent thousands of letters and made thousands of calls over the years, comforting me during declines in the market and reminding me that the future will be fine.

To Holy God for all the incredible blessings I have been given in my life.

Contents

Introduction to the
Millennium Edition

This book was written to offer encouragement and basic information to the individual investor. Who knew it would go through thirty printings and sell more than one million copies? As this latest edition appears eleven years beyond the first, I'm convinced that the same principles that helped me perform well at the Fidelity Magellan Fund still apply to investing in stocks today.

It's been a remarkable stretch since *One Up on Wall Street* hit the bookstores in 1989. I left Magellan in May, 1990, and pundits said it was a brilliant move. They congratulated me for getting out at the right time—just before the collapse of the great bull market. For the moment, the pessimists looked smart. The country's major banks flirted with insolvency, and a few went belly up. By early fall, war was brewing in Iraq. Stocks suffered one of their worst declines in recent memory. But then the war was won, the banking system survived, and stocks rebounded.

Some rebound! The Dow is up more than fourfold since October, 1990, from the 2,400 level to 11,000 and beyond—the best decade for stocks in the twentieth century. Nearly 50 percent of U.S. households own stocks or mutual funds, up from 32 percent in 1989. The market at large has created $25 trillion in new wealth, which is on display in every city and town. If this keeps up, somebody will write a book called *The Billionaire Next Door*.

More than $4 trillion of that new wealth is invested in mutual funds, up from $275 billion in 1989. The fund bonanza is okay by me, since I managed a fund. But it also must mean a lot of amateur stockpickers did poorly with their picks. If they'd done better on their own in this mother of all bull markets, they wouldn't have migrated to funds to the extent they have. Perhaps the information contained in this book will set some errant stockpickers on a more profitable path.

Since stepping down at Magellan, I've become an individual investor myself. On the charitable front, I raise scholarship money to send inner-city kids of all faiths to Boston Catholic schools. Otherwise, I work part-time at Fidelity as a fund trustee and as an adviser/trainer for young research analysts. Lately my leisure time is up at least thirtyfold, as I spend more time with my family at home and abroad.

Enough about me. Let's get back to my favorite subject: stocks. From the start of this bull market in August 1982, we've seen the greatest advance in stock prices in U.S. history, with the Dow up fifteenfold. In Lynch lingo that's a "fifteenbagger." I'm accustomed to finding fifteenbaggers in a variety of successful companies, but a fifteenbagger in the market at large is a stunning reward. Consider this: From the top in 1929 through 1982, the Dow produced only a fourbagger: up from 248 to 1,046 in a half century! Lately stock prices have risen faster as they've moved higher. It took the Dow $8\frac{1}{3}$ years to double from 2,500 to 5,000, and only $3\frac{1}{2}$ years to double from 5,000 to 10,000. From 1995–99 we saw an unprecedented five straight years where stocks returned 20 percent plus. Never before has the market recorded more than two back-to-back 20 percent gains.

Wall Street's greatest bull market has rewarded the believers and confounded the skeptics to a degree neither side could have imagined in the doldrums of the early 1970s, when I first took the helm at Magellan. At that low point, demoralized investors had to remind themselves that bear markets don't last forever, and those with patience held on to their stocks and mutual funds for the fifteen years it took the Dow and other averages to regain the prices reached in the mid-1960s. Today it's worth reminding ourselves that bull markets don't last forever and that patience is required in both directions.

On page 280 of this book I say the breakup of ATT in 1984 may have been the most significant stock market development of that era. Today it's the Internet, and so far the Internet has passed me by. All along I've been technophobic. My experience shows you don't have to be trendy to succeed as an investor. In fact, most great investors I know (Warren Buffett, for starters) are technophobes. They don't own what they don't understand, and neither do I. I understand Dunkin' Donuts and Chrysler, which is why both inhabited my portfolio. I understand banks, savings-and-loans, and their close relative, Fannie Mae. I don't visit the Web. I've never surfed on it or chatted across it. Without expert help (from my wife or my children, for instance) I couldn't find the Web.

Over the Thanksgiving holidays in 1997, I shared eggnog with a Web-tolerant friend in New York. I mentioned that my wife, Carolyn, liked the mystery novelist Dorothy Sayers. The friend sat down at a nearby computer and in a couple of clicks pulled up the entire list of Sayers titles, plus customer reviews and the one- to five-star ratings (on the literary Web sites, authors are rated like fund managers). I bought four Sayers novels for Carolyn, picked the gift wrapping, typed in our home address, and crossed one Christmas gift off my list. This was my introduction to Amazon.com.

Later on you'll read how I discovered some of my best stocks through eating or shopping, sometimes long before other professional stock hounds came across them. Since Amazon existed in cyberspace, and not in suburban mall space, I ignored it. Amazon wasn't beyond my comprehension—the business was as understandable as a dry cleaner's. Also, in 1997 it was reasonably priced relative to its prospects, and it was well-financed. But I wasn't flexible enough to see opportunity in this new guise. Had I bothered to do the research, I would have seen the huge market for this sort of shopping and Amazon's ability to capture it. Alas, I didn't. Meanwhile, Amazon was up tenfold (a "tenbagger" in Lynch parlance) in 1998 alone.

Amazon is one of at least five hundred "dot.com" stocks that have performed miraculous levitations. In high-tech and dot.com circles, it's not unusual for a newly launched public offering to rise tenfold in less time than it takes Stephen King to pen another thriller. These investments don't require much patience. Before the Internet came along, companies had to grow their way into the billion-dollar ranks. Now they can reach billion-dollar valuations before they've turned a profit or, in some cases, before they've collected any revenues. Mr. Market (a fictional proxy for stocks in general) doesn't wait for a newborn Web site to prove itself in real life the way, say, Wal-Mart or Home Depot proved themselves in the last generation.

With today's hot Internet stocks, fundamentals are old hat. (The term *old hat* is old hat in itself, proving that I'm old hat for bringing it up.) The mere appearance of a dot and a com, and the exciting concept behind it, is enough to convince today's optimists to pay for a decade's worth of growth and prosperity in advance. Subsequent buyers pay escalating prices based on the futuristic "fundamentals," which improve with each uptick.

Judging by the Maserati sales in Silicon Valley, dot.coms are highly rewarding to entrepreneurs who take them public and early buyers who make timely exits. But I'd like to pass along a word of caution to people who buy shares after they've levitated. Does it make sense to invest in a dot.com at prices that already reflect years of rapid earnings growth that may or may not occur? By the way I pose this, you've already figured out my answer is "no." With many of these new issues, the stock price doubles, triples, or even quadruples on the first day of trading. Unless your broker can stake your claim to a meaningful allotment of shares at the initial offering price—an unlikely prospect since Internet offerings are more coveted, even, than Super Bowl tickets— you'll miss a big percent of the gain. Perhaps you'll miss the entire gain, since some dot.coms hit high prices on the first few trading sessions that they never reach again.

If you feel left out of the dot.com jubilee, remind yourself that very few dot.com investors benefit from the full ride. It's misleading to measure the progress of these stocks from the offering price that most buyers can't get. Those who are allotted shares are lucky to receive more than a handful.

In spite of the instant gratification that surrounds me, I've continued to invest the old-fashioned way. I own stocks where results depend on ancient fundamentals: a successful company enters new markets, its earnings rise, and the share price follows along. Or a flawed company turns itself around. The typical big winner in the Lynch portfolio (I continue to pick my share of losers, too!) generally takes three to ten years or more to play out.

Owing to the lack of earnings in dot.com land, most dot.coms can't be rated using the standard price/earnings yardstick. In other words, there's no "e" in the all-important "p/e" ratio. Without a "p/e" ratio to track, investors focus on the one bit of data that shows up everywhere: the stock price! To my mind, the stock price is the least useful information you can track, and it's the most widely tracked. When *One Up* was written in 1989, a lone ticker tape ran across the bottom of the Financial News Network. Today you can find a ticker tape on a variety of channels, while others display little boxes that showcase the Dow, the S&P 500, and so forth. Channel surfers can't avoid knowing where the market closed. On the popular Internet portals, you can click on your customized portfolio and get the latest gyrations for every holding. Or you can get stock prices on 800 lines, pagers, and voice mail.

To me, this barrage of price tags sends the wrong message. If my favorite Internet company sells for $30 a share, and yours sells for $10, then people who focus on price would say that mine is the superior company. This is a dangerous delusion. What Mr. Market pays for a stock today or next week doesn't tell you which company has the best chance to succeed two to three years down the information superhighway. If you can follow only one bit of data, follow the earnings—assuming the company in question has earnings. As you'll see in this text, I subscribe to the crusty notion that sooner or later earnings make or break an investment in equities. What the stock price does today, tomorrow, or next week is only a distraction.

The Internet is far from the first innovation that changed the world. The railroad, telephone, the car, the airplane, and the TV can all lay claim to revolutionary effects on the average life, or at least on the prosperous top quarter of the global population. These new industries spawned new companies, only a few of which survived to dominate the field. The same thing likely will happen with the Internet. A big name or two will capture the territory, the way McDonald's did with burgers or Schlumberger did with oil services. Shareholders in those triumphant companies will prosper, while shareholders in the laggards, the has-beens, and the should-have-beens will lose money. Perhaps you'll be clever enough to pick the big winners that join the exclusive club of companies that earn $1 billion a year.

Though the typical dot.com has no earnings as yet, you can do a thumbnail analysis that gives a general idea of what the company will need to earn in the future to justify the stock price today. Let's take a hypothetical case: DotCom.com. First, you find the "market capitalization" ("market cap" for short) by multiplying the number of shares outstanding (let's say 100 million) by the current stock price (let's say $100 a share). One hundred million times $100 equals $10 billion, so that's the market cap for DotCom.com.

Whenever you invest in any company, you're looking for its market cap to rise. This can't happen unless buyers are paying higher prices for the shares, making your investment more valuable. With that in mind, before DotCom.com can turn into a tenbagger, its market cap must increase tenfold, from $10 billion to $100 billion. Once you've established this target market cap, you have to ask yourself: What will DotCom.com need to earn to support a $100 billion valuation? To get a ballpark answer, you can apply a generic price/earnings ratio for a fast-growing operation—in today's heady market, let's say 40 times earnings.

Permit me a digression here. On page 170 I mention how wonderful companies become risky investments when people overpay for them, using McDonald's as exhibit A. In 1972 the stock was bid up to a precarious 50 times earnings. With no way to "live up to these expectations," the price fell from $75 to $25, a great buying opportunity at a "more realistic" 13 times earnings.

On the following page I also mention the bloated 500 times earnings shareholders paid for Ross Perot's Electronic Data Systems. At 500 times earnings, I noted, "it would take five centuries to make back your investment, if the EDS earnings stayed constant." Thanks to the Internet, 500 times earnings has lost its shock value, and so has 50 times earnings or, in our theoretical example, 40 times earnings for DotCom.com.

In any event, to become a $100 billion enterprise, we can guess that DotCom.com eventually must earn $2.5 billion a year. Only thirty-three U.S. corporations earned more than $2.5 billion in 1999, so for this to happen to DotCom.com, it will have to join the exclusive club of big winners, along with the likes of Microsoft. A rare feat, indeed.

I'd like to end this brief Internet discussion on a positive note. There are three ways to invest in this trend without having to buy into a hope and an extravagant market cap. The first is an offshoot of the old "picks and shovels" strategy: During the Gold Rush, most would-be miners lost money, but people who sold them picks, shovels, tents, and blue jeans (Levi Strauss) made a nice profit. Today, you can look for non-Internet companies that indirectly benefit from Internet traffic (package delivery is an obvious example); or you can invest in manufacturers of switches and related gizmos that keep the traffic moving.

The second is the so-called "free Internet play." That's where an In-

ternet business is embedded in a non-Internet company with real earnings and a reasonable stock price. I'm not naming names—you can do
your own sleuthing—but several intriguing free plays have come to my
attention. In a typical situation, the company at large is valued, say, at
$800 million in today's market, while its fledgling Internet operation is
estimated to be worth $1 billion, before it has proven itself. If the In-
ternet operation lives up to its promise, it could prove very rewarding—that part of the company may be "spun off" so it trades as its own
stock. Or, if the Internet venture doesn't do well, the fact that it's an ad-
junct to the company's regular line of work protects investors on the
downside.

The third is the tangential benefit, where an old-fashioned "brick
and mortar" business benefits from using the Internet to cut costs,
streamline operations, become more efficient, and therefore more
profitable. A generation ago, scanners were installed in supermarkets.
This reduced pilferage, brought inventories under better control, and
was a huge boon to supermarket chains.

Going forward, the Internet and its handmaidens will create some
great success stories, but at this point we've mostly got great expectations and inefficient pricing. Companies valued at $500 million today
may triumph, while companies valued at $10 billion may not be worth
a dime. As expectations turn to reality, the winners will be more obvious than they are today. Investors who see this will have time to act on
their "edge."

Back to Microsoft, a 100-bagger I overlooked. Along with Cisco and
Intel, that high-tech juggernaut posted explosive earnings almost from
the start. Microsoft went public in 1986 at 15 cents a share. Three years
later you could buy a share for under $1, and from there it advanced
eightyfold. (The stock has "split" several times along the way, so original shares never actually sold for 15 cents—for further explanation, see
the footnote on page 34.) If you took the Missouri "show me" approach
and waited to buy Microsoft until it triumphed with Windows 95, you
still made seven times your money. You didn't have to be a program-
mer to notice Microsoft everywhere you looked. Except in the Apple
orchard, all new computers came equipped with the Microsoft operating system and Microsoft Windows. Apples were losing their appeal.
The more computers that used Windows, the more the software guys
wrote programs for Windows and not for Apple. Apple was squeezed
into a corner, where it sold boxes to 7–10 percent of the market.

Meanwhile the box makers that ran Microsoft programs (Dell, Hewlett-Packard, Compaq, IBM, and so on) waged fierce price wars to sell more boxes. This endless skirmish hurt the box makers' earnings, but Microsoft was unaffected. Bill Gates's company wasn't in the box business; it sold the "gas" that ran the boxes.

Cisco is another marquee performer. The stock price is up 480-fold since it went public in 1990. I overlooked this incredible winner for the usual reasons, but a lot of people must have noticed it. Businesses at large hired Cisco to help them link their computers into networks; then colleges hired Cisco to computerize the dorms. Students, teachers, and visiting parents could have noticed this development. Maybe some of them went home, did the research, and bought the stock.

I mention Microsoft and Cisco to add contemporary examples to illustrate a major theme of this book. An amateur investor can pick tomorrow's big winners by paying attention to new developments at the workplace, the mall, the auto showrooms, the restaurants, or anywhere a promising new enterprise makes its debut. While I'm on the subject, a clarification is in order.

Charles Barkley, a basketball player noted for shooting from the lip, once claimed he was misquoted in his own autobiography. I don't claim to be misquoted in this book, but I've been misinterpreted on one key point. Here's my disclaimer:

Peter Lynch doesn't advise you to buy stock in your favorite store just because you like shopping in the store, nor should you buy stock in a manufacturer because it makes your favorite product or a restaurant because you like the food. Liking a store, a product, or a restaurant is a good reason to get interested in a company and put it on your research list, but it's not enough of a reason to own the stock! Never invest in any company before you've done the homework on the company's earnings prospects, financial condition, competitive position, plans for expansion, and so forth.

If you own a retail company, another key factor in the analysis is figuring out whether the company is nearing the end of its expansion phase—what I call the "late innings" in its ball game. When a Radio Shack or a Toys "R" Us has established itself in 10 percent of the country, it's a far different prospect than having stores in 90 percent of the country. You have to keep track of where the future growth is coming from and when it's likely to slow down.

• • •

Nothing has occurred to shake my conviction that the typical amateur has advantages over the typical professional fund jockey. In 1989 the pros enjoyed quicker access to better information, but the information gap has closed. A decade ago amateurs could get information on a company in three ways: from the company itself, from *Value Line* or Standard & Poor's research sheets, or from reports written by in-house analysts at the brokerage firm where the amateurs kept an account. Often these reports were mailed from headquarters, and it took several days for the information to arrive.

Today an array of analysts' reports is available on-line, where any browser can call them up at will. News alerts on your favorite companies are delivered automatically to your e-mail address. You can find out if insiders are buying or selling or if a stock has been upgraded or downgraded by brokerage houses. You can use customized screens to search for stocks with certain characteristics. You can track mutual funds of all varieties, compare their records, find the names of their top ten holdings. You can click on to the "briefing book" heading that's attached to the on-line version of *The Wall Street Journal* and *Barron's,* and get a snapshot review of almost any publicly traded company. From there you can access "Zack's" and get a summary of ratings from all the analysts who follow a particular stock.

Again thanks to the Internet, the cost of buying and selling stocks has been drastically reduced for the small investor, the way it was reduced for institutional investors in 1975. On-line trading has pressured traditional brokerage houses to reduce commissions and transaction fees, continuing a trend that began with the birth of the discount broker two decades ago.

You may be wondering what's happened to my investing habits since I left Magellan. Instead of following thousands of companies, now I follow maybe fifty. (I continue to serve on investment committees at various foundations and charitable groups, but in all of these cases we hire portfolio managers and let them pick the stocks.) Trendy investors might think the Lynch family portfolio belongs in the New England Society of Antiquities. It contains some savings-and-loans that I bought at bargain-basement prices during a period when the S&Ls were unappreciated. These stocks have had a terrific run, and I'm still holding on to some of them. (Selling long-term winners subjects you to an IRS bear market a 20 percent tax on the proceeds.) I also own several growth companies that I've held since the 1980s, and a few since the 1970s. These businesses continue to prosper, yet the stocks still appear to be reasonably priced. Beyond that, I'm still harboring an ample supply of clunkers that sell for considerably less than the price I paid. I'm not keeping these disappointment companies because I'm stubborn or nostalgic. I'm keeping them because in each of these companies, the finances are in decent shape and there's evidence of better times ahead.

My clunkers remind me of an important point: You don't need to make money on every stock you pick. In my experience, six out of ten winners in a portfolio can produce a satisfying result. Why is this? Your losses are limited to the amount you invest in each stock (it can't go lower than zero), while your gains have no absolute limit. Invest $1,000 in a clunker and in the worst case, maybe you lose $1,000. Invest $1,000 in a high achiever, and you could make $10,000, $15,000, $20,000, and beyond over several years. All you need for a lifetime of successful investing is a few big winners, and the pluses from those will overwhelm the minuses from the stocks that don't work out.

Let me give you an update on two companies I don't own but that I wrote about in this book: Bethlehem Steel and General Electric. Both teach a useful lesson. I mentioned that shares of Bethlehem, an aging blue chip, had been in decline since 1960. A famous old company, it seems, can be just as unrewarding to investors as a shaky start-up. Bethlehem, once a symbol of American global clout, has continued to disappoint. It sold for $60 in 1958 and by 1989 had dropped to $17, punishing loyal shareholders as well as bargain hunters who thought they'd found a deal. Since 1989 the price has taken another fall, from $17 to the low single digits, proving that a cheap stock can always get cheaper. Someday, Bethlehem Steel may rise again. But assuming that will happen is wishing, not investing.

I recommended General Electric on a national TV show (it's been a tenbagger since), but in the book I mention that GE's size (market value $39 billion; annual profits $3 billion) would make it difficult for the company to increase those profits at a rapid rate. In fact, the company that brings good things to life has brought more upside to its shareholders than I'd anticipated. Against the odds and under the savvy leadership of Jack Welch, this corporate hulk has broken into a profitable trot. Welch, who recently announced his retirement, prodded GE's numerous divisions into peak performance, using excess cash to buy new businesses and to buy back shares. GE's triumph in the 1990s shows the importance of keeping up with a company's story.

Buying back shares brings up another important change in the market: the dividend becoming an endangered species. I write about its importance on page 204, but the old method of rewarding shareholders seems to have gone the way of the black-footed ferret. The bad part about the disappearing dividend is that regular checks in the mail gave investors an income stream and also a reason to hold on to stocks during periods when stock prices failed to reward. Yet in 1999 the dividend yield on the five hundred companies in the S&P 500 sank to an all-time low since World War II: near 1 percent.

It's true that interest rates are lower today than they were in 1989, so you'd expect yields on bonds and dividends on stocks to be lower. As stock prices rise, the dividend yield naturally falls. (If a $50 stock pays a $5 dividend, it yields 10 percent; when the stock price hits $100, it yields 5 percent.) Meanwhile companies aren't boosting their dividends the way they once did.

"What is so unusual," observed *The New York Times* (October 7, 1999), "is that the economy is doing so well even while companies are growing more reluctant to raise their dividends." In the not-so-distant past, when a mature, healthy company routinely raised the dividend, it was a sign of prosperity. Cutting a dividend or failing to raise it was a sign of trouble. Lately, healthy companies are skimping on their dividends and using the money to buy back their own shares, à la General Electric. Reducing the supply of shares increases the earnings per share, which eventually rewards shareholders, although they don't reap the reward until they sell.

If anybody's responsible for the disappearing dividend, it's the U.S. government, which taxes corporate profits, then taxes corporate dividends at the full rate, for so-called unearned income. To help their shareholders avoid this double taxation, companies have abandoned the dividend in favor of the buyback strategy, which boosts the stock price. This strategy subjects shareholders to increased capital gains taxes if they sell their shares, but long-term capital gains are taxed at half the rate of ordinary income taxes.

Speaking of long-term gains, in eleven years' worth of luncheon and dinner speeches, I've asked for a show of hands: "How many of you are long-term investors in stocks?" To date, the vote is unanimous—

everybody's a long-term investor, including day traders in the audience who took a couple of hours off. Long-term investing has gotten so popular, it's easier to admit you're a crack addict than to admit you're a short-term investor.

Stock market news has gone from hard to find (in the 1970s and early 1980s), then easy to find (in the late 1980s), then hard to get away from. The financial weather is followed as closely as the real weather: highs, lows, troughs, turbulence, and endless speculation about what's next and how to handle it. People are advised to think long-term, but the constant comment on every gyration puts people on edge and keeps them focused on the short term. It's a challenge not to act on it. If there were a way to avoid the obsession with the latest ups and downs, and check stock prices every six months or so, the way you'd check the oil in a car, investors might be more relaxed.

Nobody believes in long-term investing more passionately than I do, but as with the Golden Rule, it's easier to preach than to practice. Nevertheless, this generation of investors has kept the faith and stayed the course during all the corrections mentioned above. Judging by redemption calls from my old fund, Fidelity Magellan, the customers have been brilliantly complacent. Only a small percentage cashed out in the Saddam Hussein bear market of 1990.

Thanks to the day traders and some of the professional hedge fund managers, shares now change hands at an incredible clip. In 1989, three hundred million shares traded was a hectic session on the New York Stock Exchange; today, three hundred million is a sleepy interlude and eight hundred million is average. Have the day traders given Mr. Market the shakes? Does the brisk commerce in stock indexes have something to do with it? Whatever the cause (I see day traders as a major factor), frequent trading has made the stock markets more volatile. A decade ago stock prices moving up or down more than 1 percent in a single trading session was a rare occurrence. At present we get 1 percent moves several times a month.

By the way, the odds against making a living in the day-trading business are about the same as the odds against making a living at racetracks, blackjack tables, or video poker. In fact, I think of day trading as at-home casino care. The drawback to the home casino is the paperwork. Make twenty trades per day, and you could end up with 5,000 trades a year, all of which must be recorded, tabulated, and reported to the IRS. So day trading is a casino that supports a lot of accountants.

People who want to know how stocks fared on any given day ask, Where did the Dow close? I'm more interested in how many stocks went up versus how many went down. These so-called advance/decline numbers paint a more realistic picture. Never has this been truer than in the recent exclusive market, where a few stocks advance while the majority languish. Investors who buy "undervalued" small stocks or midsize stocks have been punished for their prudence. People are wondering: How can the S&P 500 be up 20 percent and my stocks are down? The answer is that a few big stocks in the S&P 500 are propping up the averages.

For instance, in 1998 the S&P 500 index was up 28 percent overall, but when you take a closer look, you find out the 50 biggest companies in the index advanced 40 percent, while the other 450 companies hardly budged. In the NASDAQ market, home to the Internet and its supporting cast, the dozen or so biggest companies were huge winners, while the rest of the NASDAQ stocks, lumped together, were losers. The same story was repeated in 1999, where the elite group of winners skewed the averages and propped up the multitude of losers. More than 1,500 stocks traded on the New York Stock Exchange lost money in 1999. This dichotomy is unprecedented. By the way, we tend to think the S&P 500 index is dominated by huge companies, while the NASDAQ is a haven for the smaller fry. By the late 1990s, NASDAQ's giants (Intel, Cisco, and a handful of others) dominated the NASDAQ index more than the S&P 500's giants dominated its index.

One industry that's teeming with small stocks is biotechnology. My high-tech aversion caused me to make fun of the typical biotech enterprise: $100 million in cash from selling shares, one hundred Ph.D.'s, 99 microscopes, and zero revenues. Recent developments inspire me to put in a good word for biotech—not that amateurs should pick their biotech stocks out of a barrel, but that biotech in general could play the same role in the new century as electronics played in the last. Today a long list of biotechs have revenue, and three dozen or so turn a profit, with another fifty ready to do the same. Amgen has become a genuine biotech blue chip, with earnings of $1 billion plus. One of the numerous biotech mutual funds might be worth a long-term commitment for part of your money.

Market commentators fill airspace and magazine space with comparisons between today's market and some earlier market, such as "This looks a lot like 1962," or "This reminds me of 1981," or when they're feeling very gloomy, "We're facing 1929 all over again." Lately the prevailing comparison seems to be with the early 1970s, when the smaller stocks faltered while the larger stocks (especially the highly touted "Nifty Fifty") continued to rise. Then, in the bear market of 1973–74, the Nifty Fifty fell 50–80 percent! This unsettling decline disproved the theory that big companies were bearproof.

If you owned the Nifty Fifty and held on to the lot for twenty-five years (preferably you were stranded on a desert island with no radios, TV sets, or magazines that told you to abandon stocks forever), you're not unhappy with the results. Though it took them a generation to do it, the Nifty Fifty made a full recovery and then some. By the mid-1990s the Nifty Fifty portfolio had caught up and passed the Dow and the S&P 500 in total return since 1974. Even if you bought them at sky-high prices in 1972, your choice was vindicated.

Once again, we've got the fifty largest companies selling for prices that skeptics describe as "too much to pay." Whether this latter-day Nifty Fifty will suffer a markdown on the order of the 1973–74 fire sale is anybody's guess. History tells us that corrections (declines of 10 percent or more) occur every couple of years, and bear markets (declines of 20 percent or more) occur every six years. Severe bear markets (declines of 30 percent or more) have materialized five times since the 1929–32 doozie. It's foolish to bet we've seen the last of the bears, which is why it's important not to buy stocks or stock mutual funds with money you'll need to spend in the next twelve months to pay college bills, wedding bills, or whatever. You don't want to be forced to sell in a losing market to raise cash. When you're a long-term investor, time is on your side.

The long bull market continues to hit occasional potholes. When *One Up* was written, stocks had just recovered from the 1987 crash. The worst fall in fifty years coincided with a Lynch golfing vacation in Ireland. It took nine or ten more trips (we bought a house in Ireland) to convince me that my setting foot on Irish sod wouldn't trigger another panic. I didn't feel too comfortable visiting Israel, Indonesia, or India, either. Setting foot in countries that begin with "I" made me nervous. But I made two trips to Israel and two to India and one to Indonesia, and nothing happened.

So far, 1987 hasn't been repeated, but the bears arrived in 1990, the year I left my job as manager of the Fidelity Magellan Fund. While the 1987 decline scared a lot of people (a 35 percent drop in two days can

do that), to me the 1990 episode was scarier. Why? In 1987 the economy was perking along, and our banks were solvent, so the fundamentals were positive. In 1990 the country was falling into recession,
our biggest banks were on the ropes, and we were preparing for war
with Iraq. But soon enough the war was won and recession overcome,
the banks recovered, and stocks took off on their biggest climb in modern history. More recently we've seen 10 percent declines in the major
averages in the spring of 1996, the summers of 1997 and 1998, and the
fall of 1999. August of 1998 brought the S&P 500 down 14.5 percent,
the second worst month since World War II. Nine months later stocks
were off and running again, with the S&P 500 up more than 50 percent!

What's my point in recounting all this? It would be wonderful if we
could avoid the setbacks with timely exits, but nobody has figured out
how to predict them. Moreover, if you exit stocks and avoid a decline,
how can you be certain you'll get back into stocks for the next rally?
Here's a telling scenario: If you put $100,000 in stocks on July 1, 1994,
and stayed fully invested for five years, your $100,000 grew into
$341,722. But if you were out of stocks for just thirty days over that
stretch—the thirty days when stocks had their biggest gains—your
$100,000 turned into a disappointing $153,792. By staying in the market, you more than doubled your reward.

As a very successful investor once said: "The bearish argument always sounds more intelligent." You can find good reasons to scuttle
your equities in every morning paper and on every broadcast of the
nightly news. When *One Up* became a best-seller, so did Ravi Batra's
The Great Depression of 1990. The obituary for this bull market has
been written countless times going back to its start in 1982. Among the
likely causes: Japan's sick economy, our trade deficit with China and
the world, the bond market collapse of 1994, the emerging market collapse of 1997, global warming, ozone depletion, deflation, the Gulf
war, consumer debt, and the latest, Y2K. The day after New Year's, we
discovered that Y2K was the most overrated scare since Godzilla's last
movie.

"Stocks are overpriced," has been the bears' rallying cry for several
years. To some, stocks looked too expensive in 1989, at Dow 2,600. To
others, they looked extravagant in 1992, above Dow 3,000. A chorus of
naysayers surfaced in 1995, above Dow 4,000. Someday we'll see another severe bear market, but even a brutal 40 percent sell-off would
leave prices far above the point at which various pundits called for in-

vestors to abandon their portfolios. As I've noted on prior occasions: "That's not to say there's no such thing as an overvalued market, but there's no point worrying about it."

It's often said a bull market must scale a wall of worry, and the worries never cease. Lately we've worried our way through various catastrophic "unthinkables": World War III, biological Armageddon, rogue nukes, the melting of the polar ice caps, a meteor crashing into the earth, and so on. Meanwhile we've witnessed several beneficial "unthinkables": communism falls; federal and state governments in the United States run budget surpluses; America creates seventeen million new jobs in the 1990s, more than making up for the highly publicized "downsizing" of big companies. The downsizing caused disruption and heartache to the recipients of the pink slips, but it also freed up millions of workers to move into exciting and productive jobs in fast-growing small companies.

This astounding job creation doesn't get the attention it deserves. America has the lowest unemployment rate of the past half century, while Europe continues to suffer from widespread idleness. Big European companies also have downsized, but Europe lacks the small businesses to take up the slack. They have a higher savings rate than we do, their citizens are well educated, yet their unemployment rate is more than twice the U.S. rate. Here's another astounding development: Fewer people were employed in Europe at the end of 1999 than were employed at the end of the prior decade.

The basic story remains simple and never-ending. Stocks aren't lottery tickets. There's a company attached to every share. Companies do better or they do worse. If a company does worse than before, its stock will fall. If a company does better, its stock will rise. If you own good companies that continue to increase their earnings, you'll do well. Corporate profits are up fifty-five-fold since World War II, and the stock market is up sixtyfold. Four wars, nine recessions, eight presidents, and one impeachment didn't change that.

In the following table, you'll find the names of 20 companies that made the top 100 list of winners in the U.S. stock market in the 1990s. The number in the left-hand column shows where each of these companies ranked in total return on the investor's dollar. Many high-tech enterprises (the likes of Helix, Photronics, Siliconix, Theragenics) that cracked the top 100 are omitted here, because I wanted to showcase the opportunities that the average person could have noticed, researched, and taken advantage of. Dell Computer was the biggest winner of all, and who hasn't heard of Dell? Anybody could have noticed Dell's strong sales and the growing popularity of its product. People who bought shares early were rewarded with an amazing 889-bagger: $10,000 invested in Dell from the outset generated an $8.9 million fortune. You didn't have to understand computers to see the promise in Dell, Microsoft, or Intel (every new machine came with an "Intel Inside" sticker). You didn't have to be a genetic engineer to realize that Amgen had transformed itself from a research lab into a pharmaceutical manufacturer with two best-selling drugs.

Schwab? His success was hard to miss. Home Depot? It continued to grow at a rapid clip, making the top 100 list for the second decade in a row. Harley Davidson? All those lawyers, doctors, and dentists becoming weekend Easy Riders was great news for Harley. Lowe's? Home Depot all over again. Who would have predicted two monster stocks from the same mundane business? Paychex? Small businesses everywhere were curing a headache by letting Paychex handle their payroll. My wife, Carolyn, used Paychex in our family foundation work, and I missed the clue and missed the stock.

Some of the best gains of the decade (as has been the case in prior decades) came from old-fashioned retailing. The Gap, Best Buy, Staples, Dollar General—these were all megabaggers and well-managed companies that millions of shoppers experienced firsthand. That two small banks appear on this list shows once again that big winners can come from any industry—even a stodgy slow-growth industry like banking. My advice for the next decade: Keep on the lookout for tomorrow's big baggers. You're likely to find one.

—*Peter Lynch with John Rothchild*

TWENTY BIG WINNERS IN U.S. STOCKS IN THE 1990s*

RANK BY STOCK PERFORMANCE	SYMBOL	COMPANY	BUSINESS	$10,000 INVESTED AT YEAR END 1989 PRODUCED THESE RETURNS BY YEAR END 1999
(1)	DELL	Dell Computer	Computer Manufacturer	$8.9 million
(6)	CCU	Clear Channel Comm.	Radio Stations	$8.1 million
(9)	BBY	Best Buy	Retailer	$995,000
(10)	MSFT	Microsoft	Technology	$960,000
(13)	SCH	Charles Schwab	Discount Broker	$827,000
(14)	NBTY	NBTY	Vitamins, Food Supplements	$782,000
(20)	WCOM	MCI Worldcom	Communications	$694,000
(21)	AMGN	Amgen	Biotechnology	$576,000
(30)	PPD	Prepaid Legal Services	Attorney Services	$416,000
(33)	INTC	Intel	Computer Chips	$372,000
(34)	HD	Home Depot	Building Supplies	$370,000
(40)	PAYX	Paychex	Payroll Services	$340,000
(46)	DG	Dollar General	Discount Retailer	$270,000
(49)	HDI	Harley Davidson	Motorcycles	$251,000
(52)	GPS	Gap	Retail Clothing	$232,000
(69)	SPLS	Staples	Office Supplies	$186,000
(75)	WBPR	Westernbank/Puerto Rico	Banking	$170,000
(77)	MDT	Medtronic	Medical Supplies	$168,000
(82)	ZION	Zion's Bancorp	Banking	$161,000
(87)	LOW	Lowe's Companies	Building Supplies	$152,000

* This list does not include companies that were acquired by other companies.
Source: Ned Davis Research

Prologue:
A Note from Ireland

You can't bring up the stock market these days without analyzing the events of October 16–20, 1987. It was one of the most unusual weeks I've ever experienced. More than a year later, and looking back on it with some dispassion, I can begin to separate the sensational ballyhoo from the incidents of lasting importance. What's worth remembering I remember as follows:

• On October 16, a Friday, my wife—Carolyn—and I spent a delightful day driving through County Cork, Ireland. I rarely take vacations, so the fact that I was traveling at all was extraordinary in itself.

• I didn't even once stop to visit the headquarters of a publicly traded company. Generally I'll detour 100 miles in any direction to get the latest word on sales, inventories, and earnings, but there didn't seem to be an S&P report or a balance sheet anywhere within 250 miles of us here.

• We went to Blarney Castle, where the legendary Blarney stone is lodged inconveniently in a parapet at the top of the building, several stories above the ground. You get to lie on your back, wiggle your way across the metal grating that comes between you and a fatal drop, and then while gripping a guardrail for emotional support, you kiss the legendary stone. Kissing the Blarney stone is as big a thrill as they say—especially the getting out alive.

• We recovered from the Blarney stone by spending a quiet weekend playing golf—at Waterville on Saturday and at Dooks on Sunday—and driving along the beautiful Ring of Kerry.

• On Monday, October 19, I faced the ultimate challenge, which demanded every bit of intelligence and stamina that I could muster—the eighteen holes at the Killeen course in Killarney, one of the most difficult courses in the world.

• After packing the clubs into the car, I drove with Carolyn out on the Dingle peninsula to the seaside resort of that name, where we checked into the Sceilig Hotel. I must have been tired. I never left the hotel room for the entire afternoon.

• That evening we dined with friends, Elizabeth and Peter Callery, at a famous seafood place called Doyle's. The next day, the 20th, we flew home.

THOSE PETTY UPSETS

Of course, I've left out a few petty upsets. In hindsight they hardly seem worth mentioning. One year later you're supposed to remember the Sistine Chapel, not that you got a blister from running through the Vatican. But in the spirit of full disclosure, I'll tell you what was bothering me:

• On Thursday, the day we left for Ireland after work, the Dow Jones industrial average dropped 48 points, and on Friday, the day we arrived, that same average dropped another 108.36 points. This made me wonder if we should be on vacation at all.

• I was thinking about Dow Jones and not about Blarney, even at the moment I kissed Blarney's stone. Throughout the weekend, between the rounds of golf, I sought out several phones and talked to my office about which stocks to sell, and which stocks to buy at bargain prices if the market fell further.

• On Monday, the day I played Killeen at Killarney, the aforementioned average dropped yet another 508 points.

Thanks to the time difference, I finished the round a few hours before the opening bell rang on Wall Street, or else I would probably have played worse. As it was, a sense of gloom and doom carried over from Friday, and perhaps that explained my (1) putting worse than I usually do, which in the best of times is terrible; and (2) failing to remember my score. The score that got my attention later that day was that the one million shareholders in Magellan Fund had just lost 18 percent of their assets, or $2 billion, in the Monday session.

My fixation on this mishap caused me to ignore the scenery on the way to Dingle. It could have been Forty-second and Broadway, for all I knew.

I wasn't napping all afternoon at the Sceilig Hotel, as the earlier paragraph may have implied. Instead, I was on the phone with my home office, deciding which of the 1,500 stocks in my fund should be sold to raise cash for the unusual number of fund redemptions. There was enough cash for normal circumstances, but not enough for the circumstances of Monday the 19th. At one point I couldn't decide if the world was coming to an end, if we were going into a depression, or if things weren't nearly as bad as that and only Wall Street was going out of business.

My associates and I sold what we had to sell. First we disposed of some British stocks in the London market. On Monday morning, stock prices in London were generally higher than prices in the U.S. market, thanks to a rare hurricane that had forced the London exchange to shut down on the preceding Friday, thus avoiding that day's big decline. Then we sold in New York, mostly in the early part of the session, when the Dow was down only 150 points but well on its way to the nadir of 508.

That night at Doyle's, I couldn't have told you what sort of seafood meal I ate. It's impossible to distinguish cod from shrimp when your mutual fund has lost the equivalent of the GNP of a small, seagoing nation.

We came home on the 20th because all of the above made me desperate to get back to the office. This was a possibility for which I'd been preparing since the day we arrived. Frankly, I'd let the upsets get to me.

THE LESSONS OF OCTOBER

I've always believed that investors should ignore the ups and downs of the market. Fortunately the vast majority of them paid little heed to the distractions cited above. If this is any example, less than three percent of the million account-holders in Fidelity Magellan switched out of the fund and into a money-market fund during the desperations of the week. When you sell in desperation, you always sell cheap.

Even if October 19 made you nervous about the stock market, you didn't have to sell that day—or even the next. You could gradually have reduced your portfolio of stocks and come out ahead of the panic-sellers, because, starting in December, the market rose steadily. By June of 1988 the market recovered some 400 points of the decline, or more than 23%.

To all the dozens of lessons we're supposed to have learned from October, I can add three: (1) don't let nuisances ruin a good portfolio; (2) don't let nuisances ruin a good vacation; and (3) never travel abroad when you're light on cash.

Probably I could go on for several chapters with further highlights, but I'd rather not waste your time. I prefer to write about something you might find more valuable: how to identify the superior companies. Whether it's a 508-point day or a 108-point day, in the end, superior companies will succeed and mediocre companies will fail, and investors in each will be rewarded accordingly.

But as soon as I remember what I ate at Doyle's, I'll let you know.

Introduction: The Advantages of Dumb Money

This is where the author, a professional investor, promises the reader that for the next 300 pages he'll share the secrets of his success. But rule number one, in my book, is: Stop listening to professionals! Twenty years in this business convinces me that any normal person using the customary three percent of the brain can pick stocks just as well, if not better, than the average Wall Street expert.

I know you don't expect the plastic surgeon to advise you to do your own facelift, nor the plumber to tell you to install your own hot-water tank, nor the hairdresser to recommend that you trim your own bangs, but this isn't surgery or plumbing or hairdressing. This is investing, where the smart money isn't so smart, and the dumb money isn't really as dumb as it thinks. Dumb money is only dumb when it listens to the smart money.

In fact, the amateur investor has numerous built-in advantages that, if exploited, should result in his or her outperforming the experts, and also the market in general. Moreover, when you pick your own stocks, you ought to outperform the experts. Otherwise, why bother?

I'm not going to get carried away and advise you to sell all your mutual funds. If that started to happen on any large scale, I'd be out of a job. Besides, there's nothing wrong with mutual funds, especially the ones that are profitable to the investor. Honesty and not immodesty compels me to report that millions of amateur investors have been well-rewarded for investing in Fidelity Magellan, which is why I was invited to write this book in the first place. The mutual fund is a wonderful invention for people who have neither the time nor the inclination to test their wits against the stock market, as well as for people with small amounts of money to invest who seek diversification.

It's when you've decided to invest on your own that you ought to try going it alone. That means ignoring the hot tips, the recommendations from brokerage houses, and the latest "can't miss" suggestion from your favorite newsletter—in favor of your own research. It means ignoring the stocks that you hear Peter Lynch, or some similar authority, is buying.

There are at least three good reasons to ignore what Peter Lynch is buying: (1) he might be wrong! (A long list of losers from my own portfolio constantly reminds me that the so-called smart money is exceedingly dumb about 40 percent of the time); (2) even if he's right, you'll never know when he's changed his mind about a stock and sold; and (3) you've got better sources, and they're all around you. What makes them better is that you can keep tabs on them, just as I keep tabs on mine.

If you stay half-alert, you can pick the spectacular performers right from your place of business or out of the neighborhood shopping mall, and long before Wall Street discovers them. It's impossible to be a credit-card-carrying American consumer without having done a lot of fundamental analysis on dozens of companies—and if you work in the industry, so much the better. This is where you'll find the tenbaggers. I've seen it happen again and again from my perch at Fidelity.

THOSE WONDERFUL TENBAGGERS

In Wall Street parlance a "tenbagger" is a stock in which you've made ten times your money. I suspect this highly technical term has been borrowed from baseball, which only goes up to a fourbagger, or home run. In my business a fourbagger is nice, but a tenbagger is the fiscal equivalent of two home runs and a double. If you've ever had a tenbagger in the stock market, you know how appealing it can be.

I developed a passion for making ten times my money early in my investing career. The first stock I ever bought, Flying Tiger Airlines, turned out to be a multibagger that put me through graduate school. In the last decade the occasional five- and tenbagger, and the rarer twentybagger, has helped my fund outgain the competition—and I own 1,400 stocks. In a small portfolio even one of these remarkable performers can transform a lost cause into a profitable one. It's amazing how this works.

The effect is most striking in weak stock markets—yes, there are tenbaggers in weak markets. Let's go back to 1980, two years before the dawn of the great bull market. Suppose you invested $10,000 in the following ten stocks on December 22, 1980, and held them until October 4, 1983. That's Strategy A. Strategy B is the same, except that you added an eleventh stock, Stop & Shop, which turned out to be the tenbagger.

The result from Strategy A is that your $10,000 would have increased to $13,040 for a mediocre 30.4% total return over nearly three years (the S&P 500 offered a total return of 40.6% in the same period). You'd have a perfect right to look at this and say: "Big deal. Why don't I leave the investing to the pros." But if you added Stop & Shop, your $10,000 would have more than doubled to $21,060, giving you a total return of 110.6% and a chance to brag on Wall Street (see page 34).

Furthermore, if you had added to your position in Stop & Shop as you saw the company's prospects improving, your overall return might have been twice again as high.

To make this spectacular showing, you only had to find one big winner out of eleven. The more right you are about any one stock, the more wrong you can be on all the others and still triumph as an investor.

APPLES AND DONUTS

You may have thought that a tenbagger can only happen with some wild penny stock in some weird company like Braino Biofeedback or Cosmic R and D, the kind of stock that sensible investors avoid. Actually there are numerous tenbaggers in companies you'll recognize: Dunkin' Donuts, Wal-Mart, Toys "R" Us, Stop & Shop, and Subaru, to mention a few. These are companies whose products you've admired and enjoyed, but who would have suspected that if you'd bought the Subaru stock along with the Subaru car, you'd be a millionaire today?

Yet it's true. This serendipitous calculation is based on several assumptions: first, that you bought the stock at its low of $2 a share in

Strategy A Portfolio

	BOUGHT	SOLD	% CHANGE
Bethlehem Steel	$25⅛	$23⅛	−8.0%
Coca-Cola	32¾	52½	+60.3%
General Motors	46⅞	74⅜	+58.7%
W. R. Grace	53⅞	48¾	−9.5%
Kellogg	18⅜	29⅞	+62.6%
Mfrs. Hanover	33	39⅛	+18.5%
Merck	80	98⅛	+22.7%
Owens Corning	26⅞	35¾	+33.0%
Phelps Dodge	39⅝	24¼	−38.8%
Schlumberger (adjusted for splits)	81⅞	51¾	−36.8%
			+162.7%

Strategy B
All of the above, plus

	BOUGHT	SOLD	% CHANGE
Stop & Shop	$6	$60	+900.0%

1977; second, that you sold at the high in 1986, which would have amounted to $312 a share, unadjusted for an 8-for-1 split.* That's a 156-bagger, and the fiscal equivalent of 39 home runs, so if you'd invested $6,410 in the stock (certainly in the price range of a car), you'd come out with $1 million exactly. Instead of owning a battered trade-in, you'd now have enough money to be able to afford a mansion and a couple of Jaguars in the garage.

You would have been unlikely to make a million dollars by investing

---

* Throughout this book we're going to be faced with the complication that occurs when companies split their shares—two-for-one, three-for-one, etc. If you invest $1,000 in 100 shares of Company X, a $10 stock, and there's a two-for-one split, then suddenly you own 200 shares of a $5 stock. Two years later, let's say, the stock price has risen to $10 a share and you've doubled your money. Yet to a person who didn't know about the split, it would appear as if you'd made nothing—the stock you bought for $10 is still selling for $10.

In the case of Subaru the stock never actually sold for $312. There had been an eight-for-one split just before the high, so the stock was actually at $39 ($312÷8) at the time. To conform with this price, all presplit levels must be divided by 8. In particular, the $2 low in 1977 is now a "split-adjusted" 25 cents per share ($2÷8 = $0.25), although the stock never actually sold for 25 cents.

Companies generally prefer not to have their share prices too high in absolute dollar terms, which is one reason why stock splits are declared.

as much in Dunkin' Donuts stock as you spent on the donuts—how many donuts can a person eat? But if along with the two dozen donuts you bought every week for a year in 1982 (a $270 total outlay) you had invested an equal amount in shares, then four years later the shares would have been worth $1,539 (a sixbagger). A $10,000 investment in Dunkin' Donuts would have resulted in a $47,000 gain in four years.

If, in 1976, you'd have bought ten pairs of jeans at The Gap for $180, the jeans would have worn out by now, but ten shares of Gap stock purchased for the same $180 ($18 per share was the initial offering price) was worth $4,672.50 at the market high in 1987. A $10,000 investment in The Gap would have resulted in a $250,000 gain.

If during 1973 you'd have spent 31 nights on business trips at La Quinta Motor Inns (paying $11.98 per night for the room), and you matched the $371.38 room bill with an equal purchase of La Quinta stock (23.21 shares), your shares would have been worth $4,363.08 ten years later. A $10,000 investment in La Quinta would have resulted in a $107,500 gain.

If during 1969 you found yourself having to pay for a traditional burial ($980) of a loved one from one of the many funeral outlets owned by Service Corporation International, and somehow in spite of your grief you managed to invest another $980 in SCI stock, your 70 shares would have been worth $14,352.19 in 1987. A $10,000 investment in SCI would have resulted in a $137,000 gain.

If back in 1982, during the same week you bought that first $2,000 Apple computer so your children could improve their grades and get into college, you'd put another $2,000 into Apple stock, then by 1987 those shares in Apple were worth $11,950, or enough to pay for a year at college.

THE POWER OF COMMON KNOWLEDGE

To get these spectacular returns you had to buy and sell at exactly the right time. But even if you missed the highs or the lows, you would have done better to have invested in any of the familiar companies mentioned above than in some of the esoteric enterprises that neither of us understands.

There's a famous story about a fireman from New England. Apparently back in the 1950s he couldn't help noticing that a local Tambrands plant (then the company was called Tampax) was expanding at a furious pace. It occurred to him that they wouldn't be expanding so fast unless they were prospering, and on that assumption he and his family invested $2,000. Not only that, they put in another $2,000 each year for the next five years. By 1972 the fireman was a millionaire—and he hadn't even bought any Subaru.

Whether or not our fortunate investor asked any brokers or other experts for advice I'm not certain, but many would have told him his theory was flawed, and if he knew what was good for him, he'd stick with the blue chips the institutions were buying, or with the hot electronics issues that were popular at the time. Luckily the fireman kept his own counsel.

You might have assumed it's the sophisticated and high-level gossip that experts hear around the Quotron machines that gives us our best investment ideas, but I get many of mine the way the fireman got his. I talk to hundreds of companies a year and spend hour after hour in heady powwows with CEOs, financial analysts, and my colleagues in the mutual-fund business, but I stumble onto the big winners in extracurricular situations, the same way you could:

Taco Bell, I was impressed with the burrito on a trip to California; La Quinta Motor Inns, somebody at the rival Holiday Inn told me about it; Volvo, my family and friends drive this car; Apple Computer, my kids had one at home and then the systems manager bought several for the office; Service Corporation International, a Fidelity electronics analyst (who had nothing to do with funeral homes, so this wasn't his field) found on a trip to Texas; Dunkin' Donuts, I loved the coffee; and recently the revamped Pier 1 Imports, recommended by my wife. In fact, Carolyn is one of my best sources. She's the one who discovered L'eggs.

L'eggs is the perfect example of the power of common knowledge. It turned out to be one of the two most successful consumer products of the seventies. In the early part of that decade, before I took over Fidelity Magellan, I was working as a securities analyst at the firm. I knew the textile business from having traveled the country visiting textile plants, calculating profit margins, price/earnings ratios, and the esoterica of warps and woofs. But none of this information was as valuable as Carolyn's. I didn't find L'eggs in my research, she found it by going to the grocery store.

Right there in a freestanding metal rack near the checkout counter was a new display of women's panty hose, packaged in colorful plastic eggs. The company, Hanes, was test-marketing L'eggs at several sites around the country, including suburban Boston. When Hanes interviewed hundreds of women leaving the test supermarkets and asked them if they'd just bought panty hose, a high percentage answered yes. Yet most of them couldn't recall the name of the brand. Hanes was ecstatic. If a product becomes a best-seller without brand-name recognition, imagine how it will sell once the brand is publicized.

Carolyn didn't need to be a textile analyst to realize that L'eggs was a superior product. All she had to do was buy a pair and try them on. These stockings had what they call a heavier denier, which made them less likely to develop a run than the normal stockings. They also fit very well, but the main attraction was convenience. You could pick up L'eggs right next to the bubble gum and the razor blades, and without having to make a special trip to the department store.

Hanes already sold its regular brand of stockings in the department stores and the specialty stores. However, the company had determined that women customarily visit one or the other every six weeks, on average, whereas they go to the grocery store twice a week, which gives them twelve chances to buy L'eggs for every one chance to buy the regular brand. Selling stockings in the grocery store was an immensely popular idea. You could have figured that out by seeing the number of women with plastic eggs in their grocery carts at the checkout counter. You could just imagine how many L'eggs were going to be sold nationwide, after the word got out.

How many women who bought panty hose, store clerks who saw the women buying panty hose, and husbands who saw the women coming home with the panty hose knew about the success of L'eggs? Millions. Two or three years after the product was introduced, you could have walked into any one of thousands of supermarkets and realized that this was a best-seller. From there, it was easy enough to find out that L'eggs was made by Hanes and that Hanes was listed on the New York Stock Exchange.

Once Carolyn alerted me to Hanes, I did the customary research into the story. The story was even better than I'd thought, so with the same confidence as the fireman who bought Tambrands, I recommended the stock to Fidelity's portfolio managers. Hanes turned out to be a sixbagger before it was taken over by Consolidated Foods, now Sara Lee. L'eggs still makes a lot of money for Sara Lee and has grown consistently over the past decade. I'm convinced Hanes would have been a 50-bagger if it hadn't been bought out.

The beauty of L'eggs is that you didn't have to know about it from the outset. You could have bought Hanes stock the first year, the second year, or even the third year after L'eggs went nationwide and you'd have tripled your money at least. But a lot of people didn't, especially husbands. Husbands (usually also known as the Designated Investors) probably were too busy buying solar-energy stocks or satellite-dish company stocks and losing their collective shirts.

Consider my friend Harry Houndstooth—whose name I've changed to protect the unfortunate. Actually there's a little bit of Houndstooth in all of us. This Designated Investor (each family seems to have one) has just spent the morning reading *The Wall Street Journal,* plus a $250-a-year stock market newsletter to which he subscribes. He's looking for another exciting stock play, something with limited risk but big potential on the upside. In both the *Journal* and his newsletter there's a favorable mention of Winchester Disk Drives, a headstrong little firm with a dandy future.

Houndstooth doesn't know a disk drive from a clay pigeon, but he calls his broker and learns that Merrill Lynch has put Winchester on its "aggressive buy" list.

All this can't be pure coincidence, thinks Houndstooth. He is soon convinced that putting $3,000 of his hard-earned money into Winchester is a very clever idea. After all, he's done the research!

Houndstooth's wife, Henrietta—also known as the Person Who Doesn't Understand the Serious Business of Money (these roles could be reversed, but usually aren't)—has just returned from the shopping mall where she's discovered a wonderful new women's apparel store called The Limited. The place is mobbed with customers. She can't wait to tell her husband about the friendly salespeople and the terrific bargains. "I bought Jennifer's entire fall wardrobe," she exclaims. "Only two hundred and seventy-five dollars."

"Two hundred and seventy-five dollars?" grouses the Designated Investor. "While you've been out squandering money, I've been home figuring out how to make it. Winchester Disk Drives is the answer. As near to a sure thing as you could get. We're putting three thousand dollars into it."

"I hope you know what you're doing," says the Person Who Doesn't Understand the Serious Business of Money. "Remember Havalight

Photo Cell? That sure thing went from seven dollars to three dollars and fifty cents. We lost fifteen hundred dollars."

"Yeah, but that was Havalight. This is Winchester. *The Wall Street Journal* calls disk drives one of the major growth industries of this decade. Why should we be the only ones not to get in on it?"

The rest of the story is easy to imagine. Winchester Disk Drives has a bad quarter, or there's unexpected competition in the disk drive industry, and the stock price drops from $10 to $5. Since the Designated Investor has no possible way to understand what any of this means, he decides the prudent thing is to sell out, delighted that he only lost another $1,500—or a little more than five sets of Jennifer's wardrobes.

Meanwhile, unbeknownst to Houndstooth, the stock price of The Limited, the store that impressed his wife, Henrietta, has been moving steadily higher, from less than 50 cents a share (adjusted for splits) in December, 1979, to $9 in 1983—already a twentybagger to there—and even if he'd bought it at the $9 price (and suffered through one drop back to $5), he'd have made more than five times his money as the stock soared to $52⅞. That's over a 100-bagger from the beginning, so if Houndstooth had invested $10,000 early enough, he would have made over a million dollars on the stock.

More realistically, if Mrs. Houndstooth had matched the $275 she put into the wardrobe with another $275 put into the stock, it's conceivable that even her tiny investment would have paid for a semester's tuition for her daughter.

But our Designated Investor, who had plenty of time to buy into The Limited even after he sold out on Winchester, continued to ignore the great spousal tip. By then there were four hundred Limited stores in the country, and most of them crowded, but Houndstooth was too busy to notice. He was following what Boone Pickens was doing with Mesa Petroleum.

Sometime near the end of 1987, and probably just before the 508-point jiggle, Houndstooth finally discovers that The Limited is on his brokerage firm's buy list. Furthermore, there have been promising articles in three different magazines, the stock has become a darling of the big institutions, and there are thirty analysts on the trail. It occurs to the Designated Investor that this is a solid, respectable buy.

"Funny thing," he mutters one day to his wife. "Remember that store you like, The Limited? Turns out to be a public company. That means we can buy the stock. Pretty good stock, to boot, judging by the special

I just saw on PBS. I heard *Forbes* even had a cover story on it. Anyway, the smart money can't get enough of it. Gotta be worth at least a couple of thousand from the retirement fund."

"We still got a couple of thousand in the retirement fund?" asks the skeptical Henrietta.

"Of course we do," blusters the Designated Investor. "And it'll soon be more, thanks to your favorite store."

"But I don't shop at The Limited anymore," Henrietta says. "The merchandise is overpriced and no longer unique. Other stores carry the same thing now."

"What's that got to do with anything," bellows our Designated Investor. "I'm not talking about shopping. I'm talking about investing."

Houndstooth buys the stock at $50, near the all-time 1987 high. Soon the price begins to fall to $16, and about halfway down, he sells out, delighted once again to have limited his losses.

IS THIS A PUBLIC COMPANY?

I'm a fine one to chide Houndstooth for missing The Limited. I didn't buy any shares on the way up, either, and my wife saw the same crowds at the shopping mall as his wife did. I, too, bought into The Limited when the story got popular and the fundamentals had begun to deteriorate, and I'm still holding on at a loss.

Actually I could go on for several pages about the tenbaggers I've missed, and more sorry examples will crop up further along in the book. When it comes to ignoring promising opportunities, I'm as adept as the next person. Once I was standing on the greatest asset play of the century, the Pebble Beach golf course, and it never occurred to me to ask if it was a public company. I was too busy asking about the distance between the tees and the greens.

Luckily there are enough tenbaggers around so that both of us could fail to notice the majority and we'll still hit our share. In a large portfolio such as mine I have to hit several before it makes an appreciable difference. In a small portfolio such as yours, you only have to hit one.

Moreover, the nice thing about investing in familiar companies such as L'eggs or Dunkin' Donuts is that when you try on the stockings or sip the coffee, you're already doing the kind of fundamental analysis that they pay Wall Street analysts to do. Visiting stores and testing products is one of the critical elements of the analyst's job.

During a lifetime of buying cars or cameras, you develop a sense of what's good and what's bad, what sells and what doesn't. If it's not cars you know something about, you know something about something else, and the most important part is, you know it before Wall Street knows it. Why wait for the Merrill Lynch restaurant expert to recommend Dunkin' Donuts when you've already seen eight new franchises opening up in your area? The Merrill Lynch restaurant analyst isn't going to notice Dunkin' Donuts (for reasons I'll soon explain) until the stock has quintupled from $2 to $10, and you noticed it when the stock was at $2.

GIGGING THE GIGAHERTZ

Among amateur investors, for some reason it's not considered sophisticated practice to equate driving around town eating donuts with the initial phase of an investigation into equities. People seem more comfortable investing in something about which they are entirely ignorant. There seems to be an unwritten rule on Wall Street: If you don't understand it, then put your life savings into it. Shun the enterprise around the corner, which can at least be observed, and seek out the one that manufactures an incomprehensible product.

I heard about one such opportunity just the other day. According to a report somebody left on my desk, this was a fantastic chance to invest in a company that makes the "one megabit S-Ram, C-mos (complementary metal oxide semiconductor); bipolar risc (reduced instructive set computer), floating point, data I/O array processor, optimizing compiler, 16-bytes dual port memory, unix operating system, whetstone megaflop polysilicon emitter, high band width, six gigahertz, double metalization communication protocol, asynchronous backward compatibility, peripheral bus architecture, four-way interleaved memory and 15 nanoseconds capability."

Gig my gigahertz and whetstone my megaflop, if you couldn't tell if that was a racehorse or a memory chip you should stay away from it, even though your broker will be calling to recommend it as the opportunity of the decade to make countless nanobucks.

A POX ON THE CABBAGE PATCH

Does that mean I think you ought to buy shares in every new fast-food franchise, every business that has a hot product, or every public company that opens an outlet in the local mall? If it were that simple, I wouldn't have lost money on Bildner's, the yuppie 7-Eleven right across the street from my office. If only I'd stuck to the sandwiches and not to the stock, fifty shares of which would scarcely buy you a tuna on rye. More on this later.

And how about Coleco? Just because the Cabbage Patch doll was the best-selling toy of this century, it couldn't save a mediocre company with a bad balance sheet, and although the stock rose dramatically for a year or so, spurred on first by home video games and then by the Cabbage Patch enthusiasm, eventually it dropped from a high of $65 in 1983 to a recent $1¾ as the company went into Chapter 11, filing for bankruptcy in 1988.

Finding the promising company is only the first step. The next step is doing the research. The research is what helps you to sort out Toys "R" Us from Coleco, Apple Computer from Televideo, or Piedmont Airlines from People Express. Now that I mention it, I wish I'd done more checking into what was happening at People Express. Maybe then I wouldn't have bought that one, either.

All my failures notwithstanding, during the twelve years I've managed Fidelity Magellan, it has risen over twentyfold per share—partly thanks to some of the little-known and out-of-favor stocks I've been able to discover and then research on my own. I'm confident that any investor can benefit from the same tactics. It doesn't take much to outsmart the smart money, which, as I've said, isn't always very smart.

This book is divided into three sections. The first, Preparing to Invest (Chapters 1 through 5), deals with how to assess yourself as a stockpicker, how to size up the competition (portfolio managers, institutional investors, and other Wall Street experts), how to evaluate whether stocks are riskier than bonds, how to examine your financial needs, and how to develop a successful stockpicking routine. The second, Picking Winners (Chapters 6 through 15), deals with how to find the most promising opportunities, what to look for in a company and what to avoid, how to use brokers, annual reports, and other resources to best advantage, and what to make of the various numbers (p/e ratio, book value, cash flow) that are often mentioned in technical evaluations of stocks. The third, The Long-term View (Chapters 16 through 20), deals with how to design a portfolio, how to keep tabs on companies in which you've taken an interest, when to buy and when to sell, the follies of options and futures, and some general observations about the health of Wall Street, American enterprise, and the stock market— things I've noticed in twenty-odd years of investing.

Part I

PREPARING TO INVEST

Before you think about buying stocks, you ought to have made some basic decisions about the market, about how much you trust corporate America, about whether you need to invest in stocks and what you expect to get out of them, about whether you are a short- or long-term investor, and about how you will react to sudden, unexpected, and severe drops in price. It's best to define your objectives and clarify your attitudes (do I really think stocks are riskier than bonds?) beforehand, because if you are undecided and lack conviction, then you are a potential market victim, who abandons all hope and reason at the worst moment and sells out at a loss. It is personal preparation, as much as knowledge and research, that distinguishes the successful stockpicker from the chronic loser. Ultimately it is not the stock market nor even the companies themselves that determine an investor's fate. It is the investor.

1

The Making of
a Stockpicker

There's no such thing as a hereditary knack for pick-ing stocks. Though many would like to blame their losses on some inbred tragic flaw, believing somehow that others are just born to invest, my own history refutes it. There was no ticker tape above my cradle, nor did I teethe on the stock pages in the precocious way that baby Pelé supposedly bounced a soccer ball. As far as I know, my father never left the pacing area to check on the price of General Motors, nor did my mother ask about the ATT dividend between contractions.

Only in hindsight can I report that the Dow Jones industrial average was down on January 19, 1944, the day I was born, and declined further the week I was in the hospital. Though I couldn't have suspected it then, this was the earliest example of the Lynch Law at work. The Lynch Law, closely related to the Peter Principle, states: Whenever Lynch advances, the market declines. (The latest proof came in the summer of 1987, when just after the publisher and I reached an agreement to produce this book, a high point in my career, the market lost 1,000 points in two months. I'll think twice before attempting to sell the movie rights.)

Most of my relatives distrusted the stock market, and with good reason. My mother was the youngest of seven children, which meant that my aunts and uncles were old enough to have reached adulthood during the Great Depression, and to have had firsthand knowledge of the Crash of '29. Nobody was recommending stocks around our household.

The only stock purchase I ever heard about was the time my grandfather, Gene Griffin, bought Cities Service. He was a very conservative investor, and he chose Cities Service because he thought it was a water utility. When he took a trip to New York and discovered it was an oil company, he sold immediately. Cities Service went up fiftyfold after that.

Distrust of stocks was the prevailing American attitude throughout the 1950s and into the 1960s, when the market tripled and then doubled again. This period of my childhood, and not the recent 1980s, was truly the greatest bull market in history, but to hear it from my uncles, you'd have thought it was the craps game behind the pool hall. "Never get involved in the market," people warned. "It's too risky. You'll lose all your money."

Looking back on it, I realize there was less risk of losing all one's money in the stock market of the 1950s than at any time before or since. This taught me not only that it's difficult to predict markets, but also that small investors tend to be pessimistic and optimistic at precisely the wrong times, so it's self-defeating to try to invest in good markets and get out of bad ones.

My father, an industrious man and former mathematics professor who left academia to become the youngest senior auditor at John Hancock, got sick when I was seven and died of brain cancer when I was ten. This tragedy resulted in my mother's having to go to work (at Ludlow Manufacturing, later acquired by Tyco Labs), and I decided to help out by getting a part-time job myself. At the age of eleven I was hired as a caddy. That was on July 7, 1955, a day the Dow Jones fell from 467 to 460.

To an eleven-year-old who'd already discovered golf, caddying was an ideal occupation. They paid me for walking around a golf course. In one afternoon I would outearn delivery boys who tossed newspapers onto lawns at six A.M. for seven days in a row. What could be better than that?

In high school I began to understand the subtler and more important advantages of caddying, especially at an exclusive club such as Brae Burn, outside of Boston. My clients were the presidents and CEOs of major corporations: Gillette, Polaroid, and more to the point, Fidelity. In helping D. George Sullivan find his ball, I was helping myself find a career. I'm not the only caddy who learned that the quickest route to the boardroom was through the locker room of a club like Brae Burn.

If you wanted an education in stocks, the golf course was the next best thing to being on the floor of a major exchange. Especially after they'd sliced or hooked a drive, club members enthusiastically described their latest triumphant investment. In a single round of play I might give out five golf tips and get back five stock tips in return.

Though I had no funds to invest in stock tips, the happy stories I heard on the fairways made me rethink the family position that the stock market was a place to lose money. Many of my clients actually seemed to have made money in the stock market, and some of the positive evidence actually trickled down to me.

A caddy quickly learns to sort his golfers into a caste system, beginning with the rare demigods (great golfer, great person, great tipper), moving down through the so-so golfers and so-so tippers, and eventually hitting bottom with the terrible golfer, terrible person, terrible tipper—a dreaded untouchable of the links. Mostly I caddied for average golfers and average spenders, but if it came down to a choice between a bad round with a big tipper, or a great round with a bad tipper, I learned to opt for the former. Caddying reinforced the notion that it helps to have money.

I continued to caddy throughout high school and into Boston College, where the Francis Ouimet Caddy Scholarship helped pay the bills. In college, except for the obligatory courses, I avoided science, math, and accounting—all the normal preparations for business. I was on the arts side of school, and along with the usual history, psychology, and political science, I also studied metaphysics, epistemology, logic, religion, and the philosophy of the ancient Greeks.

As I look back on it now, it's obvious that studying history and philosophy was much better preparation for the stock market than, say, studying statistics. Investing in stocks is an art, not a science, and people who've been trained to rigidly quantify everything have a big disadvantage. If stockpicking could be quantified, you could rent time on the nearest Cray computer and make a fortune. But it doesn't work that way. All the math you need in the stock market (Chrysler's got $1 billion in cash, $500 million in long-term debt, etc.) you get in the fourth grade.

Logic is the subject that's helped me the most in picking stocks, if only because it taught me to identify the peculiar illogic of Wall Street. Actually Wall Street thinks just as the Greeks did. The early Greeks used to sit around for days and debate how many teeth a horse has. They thought they could figure it out by just sitting there, instead of checking the horse. A lot of investors sit around and debate whether a stock is going up, as if the financial muse will give them the answer, instead of checking the company.

In centuries past, people hearing the rooster crow as the sun came up decided that the crowing caused the sunrise. It sounds silly now, but every day the experts confuse cause and effect on Wall Street in offering some new explanation for why the market goes up: hemlines are up, a certain conference wins the Super Bowl, the Japanese are unhappy, a trendline has been broken, Republicans will win the election, stocks are "oversold," etc. When I hear theories like these, I always remember the rooster.

In 1963, my sophomore year in college, I bought my first stock—Flying Tiger Airlines for $7 a share. Between the caddying and a scholarship I'd covered my tuition, living at home reduced my other expenses, and I had already upgraded myself from an $85 car to a $150 car. After all the tips that I'd had to ignore, I finally was rich enough to invest!

Flying Tiger was no wild guess. I picked it on the basis of some dogged research into a faulty premise. In one of my classes I'd read an article on the promising future of air freight, and it said that Flying Tiger was an air freight company. That's why I bought the stock, but that's not why the stock went up. It went up because we got into the Vietnam War and Flying Tiger made a fortune shunting troops and cargo in and out of the Pacific.

In less than two years Flying Tiger hit $32¾ and I had my first five-bagger. Little by little I sold it off to pay for graduate school. I went to Wharton on a partial Flying Tiger scholarship.

If your first stock is as important to your future in finance as your first love is to your future in romance, then the Flying Tiger pick was a very lucky thing. It proved to me that the big-baggers existed, and I was sure there were more of them from where this one had come.

During my senior year at Boston College I applied for a summer job at Fidelity, at the suggestion of Mr. Sullivan, the president—the hapless golfer, great guy, and good tipper for whom I'd caddied. Fidelity was the New York Yacht Club, the Augusta National, the Carnegie Hall, and the Kentucky Derby. It was the Cluny of investment houses, and like that great medieval abbey to which monks were flattered to be called, what devotee of balance sheets didn't dream of working here? There were one hundred applications for three summer positions.

Fidelity had done such a good job selling America on mutual funds that even my mother was putting $100 a month into Fidelity Capital. That fund, run by Gerry Tsai, was one of the two famous go-go funds of this famous go-go era. The other was Fidelity Trend, run by Edward C. Johnson III, also known as Ned. Ned Johnson was the son of the fabled Edward C. Johnson II, also known as Mister Johnson, who founded the company.

Ned Johnson's Fidelity Trend and Gerry Tsai's Fidelity Capital outperformed the competition by a big margin and were the envy of the industry over the period from 1958 to 1965. With these sorts of people training and supporting me, I felt as if I understood what Isaac Newton was talking about when he said: "If I have seen further . . . it is by standing upon the shoulders of Giants."

Long before Ned's great successes, his father, Mister Johnson, had changed America's mind about investing in stocks. Mister Johnson believed that you invest in stocks not to preserve capital, but to make money. Then you take your profits and invest in more stocks, and make even more money. "Stocks you trade, it's wives you're stuck with," said the always quotable Mister Johnson. He wouldn't have won any awards from *Ms.* magazine.

I was thrilled to be hired at Fidelity, and also to be installed in Gerry Tsai's old office, after Tsai had departed for the Manhattan Fund in New York. Of course the Dow Jones industrials, at 925 when I reported for work the first week of May, 1966, had fallen below 800 by the time I headed off to graduate school in September, just as the Lynch Law would have predicted.

RANDOM WALK AND MAINE SUGAR

Summer interns such as me, with no experience in corporate finance or accounting, were put to work researching companies and writing reports, the same as the regular analysts. The whole intimidating business was suddenly demystified—even liberal arts majors could analyze a stock. I was assigned to the paper and publishing industry and set out across the country to visit companies such as Sorg Paper and International Textbook. Since the airlines were on strike, I traveled by bus. By the end of the summer the company I knew most about was Greyhound.

After that interlude at Fidelity, I returned to Wharton for my second year of graduate school more skeptical than ever about the value of academic stock-market theory. It seemed to me that most of what I learned at Wharton, which was supposed to help you succeed in the investment business, could only help you fail. I studied statistics, advanced calculus, and quantitative analysis. Quantitative analysis taught me that the things I saw happening at Fidelity couldn't really be happening.

I also found it difficult to integrate the efficient-market hypothesis (that everything in the stock market is "known" and prices are always "rational") with the random-walk hypothesis (that the ups and downs of the market are irrational and entirely unpredictable). Already I'd seen enough odd fluctuations to doubt the rational part, and the success of the great Fidelity fund managers was hardly unpredictable.

It also was obvious that Wharton professors who believed in quantum analysis and random walk weren't doing nearly as well as my new colleagues at Fidelity, so between theory and practice, I cast my lot with the practitioners. It's very hard to support the popular academic theory that the market is irrational when you know somebody who just made a twentyfold profit in Kentucky Fried Chicken, and furthermore, who explained in advance why the stock was going to rise. My distrust of theorizers and prognosticators continues to the present day.

Some Wharton courses were rewarding, but even if they'd all been worthless, the experience would have been worth it, because I met Carolyn on the campus. (We got married while I was in the Army, on May 11, 1968, a Saturday when the market was closed, and we had a week-long honeymoon during which the Dow Jones lost 13.93 points—not that I was paying attention. This is something I looked up later.)

After finishing that second year at Wharton, I reported to the Army to serve my two-year hitch required under the ROTC program. From 1967 to 1969, I was a lieutenant in the artillery, sent first to Texas and later to Korea—a comforting assignment considering the alternative. Lieutenants in the artillery mostly wound up in Vietnam. The only drawback to Korea was that it was far away from the stock exchange, and as far as I knew, there was no stock market in Seoul. By this time I was suffering from Wall Street withdrawal.

I made up for lost time during infrequent leaves, when I'd rush home to buy the various hot stocks that friends and colleagues recommended. They were buying high-flying issues that kept going up, but for me they suggested conservative issues that kept going down. Actually I made some money in Ranger Oil, but I lost more in Maine Sugar, a sure-win situation that flopped.

The Maine Sugar people had gone around to all the Maine potato farmers to convince them to grow sugar beets in the off-season. This was going to be extremely profitable for Maine Sugar, not to mention for the Maine farmers. By planting the sugar beets—the perfect companion crop to potatoes—farmers could make extra money and revitalize the soil at the same time. Moreover, Maine Sugar was footing the bill for planting the beets. All the farmers had to do was haul the grown-up beets to the huge new refinery that Maine Sugar had just built.

The hitch was that these were Maine farmers, and Maine farmers are very cautious. Instead of planting hundreds of acres of sugar beets, the first year they tried it on a quarter acre, and then when that worked, they expanded to a half acre, and by the time they got to a full acre, the refinery was shut for lack of business and Maine Sugar went bankrupt. The stock fell to six cents, so one share could buy you six gumballs from a Lions Club machine.

After the Maine Sugar fiasco I vowed never to buy another stock that depended on Maine farmers' chasing after a quick buck.

I returned from Korea in 1969, rejoined Fidelity as a permanent employee and research analyst, and the stock market promptly plummeted. (Lynch Law theorists take note.) In June of 1974, I was promoted from assistant director of research to director of research, and the Dow Jones lost 250 points in the next three months. In May of 1977, I took over the Fidelity Magellan fund. The market stood at 899 and promptly began a five-month slide to 801.

Fidelity Magellan had $20 million in assets. There were only 40 stocks in the portfolio, and Ned Johnson, Fidelity's head man, recommended that I reduce the number to 25. I listened politely and then went out and raised the number to 60 stocks, six months later to 100 stocks, and soon after that, to 150 stocks. I didn't do it to be contrary. I did it because when I saw a bargain I couldn't resist buying it, and in those days there were bargains everywhere.

The open-minded Ned Johnson watched me from a distance and cheered me on. Our methods were different, but that didn't stop him from accepting mine—at least as long as I was getting good results.

My portfolio continued to grow, to the point that I once owned 150 S&L stocks alone. Instead of settling for a couple of savings-and-loans, I bought them across the board (after determining, of course, that each was a promising investment in itself). It wasn't enough to invest in one convenience store. Along with Southland, the parent company at 7-Eleven, I couldn't resist buying Circle K, National Convenience, Shop and Go, Hop-In Foods, Fairmont Foods, and Sunshine Junior, to mention a few. Buying hundreds of stocks certainly wasn't Ned Johnson's idea of how to run an equity fund, but I'm still here.

Soon enough I became known as the Will Rogers of equities, the man who never saw a stock he didn't like. They're always making jokes about it in *Barron's*—can you name one stock that Lynch doesn't own? Since I own 1,400 at present, I suppose they have a point. Certainly I can name plenty of stocks I wish I hadn't owned.

Meanwhile, however, the assets in Fidelity Magellan have grown to $9 billion, which makes this fund as large as the gross national product of half of Greece. In terms of return on investment, Fidelity Magellan has done much better than Greece over the eleven years, although Greece has an enviable record over the preceding 2,500.

As for Will Rogers, he may have given the best bit of advice ever uttered about stocks: "Don't gamble; take all your savings and buy some good stock and hold it till it goes up, then sell it. If it don't go up, don't buy it."

2

The Wall Street
Oxymorons

To the list of famous oxymorons—military intel-
ligence, learned professor, deafening silence, and jumbo shrimp—I'd
add professional investing. It's important for amateurs to view the profession with a properly skeptical eye. At least you'll realize whom
you're up against. Since 70 percent of the shares in major companies
are controlled by institutions, it's increasingly likely that you're competing against oxymorons whenever you buy or sell shares. This is a
lucky break for you. Given the numerous cultural, legal, and social barriers that restrain professional investors (many of which we've nailed up
ourselves), it's amazing that we've done as well as we have, as a group.

Of course, not all professionals are oxymoronic. There are great
fund managers, innovative fund managers, and maverick fund managers who invest as they please. John Templeton is one of the best. He
is a pioneer in the global market, one of the first to make money all
around the world. His shareholders avoided the 1972–74 collapse in
the U.S. because he had cleverly placed most of his fund's assets in
Canadian and Japanese stocks. Not only that, he was one of the first to
take advantage of the fact that the Japanese Dow Jones (the Nikkei average) is up seventeenfold from 1966 to 1988, while the U.S. Dow
Jones has only doubled.

Max Heine (now deceased) at Mutual Shares fund was another ingenious freethinker. His protégé, Michael Price, who took over after
Heine's death, has continued the tradition of buying asset-rich companies at fifty cents on the dollar and then waiting for the marketplace to
pay the full amount. He's done a brilliant job. John Neff is a champion
investor in out-of-favor stocks, for which he's constantly sticking his
neck out. Ken Heebner at Loomis-Sayles sticks his neck out, too, and
the results have been remarkable.

Peter deRoeth is another friend who has done extremely well with
small stocks. DeRoeth is a Harvard Law School graduate who developed an incurable passion for equities. He's the one who gave me Toys
"R" Us. The secret of his success is that he never went to business
school—imagine all the lessons he never had to unlearn.

George Soros and Jimmy Rogers made their millions by taking esoteric positions I couldn't begin to explain—shorting gold, buying puts,
hedging Australian bonds. And Warren Buffett, the greatest investor of
them all, looks for the same sorts of opportunities I do, except that
when he finds them, he buys the whole company.

These notable exceptions are entirely outnumbered by the run-of-
the-mill fund managers, dull fund managers, comatose fund managers,
sycophantic fund managers, timid fund managers, plus other assorted
camp followers, fuddy-duddies, and copycats hemmed in by the rules.

You have to understand the minds of the people in our business. We
all read the same newspapers and magazines and listen to the same
economists. We're a very homogeneous lot, quite frankly. There aren't
many among us who walked in off the beach. If there are any high
school dropouts running an equity mutual fund, I'd be surprised. I
doubt there are any ex-surfers or former truck drivers, either.

You won't find many well-scrubbed adolescents in our ranks. My
wife once did some research into the popular theory that great inventions and great ideas come to people before they reach thirty. On the
other hand, since I'm now forty-five and still running Fidelity Magellan,
I'm eager to report that great investing has nothing to do with youth—
and that the middle-aged investor who has lived through several kinds
of markets may have an advantage over the youngster who hasn't.

Nevertheless, with the vast majority of the fund managers being
middle-aged, it cuts out all the potential genius on the earlier and the
later ends of the geriatric spectrum.

STREET LAG

With every spectacular stock I've managed to ferret out, the virtues seemed so obvious that if 100 professionals had been free to add it to their portfolios, I'm convinced that 99 would have done so. But for reasons I'm about to describe, they couldn't. There are simply too many obstacles between them and the tenbaggers.

Under the current system, a stock isn't truly attractive until a number of large institutions have recognized its suitability and an equal number of respected Wall Street analysts (the researchers who track the various industries and companies) have put it on the recommended list. With so many people waiting for others to make the first move, it's amazing that anything gets bought.

The Limited is a good example of what I call Street lag. When the company went public in 1969, it was all but unknown to the large institutions and the big-time analysts. The underwriter of the offering was a small firm called Vercoe & Co., located in Columbus, Ohio, where the headquarters of The Limited can also be found. Peter Halliday, a high school classmate of Limited chairman Leslie Wexner, was Vercoe's sales manager back then. Halliday attributed the disinterest of Wall Street to the fact that Columbus, Ohio, was not exactly a corporate Mecca at the time.

A lone analyst (Susie Holmes of White, Weld) followed the company for a couple of years before a second analyst, Maggie Gilliam for First Boston, took official notice of The Limited in 1974. Even Maggie Gilliam might not have discovered it if she hadn't stumbled onto the Limited store at Chicago's Woodfield Mall during a snow emergency at O'Hare airport. To her credit, she paid attention to her amateur's edge.

The first institution which bought shares in The Limited was T. Rowe Price New Horizons Fund, and that was in the summer of 1975. By then there were one hundred Limited stores open for business across the country. Thousands of observant shoppers could have initiated their own coverage during this period. Still, by 1979, only two institutions owned Limited stock, accounting for 0.6 percent of the outstanding shares. Employees and executives in the company were heavy owners—usually a good sign, as we'll discuss later.

In 1981 there were four hundred Limited stores doing a thriving business and only six analysts followed the stock. This was seven years after Ms. Gilliam's discovery. By 1983, when the stock hit its intermittent high of $9, long-term investors were up eighteenfold from 1979, when the shares had sold for 50 cents, adjusted for splits.

Yes, I know that the price fell nearly in half, to $5 a share in 1984, but the company was still doing well, so that gave investors another chance to buy in. (As I'll explain in later chapters, if a stock is down but the fundamentals are positive, it's best to hold on and even better to buy more.) It wasn't until 1985, with the stock back up to $15, that analysts joined the celebration. In fact, they were falling all over one another to put The Limited on their buy lists, and aggressive institutional buying helped send the shares on a ride all the way up to $52⅞—way beyond what the fundamentals would have justified. By then, there were more than thirty analysts on the trail (thirty-seven as of this writing), and many had arrived just in time to see The Limited drop off the edge.

My favorite funeral home company, Service Corporation International, had its first public offering in 1969. Not a single analyst paid the slightest heed for the next ten years! The company made great efforts to get Wall Street's attention, and finally it got noticed by a small investment outfit called Underwood, Neuhaus. Shearson was the first major brokerage firm to show an interest, and that was in 1982. By then the stock was a fivebagger.

True, you could have more than doubled your money once again by buying SCI at $12 a share in 1983 and selling it at the $30⅜ high in 1987, but that's not quite as exciting as the fortybagger you'd have had if you'd invested back in 1978.

Thousands of people had to be familiar with this company if for no other reason than they'd been to a funeral, and the fundamentals were good all along. It turns out that the Wall Street oxymorons overlooked SCI because funeral services didn't fall into any of the standard industry classifications. It wasn't exactly a leisure business and it wasn't a consumer durable, either.

Throughout the decade of the 1970s, when Subaru was making its biggest moves, only three or four major analysts kept tabs on it. Dunkin' Donuts was a 25-bagger between 1977 and 1986, yet only two major firms follow it even today. Neither was interested five years ago. Only a few regional brokerages, such as Adams, Harkness, and Hill in Boston, got on to this profitable story, but you could have initiated coverage on your own, after you'd eaten the donuts.

Pep Boys, a stock I'll be mentioning again, sold for less than $1 a share in 1981 and hit $9½ in 1985 before it caught the attention of three analysts. Stop & Shop soared from $5 to $50 as the ranks of its analysts swelled from one to four.

I could go on, but I think we both get the point. Contrast the above with the fifty-six brokerage analysts who normally cover IBM or the forty-four who cover Exxon.

INSPECTED BY 4

Whoever imagines that the average Wall Street professional is looking for reasons to buy exciting stocks hasn't spent much time on Wall Street. The fund manager most likely is looking for reasons *not* to buy exciting stocks, so that he can offer the proper excuses if those exciting stocks happen to go up. "It was too small for me to buy" heads a long list, followed by "there was no track record," "it was in a nongrowth industry," "unproven management," "the employees belong to a union," and "the competition will kill them," as in "Stop & Shop will never work, the 7-Elevens will kill them," or "Pic 'N' Save will never work, Sears will kill them," or "Agency Rent-A-Car hasn't got a chance against Hertz and Avis." These may be reasonable concerns that merit investigation, but often they're used to fortify snap judgments and wholesale taboos.

With survival at stake, it's the rare professional who has the guts to traffic in an unknown La Quinta. In fact, between the chance of making an unusually large profit on an unknown company and the assurance of losing only a small amount on an established company, the normal mutual-fund manager, pension-fund manager, or corporate-portfolio manager would jump at the latter. Success is one thing, but it's more important not to look bad if you fail. There's an unwritten rule on Wall Street: "You'll never lose your job losing your client's money in IBM."

If IBM goes bad and you bought it, the clients and the bosses will ask: "What's wrong with that damn IBM lately?" But if La Quinta Motor Inns goes bad, they'll ask: "What's wrong with you?" That's why security-conscious portfolio managers don't buy La Quinta Motor Inns when two analysts cover the stock and it sells for $3 a share. They don't buy Wal-Mart when the stock sells for $4, and it's a dinky store in a dinky little town in Arkansas, but soon to expand. They buy Wal-Mart when there's an outlet in every large population center in America, fifty analysts follow the company, and the chairman of Wal-Mart is featured in *People* magazine as the eccentric billionaire who drives a pickup truck to work. By then the stock sells for $40.

The worst of the camp-following takes place in the bank pension-fund departments and in the insurance companies, where stocks are bought and sold from preapproved lists. Nine out of ten pension managers work from such lists, as a form of self-protection from the ruination of "diverse performance." "Diverse performance" can cause a great deal of trouble, as the following example illustrates.

Two company presidents, Smith and Jones, both of whom have pension accounts managed by the National Bank of River City, are playing golf together, as they always do. While waiting to tee off, they chat about important things such as pension accounts, and soon they discover that while Smith's account is up 40 percent for the year, Jones's account is up 28 percent. Both men ought to be satisfied, but Jones is livid. Early Monday morning he's on the phone with an officer of the bank, demanding to know why his money has underperformed Smith's money, when, after all, both accounts are handled by the same pension department. "If it happens again," Jones blusters, "we're pulling our money out."

This unpleasant problem for the pension department is soon avoided if the managers of various accounts pick stocks from the same approved batch. That way, it's very likely that both Smith and Jones will enjoy the same result, or at least the difference will not be great enough to make either of them mad. Almost by definition the result will be mediocre, but acceptable mediocrity is far more comfortable than diverse performance.

It would be one thing if an approved list were made up of, say, thirty ingenious selections, each chosen via the independent thinking of a different analyst or fund manager. Then you might have a dynamic portfolio. But the way it usually works is that each stock on the list has to be acceptable to all thirty managers, and if no great book or symphony was ever written by committee, no great portfolio has ever been selected by one, either.

I am reminded here of the Vonnegut short story in which various highly talented practitioners are deliberately held back (the good dancers wear weights, the good artists have their fingers tied together, etc.) so as not to upset the less skillful.

I'm also reminded of the little slips of paper that say "Inspected by 4" that are stuck inside the pockets of new shirts. The "Inspected by 4" method is how stocks are selected from the lists. The would-be decision-makers hardly know what they are approving. They don't travel around visiting companies or researching new products, they just take what they're given and pass it along. I think of this every time I buy shirts.

It's no wonder that portfolio managers and fund managers tend to be squeamish in their stock selections. There's about as much job security in portfolio management as there is in go-go dancing and football coaching. Coaches can at least relax between seasons. Fund managers can never relax because the game is played year-round. The wins and losses are reviewed after every third month, by clients and bosses who demand immediate results.

It's a bit more comfortable on my side of the business, working for the general public, than it is for the managers who pick stocks for their fellow professionals. Shareholders at Fidelity Magellan tend to be smaller investors who are perfectly free to sell out at any time, but they don't review my portfolio stock-by-stock to second-guess my selections. That's what happens, though, to Mr. Boon Doggle over at Blind Trust, the bank that's been hired to handle the pension accounts for White Bread, Inc.

Boon Doggle knows his stocks. He's been a portfolio manager at Blind Trust for seven years, and during that time he's made some very inspired decisions. All he wants is to be left alone to do his job. On the other hand, Sam Flint, vice president at White Bread, also thinks he knows his stocks, and every three months he casts a critical eye over Boon Doggle's selections on White Bread's behalf. Between these strenuous three-month checkups, Flint calls Doggle twice a day for an update. Doggle is so sick of Flint he wishes he'd never heard of him or of White Bread. He wastes so many hours talking to Flint about picking good stocks that he has no time left to do his job.

Fund managers in general spend a quarter of their working hours explaining what they just did—first to their immediate bosses in their own trust department, and then to their ultimate bosses, the clients like Flint at White Bread. There's an unwritten rule that the bigger the client, the more talking the portfolio manager has to do to please him. There are notable exceptions—Ford Motor, Eastman Kodak, and Eaton to name a few—but in general, it's true.

Let's say that the supercilious Flint, in reviewing Doggle's recent results for the pension fund, sees Xerox in the portfolio. Xerox currently sells for $52 a share. Flint looks across to the cost column and sees that Xerox was purchased for the fund at $32 per share. "Terrific," Flint enthuses. "I couldn't have done better myself."

The next stock Flint sees is Sears. The current price is $34⅞ and the original price was $25. "Excellent," he exclaims to Doggle. Fortunately for Doggle there is no date attached to these purchases, so Flint never realizes that Xerox and Sears have been in the portfolio since 1967, when bell-bottom pants were the national rage. Given how long Xerox has been sitting there, the return on equity is worse than it would have been in a money-market fund, but Flint doesn't see that.

Then Flint moves along to Seven Oaks International, which happens to be one of my all-time favorite picks. Ever wonder what happens to all those discount coupons—fifteen cents off Heinz ketchup, twenty-five cents off Windex, etc.—after you clip them from the newspapers and then turn them in at your supermarket checkout counter? Your supermarket wraps them up and sends them off to the Seven Oaks plant in Mexico, where piles of coupons are collated, processed, and cleared for payment, much as a check is cleared through the Federal Reserve banks. Seven Oaks makes a lot of money doing this boring job, and the shareholders are well-rewarded. It's exactly the kind of obscure, boring, and highly profitable company with an inscrutable name that I like to own.

Flint has never heard of Seven Oaks, and the only thing he knows about it is what he sees on the record—it was bought for the fund at $10 a share, and now it's selling for $6. "What's this?" Flint inquires. "It's down forty percent!" Doggle has to spend the rest of the meeting defending this one stock. After two or three similar episodes, he vows never to buy another off-beat company and to stick to the Xeroxes and the Searses. He also decides to sell Seven Oaks at the earliest opportunity so that the memory of it will be expunged forever from his list.

Reverting to "group think," and reminding himself that it's safer to pick companies in a crowd, he ignores the words of wisdom that came either from Aeschylus the playwright, Goethe the author, or Alf, the TV star from outer space:

> *Two's a company, three's a crowd*
> *Four is two companies*
> *Five is a company and a crowd*

Six is two crowds
Seven is one crowd and two companies
Eight is either four companies or two crowds and a company
Nine is three crowds
Ten is either five companies or two companies and two crowds

Even if there's nothing terribly wrong with the fundamentals of Seven Oaks (I don't think there is because I still own a small amount of it), and later it turns into a tenbagger, the stock will be sold out of White Bread's pension account because Flint doesn't like it, just as surely as stocks that ought to be sold will be kept. In our business the indiscriminate selling of current losers is called "burying the evidence."

Among the seasoned portfolio managers, burying the evidence is done so quickly and efficiently that I suspect it's already become a survival mechanism, and it will probably be inbred so that future generations can do it without hesitation, the way that ostriches have learned to stick their heads in the sand.

As it is, if Boon Doggle doesn't bury the evidence himself at the first opportunity, then he'll be fired, and the whole portfolio will be turned over to a successor who will bury it. A successor always wants to start off with a positive feeling, which means keep the Xerox and wipe out the Seven Oaks.

Before too many of my colleagues cry "foul," let me once again praise the notable exceptions. The portfolio departments of many regional banks outside of New York City have done an outstanding job picking stocks for an extended period of time. Many corporations, especially the medium-sized ones, have distinguished themselves in managing their pension money. A nationwide review would certainly turn up dozens of outstanding stockpickers who work for insurance funds, pension funds, and trust accounts.

OYSTERS ROCKEFELLER

Whenever fund managers do decide to buy something exciting (against all the social and political obstacles), they may be held back by various written rules and regulations. Some bank trust departments simply won't allow the buying of stocks in any companies with unions. Others won't invest in nongrowth industries or in specific industry groups, such as electric utilities or oil or steel. Sometimes it gets to the point that the fund manager can't buy shares in any company whose name begins with *r*, or perhaps the shares must be acquired only in months that have an *r* in their name, a rule that's been borrowed from the eating of oysters.

If it's not the bank or the mutual fund making up rules, then it's the SEC. For instance, the SEC says a mutual fund such as mine cannot own more than ten percent of the shares in any given company, nor can we invest more than five percent of the fund's assets in any given stock.

The various restrictions are well-intentioned, and they protect against a fund's putting all its eggs in one basket (more on this later) and also against a fund's taking over a company à la Carl Icahn (more on that later, too). The secondary result is that the bigger funds are forced to limit themselves to the top 90 to 100 companies, out of the 10,000 or so that are publicly traded.

Let's say you manage a $1-billion pension fund, and to guard against diverse performance, you're required to choose from a list of 40 approved stocks, via the Inspected by 4 method. Since you're only allowed to invest five percent of your total stake in each stock, you've got to buy at least 20 stocks, with $50 million in each. The most you can have is 40 stocks, with $25 million in each.

In that case you have to find companies where $25 million will buy less than ten percent of the outstanding shares. That cuts out a lot of opportunities, especially in the small fast-growing enterprises that tend to be the tenbaggers. For instance, you couldn't have bought Seven Oaks International or Dunkin' Donuts under these rules.

Some funds are further restricted with a market-capitalization rule: they don't own a stock in any company below, say, a $100-million size. (Size is measured by multiplying the number of outstanding shares by the current stock price.) A company with 20 million shares outstanding that sell for $1.75 a share has a market cap of $35 million and must be avoided by the fund. But once the stock price has tripled to $5.25, that same company has a market cap of $105 million and suddenly it's suitable for purchase. This results in a strange phenomenon: large funds are allowed to buy shares in small companies only when the shares are no bargain.

By definition, then, the pension portfolios are wedded to the ten-percent gainers, the plodders, and the regular Fortune 500 bigshots that offer few pleasant surprises. They almost have to buy the IBMs, the Xeroxes, and the Chryslers, but they'll probably wait to buy Chrysler until it's fully recovered and priced accordingly. The well-respected and highly competent money management firm of Scudder, Stevens, and Clark stopped covering Chrysler altogether right before the bottom ($3½) and didn't resume coverage until the stock hit $30.

No wonder so many pension-fund managers fail to beat the market averages. When you ask a bank to handle your investments, mediocrity is all you're going to get in a majority of the cases.

Equity mutual funds such as mine are less restricted. I don't have to buy stocks from a fixed menu, and there's no Mr. Flint hovering over my shoulder. That's not to say that my bosses and overseers at Fidelity don't monitor my progress, ask me challenging questions, and periodically review my results. It's just that nobody tells me I must own Xerox, or that I can't own Seven Oaks.

My biggest disadvantage is size. The bigger the equity fund, the harder it gets for it to outperform the competition. Expecting a $9-billion fund to compete successfully against an $800-million fund is the same as expecting Larry Bird to star in basketball games with a five-pound weight strapped to his waist. Big funds have the same built-in handicaps as big anythings—the bigger it is, the more energy it takes to move it.

Yet even at $9 billion, Fidelity Magellan has continued to compete successfully. Every year some new soothsayer says it can't go on like this, and every year so far it has. Since June, 1985, when Magellan became the country's largest fund, it has outperformed 98 percent of general equity mutual funds.

For this, I have to thank Seven Oaks, Chrysler, Taco Bell, Pep Boys, and all the other fast growers, turnaround opportunities, and out-of-favor enterprises I've found. The stocks I try to buy are the very stocks that traditional fund managers try to overlook. *In other words, I continue to think like an amateur as frequently as possible.*

GOING IT ALONE

You don't have to invest like an institution. If you invest like an institution, you're doomed to perform like one, which in many cases isn't very well. Nor do you have to force yourself to think like an amateur if you already are one. If you're a surfer, a trucker, a high school dropout, or an eccentric retiree, then you've got an edge already. That's where the tenbaggers come from, beyond the boundaries of accepted Wall Street cogitation.

When you invest, there's no Flint around to criticize your quarterly results or your semiannual results, or to grill you as to why you bought Agency Rent-A-Car instead of IBM. Well, maybe there's a spouse and perhaps a stockbroker with whom you are forced to converse, but a stockbroker will be quite sympathetic to your odd choices and certainly isn't going to fire you for picking Seven Oaks—as long as you're paying the commissions. And hasn't the spouse (the Person Who Doesn't Understand the Serious Business of Money) already proven a faith in your investment schemes by allowing you to continue to make mistakes?

(In the unlikely event that your mate is dismayed at your stock selections, you could always hide the monthly statements that arrive in the mail. I'm not endorsing this practice, only pointing out that it's one more option available to the small investor that's out of the question for the manager of an equity fund.)

You don't have to spend a quarter of your waking hours explaining to a colleague why you are buying what you are buying. There's no rule prohibiting you from buying a stock that begins with *r*, a stock that costs less than $6, or a stock in a company that's connected to the Teamsters. There's nobody to gripe, "I never heard of Wal-Mart" or "Dunkin' Donuts sounds silly—John D. Rockefeller wouldn't have invested in donuts." There's nobody to chide you for buying back a stock at $19 that you earlier sold at $11—which may be a perfectly sensible move. Professionals could never buy back a stock at $19 that they sold at $11. They'd have their Quotrons confiscated for doing that.

You're not forced to own 1,400 different stocks, nor is anyone going to tell you to sprinkle your money on 100 issues. You're free to own one stock, four stocks, or ten stocks. If no company seems attractive on the fundamentals, you can avoid stocks altogether and wait for a better opportunity. Equity fund managers do not have that luxury, either. We can't sell everything, and when we try, it's always all at once, and then there's nobody buying at decent prices.

Most important, you can find terrific opportunities in the neighborhood or at the workplace, months or even years before the news has reached the analysts and the fund managers they advise.

Then again, maybe you shouldn't have anything to do with the stock market, ever. That's an issue worth discussing in some detail, because the stock market demands conviction as surely as it victimizes the unconvinced.

3

Is This Gambling,
or What?

"Gentlemen prefer bonds."

—*Andrew Mellon*

After major upsets such as the Hiccup of Last October, some investors have taken refuge in bonds. This issue of stocks versus bonds is worth resolving right up front, and in a calm and dignified manner, or else it will come up again at the most frantic moments, when the stock market is dropping and people rush to the banks to sign up for CDs. Lately, just such a rush has occurred.

Investing in bonds, money-markets, or CDs are all different forms of investing in debt—for which one is paid interest. There's nothing wrong with getting paid interest, especially if it is compounded. Consider the Indians of Manhattan, who in 1626 sold all their real estate to a group of immigrants for $24 in trinkets and beads. For 362 years the Indians have been the subjects of cruel jokes because of it—but it turns out they may have made a better deal than the buyers who got the island.

At 8 percent interest on $24 (note: let's suspend our disbelief and assume they converted the trinkets to cash) compounded over all those years, the Indians would have built up a net worth just short of $30 trillion, while the latest tax records from the Borough of Manhattan show the real estate to be worth only $28.1 billion. Give Manhattan the benefit of the doubt: that $28.1 billion is the assessed value, and for all anybody knows it may be worth twice that on the open market. So Manhattan's worth $56.2 billion. Either way, the Indians could be ahead by $29 trillion and change.

Granted it's unlikely that the Indians could have gotten 8 percent interest, even at the kneecracker rates of the day, if in fact there were kneecracker rates in 1626. The pioneer borrowers were used to paying much less, but assuming the Indians could have wangled a 6 percent deal, they would have made $34.7 billion by now, and without having to maintain any property or mow Central Park. What a difference a couple of percentage points can make, compounded over three centuries.

However you figure it, there's something to be said for the supposed dupes in this transaction. Investing in debt isn't bad.

Bonds have been especially attractive in the last twenty years. Not in the fifty years before that, but definitely in the last twenty. Historically, interest rates never strayed far from 4 percent, but in the last decade we've seen long-term rates rise to 16 percent then fall to 8 percent, creating remarkable opportunities. People who bought U.S. Treasury bonds with 20-year maturities in 1980 have seen the face value of their bonds nearly double, and meanwhile they've still been collecting the 16 percent interest on their original investment. If you were smart enough to have bought 20-year T-bonds then, you've beaten the stock market by a sizable margin, even in this latest bull phase. Moreover, you've done it without having to read a single research report or having to pay a single tribute to a stockbroker.

(Long-term T-bonds are the best way to play interest rates because they aren't "callable"—or at least not until five years prior to maturity. As many disgruntled bond investors have discovered, many corporate and municipal bonds are callable much sooner, which means the debtors buy them back the minute it's advantageous to do so. Bondholders have no more choice in the matter than property owners who face a condemnation. As soon as interest rates begin to fall, causing bond investors to realize they've struck a shrewd bargain, the deal is canceled and they get their money back in the mail. On the other hand, if interest rates go in a direction that works against the bondholders, the bondholders are stuck with the bonds.

Since there's very little in the corporate bond business that isn't callable, you're advised to buy Treasuries if you hope to profit from a fall in interest rates.)

LIBERATING THE PASSBOOKS

Traditionally bonds were sold in large denominations—too large for the small investor, who could only invest in debt via the savings account, or the boring U.S. savings bonds. Then the bond funds were invented, and regular people could invest in debt right along with tycoons. After that, the money-market fund liberated millions of former passbook savers from the captivity of banks, once and for all. There ought to be a monument to Bruce Bent and Harry Browne, who dreamed up the money-market account and dared to lead the great exodus out of the Scroogian thrifts. They started it with the Reserve Fund in 1971.

My own boss, Ned Johnson, took the idea a thought further and added the check-writing feature. Prior to that, the money-market was most useful as a place where small corporations could park their weekly payroll funds. The check-writing feature gave the money-market fund universal appeal as a savings account and a checking account.

It's one thing to prefer stocks to a stodgy savings account that yields 5 percent forever, and quite another to prefer them to a money-market that offers the best short-term rates, and where the yields rise right away if the prevailing interest rates go higher.

If your money has stayed in a money-market fund since 1978, you certainly have no reason to feel embarrassed about it. You've missed a couple of major stock market declines. The worst you've ever collected is 6 percent interest, and you've never lost a penny of your principal. The year that short-term interest rates rose to 17 percent (1981) and the stock market dropped 5 percent, you made a 22 percent relative gain by staying in cash.

During the stock market's incredible surge from Dow 1775 on September 29, 1986, to Dow 2722 on August 25, 1987, let's say you never bought a single stock, and you felt dumber and dumber for having missed this once-in-a-lifetime opportunity. After a while you wouldn't even tell your friends you had all your money in a money-market—admitting to shoplifting would have been less mortifying.

But the morning after the crash, with the Dow beaten back to 1738, you felt vindicated. You avoided the whole trauma of October 19. With stock prices so drastically reduced, the money-market actually had outperformed the stock market over the entire year—6.12 percent for the money-market to 5.25 percent for the S&P 500.

THE STOCKS REBUT

But two months later the stock market had rebounded, and once again stocks were outperforming both money-market funds and long-term bonds. Over the long haul they always do. Historically, investing in stocks is undeniably more profitable than investing in debt. In fact, since 1927, common stocks have recorded gains of 9.8 percent a year on average, as compared to 5 percent for corporate bonds, 4.4 percent for government bonds, and 3.4 percent for Treasury bills.

The long-term inflation rate, as measured by the Consumer Price Index, is 3 percent a year, which gives common stocks a real return of 6.8 percent a year. The real return on Treasury bills, known as the most conservative and sensible of all places to put money, has been nil. That's right. Zippo.

The advantage of a 9.8 percent return from stocks over a 5 percent return from bonds may sound piddling to some, but consider this financial fable. If at the end of 1927 a modern Rip Van Winkle had gone to sleep for 60 years on $20,000 worth of corporate bonds, paying 5 percent compounded, he would have awakened with $373,584—enough for him to afford a nice condo, a Volvo, and a haircut; whereas if he'd invested in stocks, which returned 9.8 percent a year, he'd have $5,459,720. (Since Rip was asleep, neither the Crash of '29 nor the ripple of '87 would have scared him out of the market.)

In 1927, if you had put $1,000 in each of the four investments listed below, and the money had compounded tax-free, then 60 years later you'd have had these amounts:

Treasury bills	$ 7,400
Government bonds	13,200
Corporate bonds	17,600
Common stocks	272,000

In spite of crashes, depressions, wars, recessions, ten different presidential administrations, and numerous changes in skirt lengths, stocks in general have paid off fifteen times as well as corporate bonds, and well over thirty times better than Treasury bills!

There's a logical explanation for this. In stocks you've got the company's growth on your side. You're a partner in a prosperous and expanding business. In bonds, you're nothing more than the nearest source of spare change. When you lend money to somebody, the best you can hope for is to get it back, plus interest.

Think of the people who've owned McDonald's bonds over the years. The relationship between them and McDonald's begins and ends with the payoff of the debt, and that's not the exciting part of McDonald's. Sure, the original bondholders have gotten their money back, the same as they would have with a bank CD, but the original stockholders have gotten rich. They own the company. You'll never get a tenbagger in a bond—unless you're a debt sleuth who specializes in bonds in default.

WHAT ABOUT THE RISKS?

"Ah, yes," you say to yourself, especially after the latest drop in stock prices, "but what about the risks? Aren't stocks riskier than bonds?" Of course stocks are risky. Nowhere is it written that a stock owes us anything, as it's been proven to me on hundreds of sorry occasions.

Even blue-chip stocks held long term, supposedly the safest of all propositions, can be risky. RCA was a famous prudent investment, and suitable for widows and orphans, yet it was bought out by GE in 1986 for $66.50 a share, about the same price that it traded in 1967, and only 74 percent above its 1929 high of $38.25 (adjusted for splits). Less than one percent worth of annual appreciation is all you got in 57 years of sticking with a solid, world-famous, and successful company. Bethlehem Steel continues to sell far below its high of $60 a share reached in 1958.

Glance at a list of the original Dow Jones industrials from 1896. Who's ever heard of American Cotton Oil, Distilling and Cattle Feeding, Laclede Gas, U.S. Leather Preferred? These once-famous stocks must have vanished long ago.

Then from the 1916 list we see Baldwin Locomotive, gone by 1924; the 1925 list includes such household names as Paramount Famous Lasky and Remington Typewriter; in 1927, Remington Typewriter disappears and United Drug takes its place. In 1928, when the Dow Jones was expanded from 20 to 30 companies, the new arrivals included Nash Motors, Postum, Wright Aeronautical, and Victor Talking Machine. The latter two companies were removed by 1929—Victor Talking Machine because it had merged into RCA. (You've seen the results of sticking with that one.) In 1950, we find Corn Products Refining on the list, but by 1959 it, too, is taken off and replaced by Swift and Co.

The point is that fortunes change, there's no assurance that major companies won't become minor, and there's no such thing as a can't-miss blue chip.

Buy the right stocks at the wrong price at the wrong time and you'll suffer great losses. Look what happened in the 1972–74 market break, when conservative issues such as Bristol-Myers fell from $9 to $4, Teledyne from $11 to $3, and McDonald's from $15 to $4. These aren't exactly fly-by-night companies. Buy the wrong stocks at the right time and you'll suffer more of the same. During certain periods it seems to take forever for the theoretical 9.8 percent annual gain from stocks to show up in practice. The Dow Jones industrials reached an all-time high of 995.15 in 1966 and bounced along below that point until 1972. In turn, the high of 1972–73 wasn't exceeded until 1982.

But with the possible exception of the very short-term bonds and bond funds, bonds can be risky, too. Here, rising interest rates will force you to accept one of two unpleasant choices: suffer with the low yield until the bonds mature, or sell the bonds at a substantial discount to face value. If you are truly risk-averse, then the money-market fund or the bank is the place for you. Otherwise, there are risks wherever you turn.

Municipal bonds are thought to be as secure as cash in a strongbox, but on the rare occasion of a default, don't tell the losers that bonds are safe. (The best-known default is that of the Washington Public Power Supply System, and their infamous "Whoops" bonds.) Yes, I know bonds pay off in 99.9 percent of the cases, but there are other ways to lose money on bonds besides a default. Try holding on to a 30-year bond with a 6 percent coupon during a period of raging inflation, and see what happens to the value of the bond.

A lot of people have invested in funds that buy Government National Mortgage Association bonds (Ginnie Maes) without realizing how volatile the bond market has become. They are reassured by the ads—"100 percent government-guaranteed"—and they're right, the interest will be paid. But that doesn't protect the value of their shares in the bond fund when interest rates rise and the bond market collapses. Open the business page and look at what happens to such funds on a day that interest rates rise half a percent and you'll see what I mean. These days, bond funds fluctuate just as wildly as stock funds. The same volatility in interest rates that enables clever investors to make big profits from bonds also makes holding bonds more of a gamble.

STOCKS AND STUD POKER

Frankly, there is no way to separate investing from gambling into those neat categories that are meant to reassure us. There's simply no Chinese wall, bundling board, or any other absolute division between safe and rash places to store money. It was in the late 1920s that common stocks finally reached the status of "prudent investments," whereas previously they were dismissed as barroom wagers—and this was precisely the moment at which the overvalued market made buying stocks more wager than investment.

For two decades after the Crash, stocks were regarded as gambling by a majority of the population, and this impression wasn't fully revised until the late 1960s when stocks once again were embraced as investments, but in an overvalued market that made most stocks very risky. Historically, stocks are embraced as investments or dismissed as gambles in routine and circular fashion, and usually at the wrong times. ***Stocks are most likely to be accepted as prudent at the moment they're not.***

For years, stocks in large companies were considered "investments" and stocks in small companies "speculations," but lately small stocks have become investments and the speculating is done in futures and options. We're forever redrawing this line.

I'm always amused when people describe their investments as "conservative speculations" or else claim that they are "prudently speculating." Usually that means they hope they're investing but they're worried that they're gambling. The phrase "we're seeing one another" serves the same function for couples who can't decide if they're serious.

Once the unsettling fact of the risk in money is accepted, we can begin to separate gambling from investing not by the type of activity (buying bonds, buying stocks, betting on the horses, etc.) but by the skill, dedication, and enterprise of the participant. To a veteran handicapper with the discipline to stick to a system, betting on horses offers a relatively secure long-term return, which to him has been as reliable as owning a mutual fund, or shares in General Electric. Meanwhile, to the rash and impetuous stockpicker who chases hot tips and rushes in and out of his equities, an "investment" in stocks is no more reliable than throwing away paychecks on the horse with the prettiest mane, or the jockey with the purple silks.

(In fact, to the rash and impetuous stock player, my advice is: Forget Wall Street and take your mad money to Hialeah, Monte Carlo, Saratoga, Nassau, Santa Anita, or Baden-Baden. At least in those pleasant surroundings, when you lose, you'll be able to say you had a great time doing it. If you lose on stocks, there's no consolation in watching your broker pace around the office.

Also, when you lose mad money at the horses you simply throw your worthless tickets on the floor and you're done with it, but in stocks, options, and so forth you have to relive the painful episodes with the tax accountant every spring. It may take days of extra work to figure all this out.)

To me, an investment is simply a gamble in which you've managed to tilt the odds in your favor. It doesn't matter whether it's Atlantic City or the S&P 500 or the bond market. In fact, the stock market most reminds me of a stud poker game.

Betting on seven-card stud can provide a very consistent long-term return to people who know how to manage their cards. Four of the cards are dealt faceup, and you can not only see all of your hand but most of your opponents' hands. After the third or fourth card is dealt, it's pretty obvious who is likely to win and who is likely to lose, or else it's obvious there is no likely winner. It's the same on Wall Street. There's a lot of information in the open hands, if you know where to look for it.

By asking some basic questions about companies, you can learn which are likely to grow and prosper, which are unlikely to grow and prosper, and which are entirely mysterious. You can never be certain what will happen, but each new occurrence—a jump in earnings, the sale of an unprofitable subsidiary, the expansion into new markets—is like turning up another card. As long as the cards suggest favorable odds of success, you stay in the hand.

Anyone who plays regularly in a monthly stud poker game soon realizes that the same "lucky stiffs" always come out ahead. These are the players who undertake to maximize their return on investment by carefully calculating and recalculating their chances as the hand unfolds.

Consistent winners raise their bet as their position strengthens, and they exit the game when the odds are against them, while consistent losers hang on to the bitter end of every expensive pot, hoping for miracles and enjoying the thrill of defeat. In stud poker and on Wall Street, miracles happen just often enough to keep the losers losing.

Consistent winners also resign themselves to the fact that they'll occasionally be dealt three aces and bet the limit, only to lose to a hidden royal flush. They accept their fate and go on to the next hand, confident that their basic method will reward them over time. People who succeed in the stock market also accept periodic losses, setbacks, and unexpected occurrences. Calamitous drops do not scare them out of the game. If they've done the proper homework on H & R Block and bought the stock, and suddenly the government simplifies the tax code (an unlikely prospect, granted) and Block's business deteriorates, they accept the bad break and start looking for the next stock. They realize the stock market is not pure science, and not like chess, where the superior position always wins. If seven out of ten of my stocks perform as expected, then I'm delighted. If six out of ten of my stocks perform as expected, then I'm thankful. **Six out of ten is all it takes to produce an enviable record on Wall Street.**

Over time, the risks in the stock market can be reduced by proper play just as the risks in stud poker are reduced. With improper play (buying a stock that's overpriced) even the purchase of Bristol-Myers or Heinz can result in huge losses and wasted opportunities, as I've said. It happens to people who imagine that betting with blue chips relieves them of the need to pay attention, so they lose half their money in quick fashion and may not recoup it for another eight years. In the early 1970s millions of uninformed dollars chased overpriced opportunities and soon disappeared as a result. Does that make Bristol-Myers and McDonald's risky investments? Only because of the way people invested in them.

On the other hand, assuming you'd done the homework, putting your money on the risky and troubled General Public Utilities, the owners of the Three Mile Island nuclear problem, was far more "conservative" than an ill-timed investment in solid old Kellogg.

Not wanting to "risk" investment capital that belonged to my mother-in-law, Mrs. Charles Hoff, I once advised her to buy stock in Houston Industries, a very "safe" company. It was safe all right—the stock did nothing for more than a decade. I figured I could take more of a "gamble" with my own mother's money, so I bought her the "riskier" Consolidated Edison. It went up sixfold. Con Ed wasn't all that risky to those who had continued to monitor the fundamentals. The big winners come from the so-called high-risk categories, but the risks have more to do with the investors than with the categories.

The greatest advantage to investing in stocks, to one who accepts the uncertainties, is the extraordinary reward for being right. This is borne out in the mutual fund returns calculated by the Johnson Chart Service of Buffalo, New York. There's a very interesting correlation here: the "riskier" the fund, the better the payoff. If you'd put $10,000 into the average bond fund in 1963, fifteen years later you'd come out with $31,338. The same $10,000 in a balanced fund (stocks and bonds) would have produced $44,343; in a growth and income fund (all stocks), $53,157; and in an aggressive growth fund (also all stocks), $76,556.

Clearly the stock market has been a gamble worth taking—as long as you know how to play the game. And as long as you own stocks, new cards keep turning up. Now that I think of it, investing in stocks isn't really like playing a seven-card stud-poker hand. It's more like playing a 70-card stud-poker hand, or if you own ten stocks, it's like playing ten 70-card hands at once.

4

Passing the Mirror Test

"Is General Electric a good investment?" isn't the first thing I'd inquire about a stock. Even if General Electric is a good investment, it still doesn't mean you ought to own it. There's no point in studying the financial section until you've looked into the nearest mirror. Before you buy a share of anything, there are three personal issues that ought to be addressed: (1) Do I own a house? (2) Do I need the money? and (3) Do I have the personal qualities that will bring me success in stocks? Whether stocks make good or bad investments depends more on your responses to these three questions than on anything you'll read in *The Wall Street Journal*.

(1) DO I OWN A HOUSE?

As they might say on Wall Street, "A house, what a deal!" Before you do invest anything in stocks, you ought to consider buying a house, since a house, after all, is the one good investment that almost everyone manages to make. I'm sure there are exceptions, such as houses built over sinkholes and houses in fancy neighborhoods that take a dive, but in 99 cases out of 100, a house will be a money-maker.

How many times have you heard a friend or an acquaintance lament: "I'm a lousy investor in my house"? I'd bet it's not often. Millions of real estate amateurs have invested brilliantly in their houses. There are sometimes families that must move quickly and are forced to sell at a loss, but it's the rare individual who manages to lose money on a string of residences one after another, the way it routinely happens with stocks. It's a rarer individual yet who gets wiped out on a house, waking up one morning to discover that the premises have declared bankruptcy or turned belly up, which is the sad fate of many equities.

It's no accident that people who are geniuses in their houses are idiots in their stocks. A house is entirely rigged in the homeowner's favor. The banks let you acquire it for 20 percent down and in some cases less, giving you the remarkable power of leverage. (True, you can buy stocks with 50 percent cash down, which is known in the trade as "buying on margin," but every time a stock bought on margin drops in price, you have to put up more cash. That doesn't happen with a house. You never have to put up more cash if the market value goes down, even if the house is located in the depressed oil patch. The real estate agent never calls at midnight to announce: "You'll have to come up with twenty thousand dollars by eleven A.M. tomorrow or else sell off two bedrooms," which frequently happens to stockholders forced to sell their shares bought on margin. This is another great advantage to owning a house.)

Because of leverage, if you buy a $100,000 house for 20 percent down and the value of the house increases by five percent a year, you are making a 25 percent return on your down payment, and the interest on the loan is tax-deductible. Do that well in the stock market and eventually you'd be worth more than Boone Pickens.

As a bonus you get a federal tax deduction on the local real estate tax on the house, plus the house is a perfect hedge against inflation and a great place to hide out during a recession, not to mention the roof over your head. Then at the end, if you decide to cash in your house, you can roll the proceeds into a fancier house to avoid paying taxes on your profit.

The customary progression in houses is as follows: You buy a small house (a starter house), then a medium-sized house, then a larger house that eventually you don't need. After the children have moved away, then you sell the big house and revert to a smaller house, making a sizable profit in the transition. This windfall isn't taxed, because the government in its compassion gives you a once-in-a-lifetime house windfall exemption. That never happens in stocks, which are taxed as frequently and as heavily as possible.

You can have a forty-year run in houses without paying taxes, culminating in the sweetheart exclusion. Or if there are any taxes to be paid, by now you are in a lower tax bracket, so they won't be so bad.

The old Wall Street adage "Never invest in anything that eats or needs repairs" may apply to racehorses, but it's malarkey when it comes to houses.

There are important secondary reasons you'll do better in houses than in stocks. It's not likely you'll get scared out of your house by reading a headline in the Sunday real estate section: "Home Prices Take Dive." They don't publish the Friday afternoon closing market price of your home address in the classifieds, nor do they run it across the ticker tape at the bottom of your TV, and newscasters do not come on with lists of the ten most active houses—"100 Orchard Lane is down ten percent today. Neighbors saw nothing unusual to account for this unexpected decline."

Houses, like stocks, are most likely to be profitable when they're held for a long period of time. Unlike stocks, houses are likely to be owned by the same person for a number of years—seven, I think, is the average. Compare this to the 87 percent of all the stocks on the New York Stock Exchange that change hands every year. People get much more comfortable in their houses than they do in their stocks. It takes a moving van to get out of a house, and only a phone call to get out of a stock.

Finally, you're a good investor in houses because you know how to poke around from the attic to the basement and ask the right questions. The skill of poking around houses is handed down. You grow up watching how your parents checked into the public services, the schools, the drainage, the septic perk test, and the taxes. You remember rules such as "Don't buy the highest-priced property on the block." You can spot neighborhoods on the way up and neighborhoods on the way down. You can drive through an area and see what's being fixed up, what's run-down, how many houses are left to renovate. Then, before you make an offer on a house, you hire experts to search for termites, roof leaks, dry rot, rusty pipes, faulty wiring, and cracks in the foundation.

No wonder people make money in the real estate market and lose money in the stock market. They spend months choosing their houses, and minutes choosing their stocks. In fact, they spend more time shopping for a good microwave oven than shopping for a good investment.

(2) DO I NEED THE MONEY?

This brings us to question two. It makes sense to review the family budget before you buy stocks. For instance, if you're going to have to pay for a child's college education in two or three years, don't put that money into stocks. Maybe you're a widow (there are always a few widows in these stock market books) and your son Dexter, now a sophomore in high school, has a chance to get into Harvard—but not on a scholarship. Since you can scarcely afford the tuition as it is, you're tempted to increase your net worth with conservative blue-chip stocks.

In this instance, even buying blue-chip stocks would be too risky to consider. Absent a lot of surprises, stocks are relatively predictable over ten to twenty years. As to whether they're going to be higher or lower in two or three years, you might as well flip a coin to decide. Blue chips can fall down and stay down over a three-year period or even a five-year period, so if the market hits a banana peel, then Dexter's going to night school.

Maybe you're an older person who needs to live off a fixed income, or a younger person who can't stand working and wants to live off a fixed income from the family inheritance. Either way, you should stay out of the stock market. There are all kinds of complicated formulas for figuring out what percentage of your assets should be put into stocks, but I have a simple one, and it's the same for Wall Street as it is for the racetrack. *Only invest what you could afford to lose without that loss having any effect on your daily life in the foreseeable future.*

(3) DO I HAVE THE PERSONAL QUALITIES IT TAKES TO SUCCEED?

This is the most important question of all. It seems to me the list of qualities ought to include patience, self-reliance, common sense, a tolerance for pain, open-mindedness, detachment, persistence, humility, flexibility, a willingness to do independent research, an equal willingness to admit to mistakes, and the ability to ignore general panic. In terms of IQ, probably the best investors fall somewhere above the bottom ten percent but also below the top three percent. The true geniuses, it seems to me, get too enamored of theoretical cogitations and are forever betrayed by the actual behavior of stocks, which is more simple-minded than they can imagine.

It's also important to be able to make decisions without complete or perfect information. Things are almost never clear on Wall Street, or when they are, then it's too late to profit from them. The scientific mind that needs to know all the data will be thwarted here.

And finally, it's crucial to be able to resist your human nature and your "gut feelings." It's the rare investor who doesn't secretly harbor the conviction that he or she has a knack for divining stock prices or gold prices or interest rates, in spite of the fact that most of us have been proven wrong again and again. It's uncanny how often people feel most strongly that stocks are going to go up or the economy is going to improve just when the opposite occurs. This is borne out by the popular investment-advisory newsletter services, which themselves tend to turn bullish and bearish at inopportune moments.

According to information published by Investor's Intelligence, which tracks investor sentiment via the newsletters, at the end of 1972, when stocks were about to tumble, optimism was at an all-time high, with only 15 percent of the advisors bearish. At the beginning of the stock market rebound in 1974, investor sentiment was at an all-time low, with 65 percent of the advisors fearing the worst was yet to come. Before the market turned downward in 1977, once again the newsletter writers were optimistic, with only 10 percent bears. At the start of the 1982 sendoff into a great bull market, 55 percent of the advisors were bears, and just prior to the big gulp of October 19, 1987, 80 percent of the advisors were bulls again.

The problem isn't that investors and their advisors are chronically stupid or unperceptive. It's that by the time the signal is received, the message may already have changed. When enough positive general financial news filters down so that the majority of investors feel truly confident in the short-term prospects, the economy is soon to get hammered.

What else explains the fact that large numbers of investors (including CEOs and sophisticated business people) have been most afraid of stocks during the precise periods when stocks have done their best (i.e., from the mid-1930s to the late 1960s) while being least afraid precisely when stocks have done their worst (i.e., early 1970s and recently in the fall of 1987). Does the success of Ravi Batra's book *The Great Depression of 1990* almost guarantee a great national prosperity?

It's amazing how quickly investor sentiment can be reversed, even when reality hasn't changed. A week or two before the Big Burp of October, business travelers were driving through Atlanta, Orlando, or Chicago, admiring the new construction and remarking to each other, "Wow. What a glorious boom." A few days later, I'm sure those same travelers were looking at those same buildings and saying: "Boy, this place has problems. How are they ever going to sell all those condos and rent all that office space?"

Things inside humans make them terrible stock market timers. The unwary investor continually passes in and out of three emotional states: concern, complacency, and capitulation. He's concerned after the market has dropped or the economy has seemed to falter, which keeps him from buying good companies at bargain prices. Then after he buys at higher prices, he gets complacent because his stocks are going up. This is precisely the time he ought to be concerned enough to check the fundamentals, but he isn't. Then finally, when his stocks fall on hard times and the prices fall to below what he paid, he capitulates and sells in a snit.

Some have fancied themselves "long-term investors," but only until the next big drop (or tiny gain), at which point they quickly become short-term investors and sell out for huge losses or the occasional minuscule profit. It's easy to panic in this volatile business. Since I've run Magellan, the fund has declined from 10 to 35 percent during eight bearish episodes, and in 1987 alone the fund was up 40 percent in August, down 11 percent by December. We finished the year with a 1 percent gain, thus barely preserving my record of never having had a down year—knock on wood. Recently I read that the price of an average stock fluctuates 50 percent in an average year. If that's true, and apparently it's been true throughout this century, then any share currently selling for $50 is likely to hit $60 and/or fall to $40 sometime in the next twelve months. In other words, the high for the year ($60) is 50 percent higher than the low ($40). If you're the kind of buyer who can't resist getting in at $50, buying more at $60 ("See, I was right, that sucker *is* going up"), and then selling out in despair at $40 ("I guess I was wrong. That sucker's going *down"*) then no shelf of how-to books is going to help you.

Some have fancied themselves contrarians, believing that they can profit by zigging when the rest of the world is zagging, but it didn't occur to them to become contrarian until that idea had already gotten so popular that contrarianism became the accepted view. The true contrarian is not the investor who takes the opposite side of a popular hot issue (i.e., shorting a stock that everyone else is buying). The true contrarian waits for things to cool down and buys stocks that nobody cares about, and especially those that make Wall Street yawn.

When E.F. Hutton talks, everybody is supposed to be listening, but that's just the problem. Everybody ought to be trying to fall asleep. When it comes to predicting the market, the important skill here is not listening, it's snoring. The trick is not to learn to trust your gut feelings, but rather to discipline yourself to ignore them. Stand by your stocks as long as the fundamental story of the company hasn't changed.

If not, your only hope for increasing your net worth may be to adopt J. Paul Getty's surefire formula for financial success: "Rise early, work hard, strike oil."

5

Is This a Good Market?
Please Don't Ask

During every question-and-answer period after I give a speech, somebody stands up and asks me if we're in a good market or a bad market. For every person who wonders if Goodyear Tire is a solid company, or well-priced at current levels, four other people want to know if the bull is alive and kicking, or if the bear has shown its grizzly face. I always tell them the only thing I know about predicting markets is that every time I get promoted, the market goes down. As soon as those words are launched from my lips, somebody else stands up and asks me when I'm due for another promotion.

Obviously you don't have to be able to predict the stock market to make money in stocks, or else I wouldn't have made any money. I've sat right here at my Quotron through some of the most terrible drops, and I couldn't have figured them out beforehand if my life had depended on it. In the middle of the summer of 1987, I didn't warn anybody, and least of all myself, about the imminent 1,000-point decline.

I wasn't the only one who failed to issue a warning. In fact, if ignorance loves company, then I was very comfortably surrounded by a large and impressive mob of famous seers, prognosticators, and other experts who failed to see it, too. "If you must forecast," an intelligent forecaster once said, "forecast often."

Nobody called to inform me of an immediate collapse in October, and if all the people who claimed to have predicted it beforehand had sold out their shares, then the market would have dropped the 1,000 points much earlier due to these great crowds of informed sellers.

Every year I talk to the executives of a thousand companies, and I can't avoid hearing from the various gold bugs, interest-rate disciples, Federal Reserve watchers, and fiscal mystics quoted in the newspapers. Thousands of experts study overbought indicators, oversold indicators, head-and-shoulder patterns, put-call ratios, the Fed's policy on money supply, foreign investment, the movement of the constellations through the heavens, and the moss on oak trees, and they can't predict markets with any useful consistency, any more than the gizzard squeezers could tell the Roman emperors when the Huns would attack.

Nobody sent up any warning flares before the 1973–74 stock market debacle, either. Back in graduate school I learned the market goes up 9 percent a year, and since then it's never gone up 9 percent in a year, and I've yet to find a reliable source to inform me how much it will go up, or simply whether it will go up or down. All the major advances and declines have been surprises to me.

Since the stock market is in some way related to the general economy, one way that people try to outguess the market is to predict inflation and recessions, booms and busts, and the direction of interest rates. True, there is a wonderful correlation between interest rates and the stock market, but who can foretell interest rates with any bankable regularity? There are 60,000 economists in the U.S., many of them employed full-time trying to forecast recessions and interest rates, and if they could do it successfully twice in a row, they'd all be millionaires by now.

They'd have retired to Bimini where they could drink rum and fish for marlin. But as far as I know, most of them are still gainfully employed, which ought to tell us something. As some perceptive person once said, if all the economists of the world were laid end to end, it wouldn't be a bad thing.

Well, maybe not *all* economists. Certainly not the ones who are reading this book, and especially not the ones like Ed Hyman at C. J. Lawrence who looks at scrap prices, inventories, and railroad car deliveries, totally ignoring Laffer curves and phases of the moon. Practical economists are economists after my own heart.

There's another theory that we have recessions every five years, but it hasn't happened that way so far. I've looked in the Constitution, and nowhere is it written that every fifth year we have to have one. Of course, I'd love to be warned before we do go into a recession, so I could adjust my portfolio. But the odds of my figuring it out are nil. Some people wait for these bells to go off, to signal the end of a recession or the beginning of an exciting new bull market. The trouble is the bells never go off. Remember, things are never clear until it's too late.

There was a 16-month recession between July, 1981, and November, 1982. Actually this was the scariest time in my memory. Sensible professionals wondered if they should take up hunting and fishing, because soon we'd all be living in the woods, gathering acorns. This was a period when we had 14 percent unemployment, 15 percent inflation, and a 20-percent prime rate, but I never got a phone call saying any of that was going to happen, either. After the fact a lot of people stood up to announce they'd been expecting it, but nobody mentioned it to me before the fact.

Then at the moment of greatest pessimism, when eight out of ten investors would have sworn we were heading into the 1930s, the stock market rebounded with a vengeance, and suddenly all was right with the world.

PENULTIMATE PREPAREDNESS

No matter how we arrive at the latest financial conclusion, we always seem to be preparing ourselves for the *last* thing that's happened, as opposed to what's going to happen next. This "penultimate preparedness" is our way of making up for the fact that we didn't see the last thing coming along in the first place.

The day after the market crashed on October 19, people began to worry that the market was *going* to crash. It had already crashed and we'd survived it (in spite of our not having predicted it), and now we were petrified there'd be a replay. Those who got out of the market to ensure that they wouldn't be fooled the next time as they had been the last time were fooled again as the market went up.

The great joke is that the next time is never like the last time, and yet we can't help readying ourselves for it anyway. This all reminds me of the Mayan conception of the universe.

In Mayan mythology the universe was destroyed four times, and every time the Mayans learned a sad lesson and vowed to be better protected—but it was always for the previous menace. First there was a flood, and the survivors remembered it and moved to higher ground into the woods, built dikes and retaining walls, and put their houses in the trees. Their efforts went for naught because the next time around the world was destroyed by fire.

After that, the survivors of the fire came down out of the trees and ran as far away from woods as possible. They built new houses out of stone, particularly along a craggy fissure. Soon enough, the world was destroyed by an earthquake. I don't remember the fourth bad thing that happened—maybe a recession—but whatever it was, the Mayans were going to miss it. They were too busy building shelters for the next earthquake.

Two thousand years later we're still looking backward for signs of the upcoming menace, but that's only if we can decide what the upcoming menace is. Not long ago, people were worried that oil prices would drop to $5 a barrel and we'd have a depression. Two years before that, those same people were worried that oil prices would rise to $100 a barrel and we'd have a depression. Once they were scared that the money supply was growing too fast. Now they're scared that it's growing too slow. The last time we prepared for inflation we got a recession, and then at the end of the recession we prepared for more recession and we got inflation.

Someday there will be another recession, which will be very bad for the stock market, as opposed to the inflation that is also very bad for the stock market. Maybe there will already have been a recession between now and the time this is published. Maybe we won't get one until 1990, or 1994. You're asking me?

THE COCKTAIL THEORY

If professional economists can't predict economies and professional forecasters can't predict markets, then what chance does the amateur investor have? You know the answer already, which brings me to my own "cocktail party" theory of market forecasting, developed over years of standing in the middle of living rooms, near punch bowls, listening to what the nearest ten people said about stocks.

In the first stage of an upward market—one that has been down awhile and that nobody expects to rise again—people aren't talking about stocks. In fact, if they lumber up to ask me what I do for a living, and I answer, "I manage an equity mutual fund," they nod politely and wander away. If they don't wander away, then they quickly change the subject to the Celtics game, the upcoming elections, or the weather. Soon they are talking to a nearby dentist about plaque.

When ten people would rather talk to a dentist about plaque than to the manager of an equity mutual fund about stocks, it's likely that the market is about to turn up.

In stage two, after I've confessed what I do for a living, the new acquaintances linger a bit longer—perhaps long enough to tell me how risky the stock market is—before they move over to talk to the dentist. The cocktail party talk is still more about plaque than about stocks. The market's up 15 percent from stage one, but few are paying attention.

In stage three, with the market up 30 percent from stage one, a crowd of interested parties ignores the dentist and circles around me all evening. A succession of enthusiastic individuals takes me aside to ask what stocks they should buy. Even the dentist is asking me what stocks he should buy. Everybody at the party has put money into one issue or another, and they're all discussing what's happened.

In stage four, once again they're crowded around me—but this time it's to tell *me* what stocks *I* should buy. Even the dentist has three or four tips, and in the next few days I look up his recommendations in the newspaper and they've all gone up. When the neighbors tell me what to buy and then I wish I had taken their advice, it's a sure sign that the market has reached a top and is due for a tumble.

Do what you want with this, but don't expect me to bet on the cocktail party theory. I don't believe in predicting markets. I believe in buying great companies—especially companies that are undervalued, and/or underappreciated. Whether the Dow Jones industrial average was at 1,000 or 2,000 or 3,000 points today, you'd be better off having owned Marriott, Merck, and McDonald's than having owned Avon Products, Bethlehem Steel, and Xerox over the last ten years. You'd also be better off having owned Marriott, Merck, or McDonald's than if you'd put the money into bonds or money-market funds over the same period.

If you had bought stocks in great companies back in 1925 and held on to them through the Crash and into the Depression (admittedly this wouldn't have been easy), by 1936 you would have been very pleased at the results.

WHAT STOCK MARKET?

The market ought to be irrelevant. If I could convince you of this one thing, I'd feel this book had done its job. And if you don't believe me, believe Warren Buffett. "As far as I'm concerned," Buffett has written, "the stock market doesn't exist. It is there only as a reference to see if anybody is offering to do anything foolish."

Buffett has turned his Berkshire Hathaway into an extraordinarily profitable enterprise. In the early 1960s it cost $7 to buy a share in his great company, and that same share is worth $4,900 today. A $2,000 investment in Berkshire Hathaway back then has resulted in a 700-bagger that's worth $1.4 million today. That makes Buffett a wonderful investor. What makes him the greatest investor of all time is that during a certain period when he thought stocks were grossly overpriced, he sold everything and returned all the money to his partners at a sizable profit to them. The voluntary returning of money that others would gladly pay you to continue to manage is, in my experience, unique in the history of finance.

I'd love to be able to predict markets and anticipate recessions, but since that's impossible, I'm as satisfied to search out profitable companies as Buffett is. I've made money even in lousy markets, and vice versa. Several of my favorite tenbaggers made their biggest moves during bad markets. Taco Bell soared through the last two recessions. The only down year in the stock market in the eighties was 1981, and yet it was the perfect time to buy Dreyfus, which began its fantastic march from $2 to $40, the twentybagger that yours truly managed to miss.

Just for the sake of argument, let's say you could predict the next economic boom with absolute certainty, and you wanted to profit from your foresight by picking a few high-flying stocks. You still have to pick the right stocks, just the same as if you had no foresight.

If you knew there was going to be a Florida real estate boom and you picked Radice out of a hat, you would have lost 95 percent of your investment. If you knew there was a computer boom and you picked Fortune Systems without doing any homework, you'd have seen it fall from $22 in 1983 to $1⅞ in 1984. If you knew the early 1980s was bullish for airlines, what good would it have done if you'd invested in People Express (which promptly bought the farm) or Pan Am (which declined from $9 in 1983 to $4 in 1984 thanks to inept management)?

Let's say you knew that steel was making a comeback, and so you took a list of steel stocks, taped it to a dart board, and threw a dart at LTV. LTV declined from $26½ to $1⅛ between 1981 and 1986, roughly the period in which Nucor, a company in the same industry, rose from $10 to $50. (I owned both, so why did I sell my Nucor and hold on to my LTV? I might as well have thrown darts, too.)

In case after case the proper picking of markets would have resulted in your losing half your assets because you'd picked the wrong stocks. If you rely on the market to drag your stock along, then you might as well take the bus to Atlantic City and bet on red or black. If you wake up in the morning and think to yourself, "I'm going to buy stocks because I think the market is going up this year," then you ought to pull the phone out of the wall and stay as far away as possible from the nearest broker. You're relying on the market to bail you out, and chances are, it won't.

If you want to worry about something, worry about whether the sheet business is getting better at West Point-Pepperell, or whether Taco Bell is doing well with its new burrito supreme. Pick the right stocks and the market will take care of itself.

That's not to say there isn't such a thing as an overvalued market, but there's no point worrying about it. The way you'll know when the market is overvalued is when you can't find a single company that's reasonably priced or that meets your other criteria for investment. The reason Buffett returned his partners' money was that he said he couldn't find any stocks worth owning. He'd looked over hundreds of individual companies and found not one he'd buy on the fundamental merits.

The only buy signal I need is to find a company I like. In that case, it's never too soon nor too late to buy shares.

What I hope you'll remember most from this section are the following points:

- Don't overestimate the skill and wisdom of professionals.
- Take advantage of what you already know.
- Look for opportunities that haven't yet been discovered and certified by Wall Street—companies that are "off the radar scope."
- Invest in a house before you invest in a stock.
- Invest in companies, not in the stock market.
- Ignore short-term fluctuations.
- Large profits can be made in common stocks.
- Large losses can be made in common stocks.

- Predicting the economy is futile.
- Predicting the short-term direction of the stock market is futile.
- The long-term returns from stocks are both relatively predictable and also far superior to the long-term returns from bonds.
- Keeping up with a company in which you own stock is like playing an endless stud-poker hand.
- Common stocks aren't for everyone, nor even for all phases of a person's life.
- The average person is exposed to interesting local companies and products years before the professionals.
- Having an edge will help you make money in stocks.
- In the stock market, one in the hand is worth ten in the bush.

Part II
PICKING
WINNERS

In this section we'll discuss how to exploit an edge, how to find the most promising investments, how to evaluate what you own and what you can expect to gain in each of six different categories of stocks, the characteristics of the perfect company, the characteristics of companies that should be avoided at all costs, the importance of earnings to the eventual success or failure of any stock, the questions to ask in researching a stock, how to monitor a company's progress, how to get the facts, and how to evaluate the important benchmarks, such as cash, debt, price/earning ratios, profit margins, book value, dividends, etc.

6

Stalking the Tenbagger

The best place to begin looking for the tenbagger is close to home—if not in the backyard then down at the shopping mall, and especially wherever you happen to work. With most of the tenbaggers already mentioned—Dunkin' Donuts, The Limited, Subaru, Dreyfus, McDonald's, Tambrands, and Pep Boys—the first sips of success were apparent at hundreds of locations across the country. The fireman in New England, the customers in central Ohio where Kentucky Fried Chicken first opened up, the mob down at Pic 'N' Save, all had a chance to say, "This is great; I wonder about the stock," long before Wall Street got its original clue.

The average person comes across a likely prospect two or three times a year—sometimes more. Executives at Pep Boys, clerks at Pep Boys, lawyers and accountants, suppliers of Pep Boys, the firm that did the advertising, sign painters, building contractors for the new stores, and even the people who washed the floors all must have observed Pep Boys' success. Thousands of potential investors got this "tip," and that doesn't even count the hundreds of thousands of customers.

At the same time, the Pep Boys employee who buys insurance for the company could have noticed that insurance prices were going up—which is a good sign that the insurance industry is about to turn around

—and so maybe he'd consider investing in the insurance suppliers. Or maybe the Pep Boys building contractors noticed that cement prices had firmed, which is good news for the companies that supply cement.

All along the retail and wholesale chains, people who make things, sell things, clean things, or analyze things encounter numerous stock-picking opportunities. In my own business—the mutual-fund industry—the salesmen, clerks, secretaries, analysts, accountants, telephone operators, and computer installers, all could scarcely have overlooked the great boom of the early 1980s that sent mutual-fund stocks soaring.

You don't have to be a vice president at Exxon to sense the growing prosperity in that company, or a turnaround in oil prices. You can be a roustabout, a geologist, a driller, a supplier, a gas-station owner, a grease monkey, or even a client at the gas pumps.

You don't have to work in Kodak's main office to learn that the new generation of inexpensive, easy-to-use, high-quality 35mm cameras from Japan is reviving the photo industry, and that film sales are up. You could be a film salesman, the owner of a camera store, or a clerk in a camera store. You could also be the local wedding photographer who notices that five or six relatives are taking unofficial pictures at weddings and making it harder for you to get good shots.

You don't have to be Steven Spielberg to know that some new blockbuster, or string of blockbusters, is going to give a significant boost to the earnings of Paramount or Orion Pictures. You could be an actor, an extra, a director, a stuntman, a lawyer, a gaffer, the makeup person, or the usher at a local cinema, where the standing-room-only crowds six weeks in a row inspire you to investigate the pros and cons of investing in Orion's stock.

Maybe you're a teacher and the school board chooses your school to test a new gizmo that takes attendance, saving the teachers thousands of wasted hours counting heads. "Who makes this gizmo?" is the first question I'd ask.

How about Automatic Data Processing, which processes nine million paychecks a week for 180,000 small and medium-sized companies? This has been one of the all-time great opportunities: The company went public in 1961 and has increased earnings every year without a lapse. The worst it ever did was to earn 11 percent more than the previous year, and that was during the 1982–83 recession when many companies reported losses.

Automatic Data Processing sounds like the sort of high-tech enterprise I try to avoid, but in reality it's not a computer company. It uses computers to process paychecks, and users of technology are the biggest beneficiaries of high-tech. As competition drives down the price of computers, a firm such as Automatic Data can buy the cheaper equipment, so its costs are continually reduced. This only adds to profits.

Without fanfare, this mundane enterprise that came public at six cents a share (adjusted for splits) now sells for $40—a 600-bagger long-term. It got as high as $54 before the October stumble. The company has twice as much cash as debt and shows no sign of slowing down.

The officers and employees of 180,000 client firms could certainly have known about the success of Automatic Data Processing, and since many of Automatic Data's biggest and best customers are major brokerage houses, so could half of Wall Street.

So often we struggle to pick a winning stock, when all the while a winning stock has been struggling to pick us.

THE TENBAGGER IN ULCERS

Can't think of any such opportunity in your own life? What if you're retired, live ten miles from the nearest traffic light, grow your own food, and don't have a television set? Well, maybe one day you have to go to a doctor. The rural existence has given you ulcers, which is the perfect introduction to SmithKline Beckman.

Hundreds of doctors, thousands of patients, and millions of friends and relatives of patients heard about the wonder drug Tagamet, which came on the market in 1976. So did the pharmacist who dispensed the pills and the delivery boy who spent half his workday delivering them. Tagamet was a boon for the afflicted, and a bonanza for investors.

A great patients' drug is one that cures an affliction once and for all, but a great investor's drug is one that the patient has to keep buying. Tagamet was one of the latter. It provided fantastic relief from the suffering from ulcers, and the direct beneficiaries had to keep taking it again and again, making indirect beneficiaries out of the shareholders of Smith-Kline Beckman, the makers of Tagamet. Thanks largely to Tagamet, the stock rose from $7½ a share in 1977 to $72 a share at the 1987 high.

These users and prescribers had a big lead on the Wall Street talent. No doubt some of the oxymorons suffered from ulcers themselves—this is an anxious business—but SmithKline must not have been included on their buy lists, because it was a year before the stock began its ascent.

During the testing period for the drug, 1974–76, the price climbed from around $4 to $7, and when the government approved Tagamet in 1977, the stock sold for $11. From there it shot up to $72 (see chart).*

Then if you missed Tagamet, you had a second chance with Glaxo and its own wonder drug for ulcers—Zantac. Zantac went through testing in the early eighties and got its U.S. approval in 1983. Zantac was just as well-received as Tagamet, and just as profitable to Glaxo. In mid-1983 Glaxo's stock sold for $7.50 and moved up to $30 in 1987.

Did the doctors who prescribed Tagamet and Zantac buy shares in SmithKline and Glaxo? Somehow I doubt that many did. It's more likely that the doctors were fully invested in oil stocks. Perhaps they heard that Union Oil of California was a takeover candidate. Meanwhile, the Union Oil executives were probably buying drug stocks, especially the hot issues like American Surgery Centers, which sold for $18.50 in 1982 and fell to 5 cents.

In general, if you polled all the doctors, I'd bet only a small percentage would turn out to be invested in medical stocks, and more would be invested in oil; and if you polled the shoe-store owners, more would be invested in aerospace than in shoes, while the aerospace engineers are more likely to dabble in shoe stocks. Why it is that stock certificates, like grasses, are always greener in somebody else's pasture I'm not sure.

Perhaps a winning investment seems so unlikely in the first place that people can best imagine it happening as far away as possible, somewhere off in the Great Beyond, just as we all imagine that perfect behavior takes place in heaven and not on earth. Therefore the doctor who understands the ethical drug business inside out is more comfortable investing in Schlumberger, an oil-service company about which he knows nothing; while the managers of Schlumberger are likely to own Johnson & Johnson or American Home Products.

True, true. You don't necessarily have to know anything about a company for its stock to go up. But the important point is that (1) the

---

* Throughout the day I'm constantly referring to stock charts. I keep a long-term chart book close to my side at the office, and another one at home, to remind me of momentous and humbling occurrences.

What most people get out of family photo albums, I get out of these wonderful publications. If my life were to flash before my eyes, I bet I'd see the chart of Flying Tiger, my first tenbagger; of Apple Computer, a stock I rediscovered thanks in part to my family; and Polaroid, which makes me remember the new camera that my wife and I took on our honeymoon. That was back in a more primitive era, when we had to let the film develop for sixty seconds before we could see the picture. Since neither of us had a watch, Carolyn used her physiology training and counted out the seconds with her pulse.

SMITHKLINE BECKMAN CORPORATION (SKB)

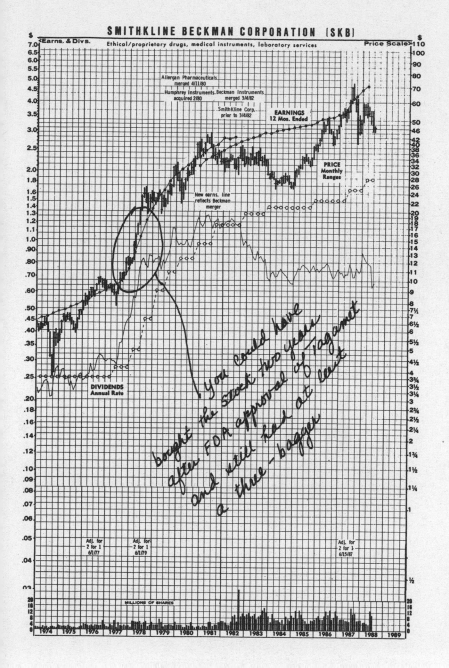

Ethical/proprietary drugs, medical instruments, laboratory services

Earns. & Divs.

Price Scale

Allergan Pharmaceuticals merged 4/11/80

Humphrey Instruments acquired 2/80 · Beckman Instruments merged 3/4/80

SmithKline Corp. prior to 3/4/82

EARNINGS
12 Mos. Ended

PRICE
Monthly
Ranges

New earns. line reflects Beckman merger

DIVIDENDS
Annual Rate

you could have bought the stock two years after FDA approval of Tagamet and still have at least a three-bagger

Adj. for 2 for 1 6/1/77

Adj. for 2 for 1 6/1/79

Adj. for 2 for 1 6/15/87

MILLIONS OF SHARES

1974 1975 1976 1977 1978 1979 1980 1981 1982 1983 1984 1985 1986 1987 1988 1989

oil experts, on average, are in a better position than doctors to decide when to buy or to sell Schlumberger; and (2) the doctors, on average, know better than oil experts when to invest in a successful drug. The person with the edge is always in a position to outguess the person without an edge—who after all will be the last to learn of important changes in a given industry.

The oilman who invests in SmithKline because his broker suggests it won't realize that patients have abandoned Tagamet and switched to a rival ulcer drug until the stock is down 40 percent and the bad news has been fully "discounted" in the price. "Discounting" is a Wall Street euphemism for pretending to have anticipated surprising developments.

On the other hand, the oilman will be among the earliest to observe the telltale signs of revival in the oil patch, a revival that will inspire Schlumberger's eventual comeback.

Though people who buy stocks about which they are ignorant may get lucky and enjoy great rewards, it seems to me they are competing under unnecessary handicaps, just like the marathon runner who decides to stake his reputation on a bobsled race.

THE DOUBLE EDGE

Here we've been talking about the oil executive and his knowledge, and lumping him and it together in the same chapter with the knowledge of the customers in the checkout line at Pep Boys. Of course it's absurd to contend that the one is equal to the other. One is a professional's understanding of the workings of an industry; the other is a consumer's awareness of a likable product. Both are useful in picking stocks, but in different ways.

The professional's edge is especially helpful in knowing when and when not to buy shares in companies that have been around awhile, especially those in the so-called cyclical industries. If you work in the chemical industry, then you'll be among the first to realize that demand for polyvinyl chloride is going up, prices are going up, and excess inventories are going down. You'll be in a position to know that no new competitors have entered the market and no new plants are under construction, and that it takes two to three years to build one. All this means higher profits for existing companies that make the product.

Or if you own a Goodyear tire store and suddenly after three years of sluggish sales you notice that you can't keep up with new orders, you've just received a strong signal that Goodyear may be on the rise. You already know that Goodyear's new high-performance tire is the best. You call up your broker and ask for the latest background information on the tire company, instead of waiting for the broker to call to tell you about Wang Laboratories.

Unless you work in some job that's related to computers, what good is a Wang tip to you? What could you possibly know that thousands of other people don't know a lot better? If the answer is "nada," then you haven't got an edge in Wang. But if you sell tires, make tires, or distribute tires, you've got an edge in Goodyear. All along the supply lines of the manufacturing industry, people who make things and sell things encounter numerous stockpicking opportunities.

It might be a service industry, the property-casualty insurance business, or even the book business where you can spot a turnaround. Buyers and sellers of any product notice shortages and gluts, price changes and shifts in demand. Such information isn't very valuable in the auto industry, since car sales are reported every ten days. Wall Street is obsessed with cars. But in most other endeavors the grassroots observer can spot a turnaround six to twelve months ahead of the regular financial analysts. This gives an incredible head start in anticipating an improvement in earnings—and earnings, as you'll see, make stock prices go higher.

It doesn't have to be a turnaround in sales that gets your attention. It may be that companies you know about have incredible hidden assets that don't show up on the balance sheet. If you work in real estate, maybe you know that a department store chain owns four city blocks in downtown Atlanta, carried on the books at pre–Civil War prices. This is a definite hidden asset, and similar opportunities might be found in gold, oil, timberland, and TV stations.

You're looking for a situation where the value of the assets per share exceeds the price per share of the stock. In such delightful instances you can truly buy a great deal of something for nothing. I've done it myself numerous times.

Thousands of employees of Storer Communications and its affiliates, plus countless others who work in cable TV or network TV, could have figured out that Storer's TV and cable properties were valued at $100 per share, while the stock was selling for $30. Executives knew this, programmers could have known it, cameramen could have known it, and even the people who come around to hook up the cable to the house could have known it. All any of them had to do was buy Storer at $30 or $35 or $40 or $50 and wait for the Wall Street experts to figure it out. Sure enough, Storer was taken private in late 1985 at $93.50 a share—which by 1988 turned out to have been a bargain price.

I could go on for the rest of the book about the edge that being in a business gives the average stockpicker. On top of that, there's the consumer's edge that's helpful in picking out the winners from the newer and smaller fast-growing companies, especially in the retail trades. Whichever edge applies, the exciting part is that you can develop your own stock detection system outside the normal channels of Wall Street, where you'll always get the news late.

MY WONDERFUL EDGE

Who could have had a greater advantage than yours truly, sitting in an office at Fidelity during the boom in financial services and in the mutual funds? This was my chance to make up for missing Pebble Beach. Perhaps I can be forgiven for that incredible asset play. Golf and sailing are my summer hobbies, but mutual funds are my regular business.

I'd been coming to work here for nearly two decades. I know half the officers in the major financial-service companies, I follow the daily ups and downs, and I could notice important trends months before the analysts on Wall Street. You couldn't have been more strategically placed to cash in on the bonanza of the early 1980s.

The people who print prospectuses must have seen it—they could hardly keep up with all the new shareholders in the mutual funds. The sales force must have seen it as they crisscrossed the country in their Winnebagos and returned with billions in new assets. The maintenance services must have seen the expansion in the offices at Federated, Franklin, Dreyfus, and Fidelity. The companies that sold mutual funds prospered as never before in their history. The mad rush was on.

Fidelity isn't a public company, so you couldn't invest in the rush here. But what about Dreyfus? Want to see a chart that doesn't stop? The stock sold for 40 cents a share in 1977, then nearly $40 a share in 1986, a 100-bagger in nine years, and much of that during a lousy stock market. Franklin was a 138-bagger, and Federated was up fiftyfold before it was bought out by Aetna. I was right on top of all of them. I knew the Dreyfus story, the Franklin story, and the Federated story from beginning to end. Everything was right, earnings were up, the momentum was obvious (see chart).

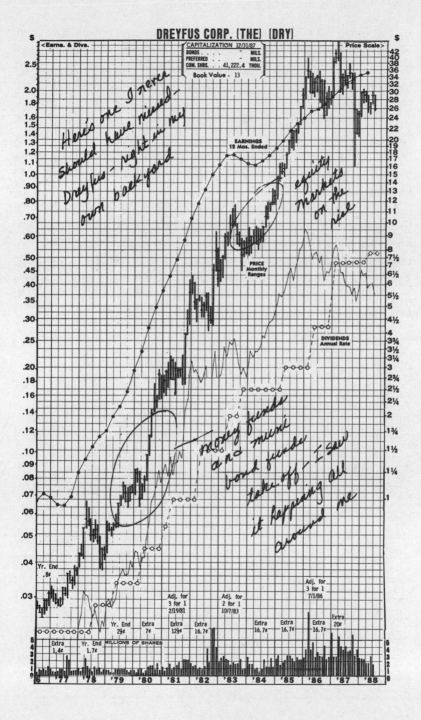

DREYFUS CORP. (THE) (DRY)

CAPITALIZATION 12/31/87
BONDS . . . — MILS.
PREFERRED . . — MILS.
COM. SHRS. . . 41,222.4 THOU.
Book Value - 13

Here's one I never should have missed — Dreyfus — right in my own backyard

equity markets on the rise

money funds and muni bond funds take off — I saw it happening all around me

EARNINGS 12 Mos. Ended

PRICE Monthly Ranges

DIVIDENDS Annual Rate

Yr. End .8¢

Adj. for 3 for 1 2/19/81

Adj. for 2 for 1 10/7/83

Adj. for 3 for 1 7/1/86

Yr. End 2½¢   Extra 7¢   Extra 12½¢   Extra 16.7¢   Extra 16.7¢   Extra 16.7¢   Extra 16.7¢   Extra 20¢

Extra 1.4¢   Yr. End 1.7¢   MILLIONS OF SHARES

How much did I make from all this? Zippo. I didn't buy a single share of any of the financial services companies; not Dreyfus, not Federated, not Franklin. I missed the whole deal and didn't realize it until it was too late. I guess I was too busy thinking about Union Oil of California, just like the doctors.

Every time I look at the Dreyfus chart, it reminds me of the advice I've been trying to give you all along: Invest in things you know about. Neither of us should let an opportunity like this one pass us by again, and I didn't. The 1987 market break gave me another chance with Dreyfus (see Chapter 17).

The list below is only a partial record of the many tenbaggers I've either neglected to buy or sold too soon during the period I've managed Magellan. With a few of them I got a small part of the gain, and with others I managed to lose money through bad timing and fuzzy thinking. You'll notice the list goes only up to *m,* but that's only because I got tired of writing them down. This being an incomplete account, you can imagine how many opportunities must be out there.

GREAT OPPORTUNITIES OVERLOOKED

AAR	Ball
Adams-Millis	Bard (CR)
Affiliated Publications	Bemis
Albertson's	Bergen Brunswig
Alexander & Baldwin	Betz Labs
Alexander's	Brunswick
Allegheny Corp.	Capital Cities
Alza	Carolina Freight
American Family	Carson Pirie Scott
American Greetings	Carter Wallace
American International	Chicago Milwaukee
Ames Department Stores	Chris-Craft
Anheuser-Busch	Commercial Metals
Automatic Data Processing	Community Psychiatric
Aydin	Cray Research

Dean Foods	Helene Curtis
Deluxe Check Printers	Hershey Foods
Dillards	Hillenbrand
Dow Jones	Hospital Corp. Amer.
Dun & Bradstreet	Houghton Mifflin
EG&G	Humana
Emerson Radio	Jostens
Ethyl	Limited (The)
Figgie International	Liz Claiborne
First Boston	Lockheed
Flightsafety Intl.	Loews
Flowers	Manor Care
Forest Labs	Marriott
Fuqua Industries	McGraw Hill
The Gap	Media General
Geico	Melville
General Cinema	Meredith
Giant Food	Molex
Handleman	Mylan
Harland (John)	

7

I've Got It, I've Got It— What Is It?

However a stock has come to your attention, whether
via the office, the shopping mall, something you ate, something you
bought, or something you heard from your broker, your mother-in-
law, or even from Ivan Boesky's parole officer, the discovery is not
a buy signal. Just because Dunkin' Donuts is always crowded or
Reynolds Metals has more aluminum orders than it can handle doesn't
mean you ought to own the stock. Not yet. What you've got so far is
simply a lead to a story that has to be developed.

In fact, you ought to treat the initial information (whatever brought
this company to your attention) as if it were an anonymous and intriguing tip, mysteriously shoved into your mailbox. This will keep you
from buying a stock just because you've seen something you like, or
worse, because of the reputation of the tipper, as in: "Uncle Harry's
buying it, and he's rich, so he must know what he's talking about." Or:
"Uncle Harry's buying it, and so am I, because his last stock tip doubled."

Developing the story is really not difficult: at most it will take a couple of hours. In the next few chapters I'm going to tell you how I do it,
and where you can find the most useful sources of information.

It seems to me that this homework phase is just as important to your success in stocks as your previous vow to ignore the short-term gyrations of the market. Perhaps some people make money in stocks without doing any of the research I'll describe, but why take unnecessary chances? ***Investing without research is like playing stud poker and never looking at the cards.***

For some reason the whole business of analyzing stocks has been made to seem so esoteric and technical that normally careful consumers invest their life savings on a whim. The same couple that spends the weekend searching for the best deal on airfares to London buys 500 shares of KLM without having spent five minutes learning about the company.

Let's go back to the Houndsteeth. They fancy themselves to be smart consumers, even going so far as to read the labels on pillowcases. They compare the weights and prices on the boxes of laundry soap to find the best buy. They calculate the watts-per-lumen of competing light bulbs, but all of their savings are dwarfed by Houndstooth's fiascoes in the stock market.

Isn't that Houndstooth over there in his recliner, reading the *Consumer Reports* article on the relative thickness and absorbency of the five popular brands of toilet paper? He's trying to figure out whether or not to switch to Charmin. But will he give equal time to reading the annual report of Procter and Gamble, the company that makes the Charmin, before he invests $5,000 in the stock? Of course not. He'll buy the stock first and later toss the Procter and Gamble annual report into the garbage can.

The Charmin syndrome is a common affliction, but it's easily cured. All you have to do is put as much effort into picking your stocks as you do into buying your groceries. Even if you already own stocks, it's useful to go through the exercise, because it's possible that some of these stocks will not and cannot live up to your expectations for them. That's because there are different kinds of stocks, and there are limits to how each kind can perform. In developing the story you have to make certain initial distinctions.

WHAT'S THE BOTTOM LINE?

Procter and Gamble is a good illustration of what I'm talking about. Remember I mentioned that L'eggs was one of the two most profitable new products of the 1970s. The other was Pampers. Any friend or relative of a baby could have realized how popular Pampers were, and right on the box it says that Pampers are made by Procter and Gamble.

But on the strength of Pampers alone, should you have rushed out to buy the stock? Not if you'd begun to develop the story. Then, in about five minutes, you would have noticed that Procter and Gamble is a huge company and that Pampers sales contribute only a small part of the earnings. Pampers made some difference to Procter and Gamble, but it wasn't nearly as consequential as what L'eggs did for a smaller outfit such as Hanes.

If you're considering a stock on the strength of some specific product that a company makes, the first thing to find out is: What effect will the success of the product have on the company's bottom line? Back in February of 1988, I recall, investors got very enthused about Retin-A, a skin cream made by Johnson & Johnson. Since 1971 this cream had been sold as an acne medicine, but a recent doctors' study suggested it might also fight skin blots and blemishes caused by the sun. The newspapers loved this story, and headline writers called it the anti-aging cream, and the "wrinkle-fighter." You would have thought that Johnson & Johnson had discovered the Fountain of Youth.

So what happens? Johnson & Johnson stock jumps $8 a share in two days (January 21–22, 1988), which adds $1.4 billion in extra market value to the company. In all this hoopla the buyers must have forgotten to notice that the previous year's sales of Retin-A brought in only $30 million a year to Johnson & Johnson, and the company still faced further FDA review on the new claims.

In another case, which happened about the same time, investors did better homework. A new medical study reported that an aspirin every other day might reduce the risk of men's getting heart attacks. The study used the Bufferin brand of aspirin made by Bristol-Myers, but Bristol-Myers stock hardly budged, moving up just 50 cents per share to $42⅞. A lot of people must have realized that domestic Bufferin sales last year were $75 million, less than 1.5 percent of Bristol-Myers's total revenues of $5.3 billion.

A somewhat better aspirin play was Sterling Drug, maker of Bayer aspirin, before it was bought out by Eastman Kodak. Sterling's aspirin sales were 6.5 percent of its total revenues, but close to 15 percent of the company's profits—aspirin was Sterling's most profitable product.

BIG COMPANIES, SMALL MOVES

The size of a company has a great deal to do with what you can expect to get out of the stock. How big is this company in which you've taken an interest? Specific products aside, big companies don't have big stock moves. In certain markets they perform well, but you'll get your biggest moves in smaller companies. You don't buy stock in a giant such as Coca-Cola expecting to quadruple your money in two years. If you buy Coca-Cola at the right price, you might triple your money in six years, but you're not going to hit the jackpot in two.

There's nothing wrong with Procter and Gamble or Coca-Cola, and recently both have been excellent performers. But you just have to know these are big companies so you won't have false hopes or unrealistic expectations.

Sometimes a series of misfortunes will drive a big company into desperate straits, and, as it recovers, the stock will make a big move. Chrysler had a big move, as did Ford and Bethlehem Steel. When Burlington Northern got depressed, the stock dropped from $12 to $6 and then climbed back to $70. But these are extraordinary situations that fall into the category of turnarounds. In the normal course of business, multibillion-dollar enterprises such as Chrysler or Burlington Northern, DuPont or Dow Chemical, Procter and Gamble or Coca-Cola, simply cannot grow fast enough to become tenbaggers.

For a General Electric to double or triple in size in the foreseeable future is mathematically impossible. GE already has gotten so big that it represents nearly one percent of the entire U.S. gross national product. Every time you spend a dollar, GE gets almost a penny of it. Think of that. In all the trillions spent annually by American consumers, nearly a penny of every dollar goes to goods or services (light bulbs, appliances, insurance, the National Broadcasting Corporation [NBC], etc.) provided by GE.

Here is a company that has done everything right—made sensible acquisitions; cut costs; developed successful new products; rid itself of bumbling subsidiaries; avoided getting suckered into the computer business (after selling its mistake to Honeywell)—and still the stock inches along. That's not GE's fault. The stock can't help but inch along since it's attached to such a huge enterprise.

GE has 900 million shares outstanding, and a total market value of $39 billion. The annual profit, more than $3 billion, is enough to qualify as a Fortune 500 company on its own. There is simply no way that GE could accelerate its growth very much without taking over the world. And since fast growth propels stock prices, it's no surprise that GE moves slowly as La Quinta soars.

Everything else being equal, you'll do better with the smaller companies. In the last decade you'd have made more money on Pic 'N' Save than on Sears, although both are retail chains. Now that Waste Management is a multibillion-dollar conglomerate, it will probably lag behind the speedy new entries in the waste-removal field. In the recent comeback of the steel industry, shareholders in the smaller Nucor have fared better than shareholders in U.S. Steel (now USX). In the earlier comeback of the drug industry, the smaller SmithKline Beckman outperformed the larger American Home Products.

THE SIX CATEGORIES

Once I've established the size of the company relative to others in a particular industry, next I place it into one of six general categories: slow growers, stalwarts, fast growers, cyclicals, asset plays, and turnarounds. There are almost as many ways to classify stocks as there are stockbrokers—but I've found that these six categories cover all of the useful distinctions that any investor has to make.

Countries have a growth rate (the GNP), industries have a growth rate, and so does an individual company. Whatever the entity, "growth" means that it does more of whatever it does this year (make cars, shine shoes, sell hamburgers) than it did last year. President Eisenhower once said that "things are more like they are now than they ever were before." That's a pretty good definition of economic growth.

Keeping track of the growth rates of industry is an industry in itself. There are endless charts, tables, and comparisons. With individual companies it's a little trickier, since growth can be measured in various ways: growth in sales, growth in profits, growth in earnings, etc. But when you hear about a "growth company," you can assume that it's expanding. There are more sales, more production, and more profits in each successive year.

The growth of an individual company is measured against the growth of the economy at large. Slow-growing companies, as you might have guessed, grow very slowly—more or less in line with the nation's GNP, which lately has averaged about three percent a year.

Fast-growing companies grow very fast, sometimes as much as 20 to 30 percent a year or more. That's where you find the most explosive stocks.

Three of my six categories have to do with growth stocks. I separate the growth stocks into slow growers (sluggards), medium growers (stalwarts), and then the fast growers—the superstocks that deserve the most attention.

THE SLOW GROWERS

Usually these large and aging companies are expected to grow slightly faster than the gross national product. Slow growers didn't start out that way. They started out as fast growers and eventually pooped out, either because they had gone as far as they could, or else they got too tired to make the most of their chances. When an industry at large slows down (as they always seem to do), most of the companies within the industry lose momentum as well.

Electric utilities are today's most popular slow growers, but throughout the 1950s and into the 1960s the utilities were fast growers, expanding at over twice the rate of GNP. They were successful companies and great stocks. As people installed central air conditioning, bought big refrigerator/freezers, and generally ran up their electric bills, electricity consumption became a high-growth industry, and the major utilities, particularly in the Sunbelt, expanded at double-digit rates. In the 1970s, as the cost of power rose sharply, consumers learned to conserve electricity, and the utilities lost their momentum.

Sooner or later every popular fast-growing industry becomes a slow-growing industry, and numerous analysts and prognosticators are fooled. There's always a tendency to think that things will never change, but inevitably they do. Alcoa once had the same kind of go-go reputation that Apple Computer has today, because aluminum was a fast-growth industry. In the twenties the railroads were the great growth companies, and when Walter Chrysler left the railroads to run an automobile plant, he had to take a cut in pay. "This isn't the railroad, Mr. Chrysler," he was told.

Then cars became the fast-growth industry, and for a time it was steel, then chemicals, then electric utilities, then computers. Now even computers are slowing down, at least in the mainframe and minicomputer parts of the business. IBM and Digital may be the slow growers of tomorrow.

It's easy enough to spot a slow-grower in the books of stock charts that your broker can provide, or that you can find at the local library. The chart of a slow grower such as Houston Industries resembles the topographical map of Delaware, which, as you probably know, has no hills. Compare this to the chart of Wal-Mart, which looks like a rocket launch, and you'll see that Wal-Mart is definitely not a slow grower (see accompanying charts).

Another sure sign of a slow grower is that it pays a generous and regular dividend. As I'll discuss more fully in Chapter 13, companies pay generous dividends when they can't dream up new ways to use the money to expand the business. Corporate managers would much prefer to expand the business, an effort that always enhances their prestige, than to pay a dividend, an effort that is mechanical and requires no imagination.

This doesn't mean that by paying a dividend the corporate directors are doing the wrong thing. In many cases it may be the best use to which the company's earnings can be put. (See Chapter 13.)

You won't find a lot of two to four percent growers in my portfolio, because if companies aren't going anywhere fast, neither will the price of their stocks. If growth in earnings is what enriches a company, then what's the sense of wasting time on sluggards?

THE STALWARTS

Stalwarts are companies such as Coca-Cola, Bristol-Myers, Procter and Gamble, the Bell telephone sisters, Hershey's, Ralston Purina, and Colgate-Palmolive. These multibillion-dollar hulks are not exactly agile climbers, but they're faster than slow growers. As you can see in the chart of Procter and Gamble, it's not as flat as the map of Delaware, but it's no Everest, either. When you traffic in stalwarts, you're more or less in the foothills: 10 to 12 percent annual growth in earnings.

Depending on when you buy them and at what price, you can make a sizable profit in stalwarts. As you can see on the Procter and Gamble chart, the stock has performed well throughout the 1980s. However, if you'd bought it back in 1963, you only made fourfold on your money. Holding a stock for twenty-five years for that kind of return isn't a very exciting prospect—since you're no better off than if you'd bought a bond or stuck with a cash fund.

In fact, when anyone brags about doubling or tripling his money on a stalwart (or on any company, for that matter), your next question

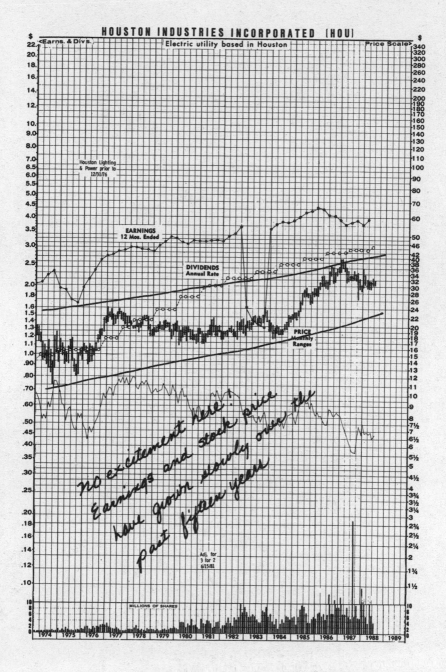

HOUSTON INDUSTRIES INCORPORATED (HOU)

Electric utility based in Houston

<Earns. & Divs.

Price Scale>

Houston Lighting
& Power prior to
12/31/76

EARNINGS
12 Mos. Ended

DIVIDENDS
Annual Rate

PRICE
Monthly
Ranges

No excitement here! Earnings and stock price have grown slowly over the past fifteen years

Adj. for
3 for 2
6/15/83

MILLIONS OF SHARES

1974 1975 1976 1977 1978 1979 1980 1981 1982 1983 1984 1985 1986 1987 1988 1989

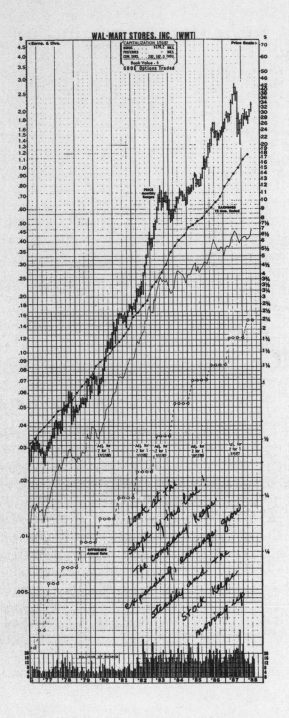

WAL-MART STORES, INC. (WMT)

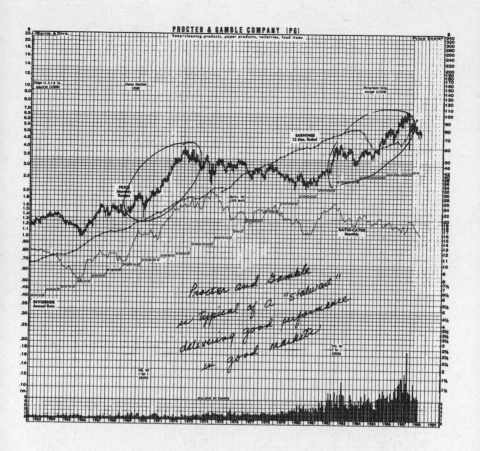

Procter and Gamble
is typical of a "stalwart"
delivering good performance
in good markets

ought to be: "And how long did you own it?" In many instances the risk
of ownership has not resulted in any advantage to the owner, who
therefore took chances for nothing.

In the market we've had since 1980 the stalwarts have been good
performers, but not the star performers. Most of these are huge companies, and it's unusual to get a tenbagger out of a Bristol-Myers or a
Coca-Cola. So if you own a stalwart like Bristol-Myers and the stock's
gone up 50 percent in a year or two, you have to wonder if maybe
that's enough and begin to think about selling. How much can you expect to squeeze out of Colgate-Palmolive? You aren't going to become
a millionaire off it the way you could have with Subaru, unless there is
some startling new development you would have heard about by now.

Fifty percent in two years is what you'd be delighted to get from

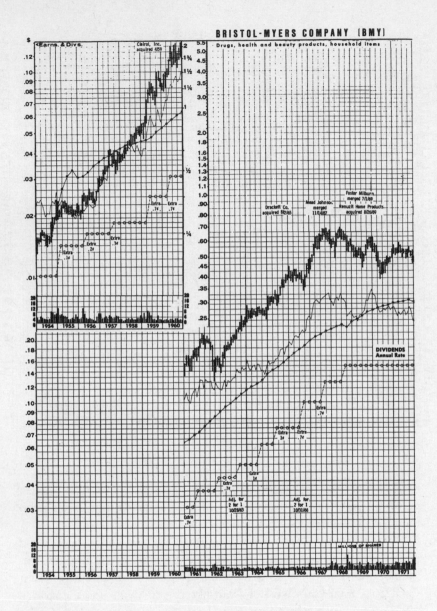

BRISTOL-MYERS COMPANY (BMY)

Colgate-Palmolive in most normal situations. With the stalwarts you
have to consider taking profits more readily than you would with a
Shoney's, or a Service Corporation International. Stalwarts are stocks
that I generally buy for a 30 to 50 percent gain, then sell and repeat the
process with similar issues that haven't yet appreciated.

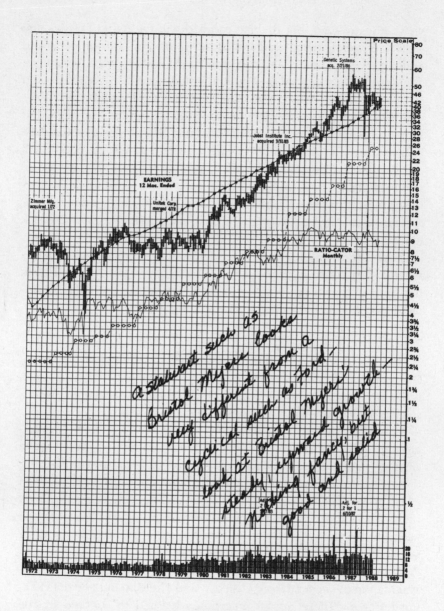

I always keep some stalwarts in my portfolio because they offer pretty good protection during recessions and hard times. You can see here that during the 1981–82 period, when the country seemed to be falling apart and the stock market fell apart with it, Bristol-Myers went sideways (see chart). It didn't do that well in the 1973–74 washout as we've already seen, but nothing escaped that bath, and besides, the stock was grossly overpriced at the time. In general, Bristol-Myers and Kellogg, Coca-Cola and MMM, Ralston Purina and Procter and Gamble, are good friends in a crisis. You know they won't go bankrupt, and soon enough they will be reassessed and their value will be restored.

Bristol-Myers has had only one down quarter in twenty years, and Kellogg hasn't had a down quarter for thirty. It's no accident that Kellogg can survive recessions. No matter how bad things get, people still eat cornflakes. They may take fewer trips, postpone the purchase of new cars, buy fewer clothes and expensive knickknacks, and order fewer lobster dinners at restaurants, but they eat just as many cornflakes as ever. Maybe they eat more cornflakes, to make up for the lack of lobsters.

People don't buy less dog food during recessions either, which is why Ralston Purina is a relatively safe stock to own. In fact, as I write this, my colleagues are flocking to the Kelloggs and the Ralston Purinas, since they're all afraid of a recession right now.

THE FAST GROWERS

These are among my favorite investments: small, aggressive new enterprises that grow at 20 to 25 percent a year. If you choose wisely, this is the land of the 10- to 40-baggers, and even the 200-baggers. With a small portfolio, one or two of these can make a career.

A fast-growing company doesn't necessarily have to belong to a fast-growing industry. As a matter of fact, I'd rather it didn't, as you'll see in Chapter 8. All it needs is the room to expand within a slow-growing industry. Beer is a slow-growing industry, but Anheuser-Busch has been a fast grower by taking over market share, and enticing drinkers of rival brands to switch to theirs. The hotel business grows at only 2 percent a year, but Marriott was able to grow 20 percent by capturing a larger segment of that market over the last decade.

The same thing happened to Taco Bell in the fast-food business, Wal-Mart in the general store business, and The Gap in the retail clothing business. These upstart enterprises learned to succeed in one place, and then to duplicate the winning formula over and over, mall by mall, city by city. The expansion into new markets results in the phenomenal acceleration in earnings that drives the stock price to giddy heights.

There's plenty of risk in fast growers, especially in the younger companies that tend to be overzealous and underfinanced. When an underfinanced company has headaches, it usually ends up in Chapter 11. Also, Wall Street does not look kindly on fast growers that run out of stamina and turn into slow growers, and when that happens, the stocks are beaten down accordingly.

I've already mentioned how electric utilities, especially the ones in the Sunbelt, went from being fast growers to being slow growers. In the 1960s plastics was a high-growth industry. Plastics were so much on people's minds that when the word "plastics" was whispered to Dustin Hoffman in the movie *The Graduate,* the word itself became a famous line. Dow Chemical got into plastics, enjoyed a vigorous growth spurt, and was beloved as a fast grower for several years. Then the growth slowed down and Dow became a sober chemical company, a sort of plodder with cyclical overtones.

Aluminum was a great growth industry even into the 1960s and so was carpets, but when these industries matured, the companies within them became GNP-type growers, and the stock market yawned.

So while the smaller fast growers risk extinction, the larger fast growers risk a rapid devaluation when they begin to falter. Once a fast grower gets too big, it faces the same dilemma as Gulliver in Lilliput. There's simply no place for it to stretch out.

But for as long as they can keep it up, fast growers are the big winners in the stock market. I look for the ones that have good balance sheets and are making substantial profits. The trick is figuring out when they'll stop growing, and how much to pay for the growth.

THE CYCLICALS

A cyclical is a company whose sales and profits rise and fall in regular if not completely predictable fashion. In a growth industry, business just keeps expanding, but in a cyclical industry it expands and contracts, then expands and contracts again.

The autos and the airlines, the tire companies, steel companies, and chemical companies are all cyclicals. Even defense companies behave like cyclicals, since their profits' rise and fall depends on the policies of various administrations.

AMR Corporation, the parent of American Airlines, is a cyclical, and so is Ford Motor, as you can see by the chart. Charts of the cyclicals look like the polygraphs of liars, or the maps of the Alps, as opposed to the maps of Delaware you get with the slow growers.

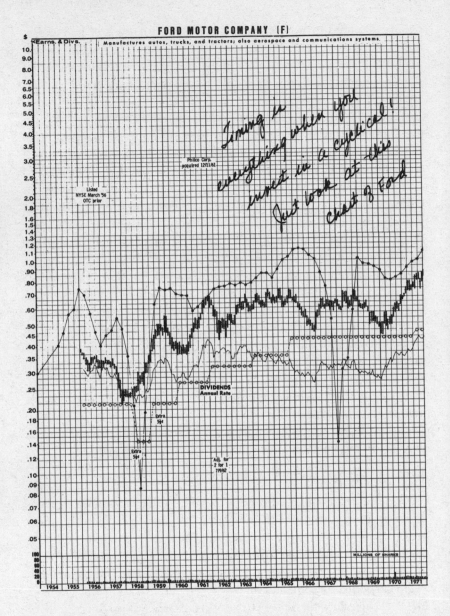

Coming out of a recession and into a vigorous economy, the cyclicals flourish, and their stock prices tend to rise much faster than the prices of the stalwarts. This is understandable, since people buy new cars and take more airplane trips in a vigorous economy, and there's greater demand for steel, chemicals, etc. But going the other direction,

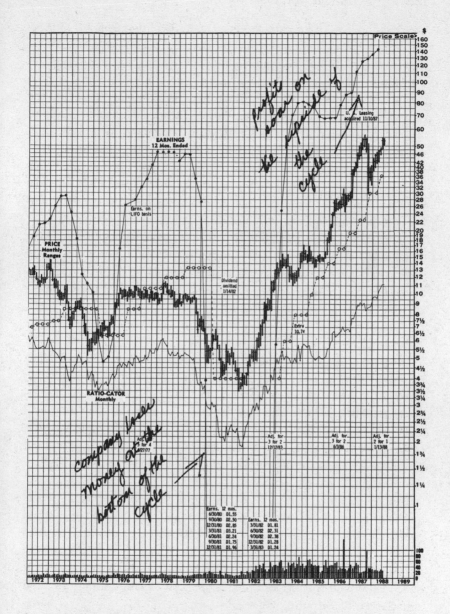

the cyclicals suffer, and so do the pocketbooks of the shareholders. You can lose more than fifty percent of your investment very quickly if you buy cyclicals in the wrong part of the cycle, and it may be years before you'll see another upswing.

Cyclicals are the most misunderstood of all the types of stocks. It is here that the unwary stockpicker is most easily parted from his money, and in stocks that he considers safe. Because the major cyclicals are large and well-known companies, they are naturally lumped together with the trusty stalwarts. Since Ford is a blue chip, one might assume that it will behave the same as Bristol-Myers, another blue chip (see charts). But this is far from the truth. Ford's stock fluctuates wildly as the company alternately loses billions of dollars in recessions and makes billions of dollars in prosperous stretches. If a stalwart such as Bristol-Myers can lose half its value in a sorry market and/or a national economic slump, a cyclical such as Ford can lose 80 percent. That's just what happened to Ford in the early 1980s. You have to know that owning Ford is different from owning Bristol-Myers.

Timing is everything in cyclicals, and you have to be able to detect the early signs that business is falling off or picking up. If you work in some profession that's connected to steel, aluminum, airlines, automobiles, etc., then you've got your edge, and nowhere is it more important than in this kind of investment.

TURNAROUNDS

Turnaround candidates have been battered, depressed, and often can barely drag themselves into Chapter 11. These aren't slow growers; these are no growers. These aren't cyclicals that rebound; these are potential fatalities, such as Chrysler. Actually Chrysler once was a cyclical that went so far down in a down cycle that people thought it would never come back up. A poorly managed cyclical is always a potential candidate for the kind of trouble that befell Chrysler and, to a slightly lesser extent, Ford.

The Penn Central bankruptcy was one of the most traumatic events that ever happened to Wall Street. That this blue chip, this grand old company, this solid enterprise, could collapse was as startling and as unexpected as the collapse of the George Washington Bridge would be. An entire generation of investors had its faith shaken—and yet once again there was opportunity in this crisis. Penn Central has been a marvelous turnaround play.

Turnaround stocks make up lost ground very quickly, as Chrysler, Ford, Penn Central, General Public Utilities, and numerous others have proven. The best thing about investing in successful turnarounds is that of all the categories of stocks, their ups and downs are least related to the general market.

I made a lot of money for my shareholders by buying Chrysler. I started buying at $6 (unadjusted for later splits) in early 1982 and watched it go up fivefold in less than two years and fifteenfold in five years. At one point I had 5% of my fund invested in Chrysler. While other stocks that I owned have risen higher, no single stock ever had the impact of Chrysler because none ever represented such a large percentage of the fund while it rose. And I didn't even buy Chrysler at the bottom!

Other more daring Chrysler fans bought in at $1.50 and made a 32-bagger out of it. Either way, Chrysler was a happy occurrence. So was Lockheed, which sold for $1 in 1973, and even after the government bailed out the company you could have bought the stock for $4 in 1977 and sold it for $60 in 1986. Lockheed was one I missed.

In absolute dollars I get my greatest profits from the revival of the Chryslers and the Penn Centrals, bigger companies in which I can buy enough shares to have a meaningful impact on my fund.

It's not easy to compile lists of failed turnarounds except from memory, because their existence is wiped out of the S&P books, the chart books, and the stockbrokers' records, and these companies are never heard from again. I could attempt to reconstruct the rather long list of the failed turnarounds I wish I hadn't bought, except the mere idea of it gives me a headache.

In spite of this, the occasional major success makes the turnaround business very exciting, and very rewarding overall.

There are several different types of turnarounds, and I've owned all of them at one time or another. There's the bail-us-out-or-else kind of turnaround such as Chrysler or Lockheed, where the whole thing depended on a government loan guarantee. There's the who-would-have-thunk-it kind of turnaround, such as Con Edison. Who would ever have believed you could lose this much money in a utility, as the stock price fell from $10 to $3 by 1974; and who would have believed you could make this much, as the price rebounded from $3 to $52 by 1987?

There's the little-problem-we-didn't-anticipate kind of turnaround, such as Three Mile Island. This was a minor tragedy perceived to be worse than it was, and in minor tragedy there's major opportunity. I made a lot of money in General Public Utilities, the owner of Three Mile Island. Anybody could have. You just had to be patient, keep up with the news, and read it with dispassion.

After the original meltdown of the nuclear unit in 1979 the situation eventually stabilized. In 1985 GPU announced it was going to start up the sister reactor that had been turned off for years after the crisis but was unaffected by it. It was a good sign for the stock that they got that sister plant back on line, and an even better sign when other utilities agreed to share in the costs of the Three Mile Island cleanup. You had almost seven years to buy the stock after the place calmed down and all this good news had come out. The low of $3\frac{3}{8}$ was reached in 1980, but you could still have gotten in for $15 a share in late 1985 and watched the stock hit $38 in October, 1988.

I try to stay away from the tragedies where the outcome is unmeasurable, such as the Bhopal disaster at the Union Carbide plant in India. This was a terrible gas leak that resulted in thousands of deaths, and how much the families would get out of Union Carbide in damages was an open question. I invested in the Johns-Manville turnaround but sold at a modest loss after realizing there was no way to predict the extent of that company's liability, either.

There's the perfectly-good-company-inside-a-bankrupt-company kind of turnaround, such as Toys "R" Us. Once Toys "R" Us was spun out on its own, away from its less successful parent, Interstate Department Stores, the result was 57 bags.

There's the restructuring-to-maximize-shareholder-values kind of turnaround, such as Penn Central. Wall Street seems to favor restructuring these days, and any director or CEO who mentions it is warmly applauded by shareholders. Restructuring is a company's way of ridding itself of certain unprofitable subsidiaries it should never have acquired in the first place. The earlier buying of these ill-fated subsidiaries, also warmly applauded, is called diversification. I call it *diworseification.*

I'll have more to say about diworseification later—most of it unflattering. The only positive aspect is that some companies that diworseify themselves into sorry shape are future candidates for turnarounds. Goodyear is coming back right now. It's gotten out of the oil business, sold off some sluggish subsidiaries, and rededicated itself to the thing it does best: making tires. Merck, having washed its hands of Calgon and a few other minor distractions, is once again concentrating on its ethical drugs. It has four new drugs in clinical trials and two that have passed FDA approval, and the earnings are picking up.

THE ASSET PLAYS

An asset play is any company that's sitting on something valuable that you know about, but that the Wall Street crowd has overlooked. With so many analysts and corporate raiders snooping around, it doesn't seem possible that there are any assets that Wall Street hasn't noticed, but believe me, there are. The asset play is where the local edge can be used to greatest advantage.

The asset may be as simple as a pile of cash. Sometimes it's real estate. I've already mentioned Pebble Beach as a great asset play. Here's why: At the end of 1976 the stock was selling for 14½ per share, which, with 1.7 million shares outstanding, meant that the whole company was valued at only $25 million. Less than three years later (May, 1979), Twentieth Century-Fox bought out Pebble Beach for $72 million, or 42½ per share. What's more, a day after buying the company, Twentieth Century turned around and sold Pebble Beach's gravel pit—just one of the company's many assets—for $30 million. In other words, the gravel pit alone was worth more than what investors in 1976 paid for the whole company. Those investors got all the adjacent land, the 2,700 acres in Del Monte Forest and the Monterey Peninsula, the 300-year-old trees, the hotel, and the two golf courses for nothing.

Whereas Pebble Beach was an over-the-counter stock, Newhall Land and Farming was on the New York Stock Exchange and very visible while it went up well over twentyfold. The company had two significant properties: the Cowell Ranch in the San Francisco Bay area, and the much larger and more valuable Newhall Ranch, thirty miles north of downtown Los Angeles. The Newhall Ranch has a planned community complete with an amusement park, a large industrial-office complex, and it is developing a major shopping mall.

Hundreds of thousands of California commuters drive by the Newhall Ranch every day. Insurance appraisers, mortgage bankers, and real estate agents involved in the various Newhall deals certainly knew of the extent of Newhall's holdings and of the general increase in California property values. How many people owned houses in the areas around the Newhall Ranch and saw the great escalation in land values, years ahead of any Wall Street analysts? How many of them considered researching this stock that has been a twenty-bagger from the early seventies and a fourbagger since 1980? If I'd lived in California, I wouldn't have missed it. At least, I hope I wouldn't have.

I once visited a mundane little Florida cattle company called Alico, run out of La Belle, a small town at the edge of the Everglades. All I saw there was scrub pine and palmetto brush, a few cows grazing around, and perhaps twenty Alico employees trying unsuccessfully to look busy. It wasn't very exciting, until you figured out that you could have bought Alico for under $20 a share, and ten years later the land alone turned out to be worth more than $200 a share. A smart codger named Ben Hill Griffin, Jr., kept buying up the stock and waiting for Wall Street to notice Alico. He must have made a fortune by now.

Many of the publicly traded railroads such as Burlington Northern, Union Pacific, and Santa Fe Southern Pacific are land rich, dating back to the nineteenth century when the government gave away half the country as a sop to the railroad tycoons. These companies have the oil and gas rights, the mineral rights, and the timber rights as well.

There are asset plays in metals and in oil, in newspapers and in TV stations, in patented drugs and even sometimes in a company's losses. That's what happened with Penn Central. After it came out of bankruptcy, Penn Central had a huge tax-loss carryforward, which meant that when it started making money again, it wouldn't have to pay taxes. In those years the corporate tax rate was 50 percent, so Penn Central was reborn with a 50 percent advantage up front.

Actually Penn Central might have been the ultimate asset play. The company had everything: tax-loss carryforward, cash, extensive land holdings in Florida, other land elsewhere, coal in West Virginia, and air rights in Manhattan. Anybody who had anything to do with Penn Central could have figured out that this was a stock worth buying. It went up eightfold.

Right now I'm holding on to Liberty Corp., an insurance company whose TV properties are worth more than the price I paid for the stock. Once you found out that the TV properties were worth $30 a share, and you saw that the stock was selling for $30 a share, you could take out your pocket calculator and subtract $30 from $30. The result was the cost of your investment in a valuable insurance business—zero.

I wish I'd bought more shares of Telecommunications, Inc., a cable company that sold for 12 cents a share in 1977 and $31 ten years later— up 250-fold. I had a very small position in this, the largest U.S. cable company, because I didn't appreciate the value of the assets. The earnings were poor and the debts were worrisome, so on the traditional measures, cable was an unattractive business. But the assets (in the form of the cable subscribers) more than made up for these negatives. All the people with an edge in the cable business could have known it; and so could I.

Regrettably, I never took more than a piddling position in the cable industry, despite the urging of Fidelity's Morris Smith, who periodically pounded on my table to convince me to buy more. He definitely was right—for the following important reason.

Fifteen years ago, each cable subscriber was worth about $200 to the buyer of a cable franchise, then ten years ago it was $400, five years ago $1,000, and now it's as high as $2,200. People in the industry keep up with these numbers, so it's not exactly esoteric information. The millions of subscribers to Telecommunications, Inc., made it a huge asset.

I think I missed all of this because cable TV didn't arrive in my town until 1986 and in my house until 1987. So I had no firsthand appreciation of worth of the industry in general. Somebody could tell me about it, just as somebody could tell you about a blind date, but until you are personally confronted with the evidence, it has no impact.

If I'd seen how my youngest daughter, Beth, loves the Disney channel, how much Annie looks forward to watching Nickelodeon, how my oldest daughter Mary appreciates MTV, how Carolyn takes to the old Bette Davis movies and I take to CNN news and cable sports, I would have understood that cable is as much of a fixture as water or electricity—the video utility. It's impossible to say enough about the value of personal experience in analyzing companies and trends.

Asset opportunities are everywhere. Sure they require a working knowledge of the company that owns the assets, but once that's understood, all you need is patience.

HIGHFLIERS TO LOW RIDERS

Companies don't stay in the same category forever. Over my years of watching stocks I've seen hundreds of them start out fitting one description and end up fitting another. Fast growers can lead exciting lives, and then they burn out, just as humans can. They can't maintain double-digit growth forever, and sooner or later they exhaust themselves and settle down into the comfortable single digits of sluggards and stalwarts. I've already seen it happen in the carpet business and in plastics, calculators and disk drives, health maintenance and computers. From Dow Chemical to Tampa Electric, the highfliers of one decade become the groundhogs of the next. Stop & Shop went from being a slow grower to a fast grower, an unusual reversal.

Advanced Micro Devices and Texas Instruments, once champion fast growers, are now regarded as cyclicals. Cyclicals with serious financial problems collapse and then reemerge as turnarounds. Chrysler was a traditional cyclical that almost went out of business, became a turnaround, then got turned around and became a cyclical again. LTV was a cyclical steel company, and now it's a turnaround.

Growth companies that can't stand prosperity foolishly diworseify and fall out of favor, which makes them into turnarounds. A fast grower such as Holiday Inn inevitably slows down, and the stock is depressed until some smart investors realize that it owns so much real estate that it's a great asset play. Look what's happened to retailers such as Federated and Allied Stores—because of the department stores they built in prime locations, and because of the shopping centers they own, they've been taken over for their assets. McDonald's is a classic fast grower, but because of the thousands of outlets it either owns or is repurchasing from the franchisees, it could be a great future asset play in real estate.

Companies such as Penn Central may fall into two categories at once, and Disney, over its lifetime, has been in every major category: years ago it had the momentum of a fast grower, which led to the size and financial strength of a stalwart, followed by a period when all those great assets in real estate, old movies, and cartoons were significant. Then, in the mid-1980s, when Disney was in a slump, you could have bought it as a turnaround.

International Nickel (which became Inco in 1976) was first a growth company, then a cyclical, and then a turnaround. One of the old-line companies in the Dow Jones average, it was one of my first successes as a young analyst at Fidelity. In December, 1970, I wrote a sell recommendation on Inco at $47⅞. The fundamentals looked bleak to me. My argument (nickel consumption slowing down, increased capacity among producers, and high labor costs at Inco) convinced Fidelity to sell the large position it held in the stock; and we even accepted a slightly lower price in order to find a buyer for our big block of shares.

The stock went sideways into April, when it still sold for $44½. I was beginning to worry that my analysis was faulty. Around me were port-folio managers who shared my concern, and that's putting it mildly. Fi-nally reality caught up with the market and the stock fell to $25 in 1971, $14 in 1978, and down to $8 in 1982. Seventeen years after the young analyst recommended the Inco sale, the older fund manager bought a large position for Fidelity Magellan as a turnaround.

SEPARATING THE DIGITALS FROM THE WAL-MARTS

If you can't figure out what category your stocks are in, then ask your broker. If a broker recommended the stocks in the first place, then you definitely ought to ask, because how else are you to know what you're looking for? Are you looking for slow growth, fast growth, re-cession protection, a turnaround, a cyclical bounce, or assets?

Basing a strategy on general maxims, such as "Sell when you double your money," "Sell after two years," or "Cut your losses by selling when the price falls ten percent," is absolute folly. It's simply impossible to find a generic formula that sensibly applies to all the different kinds of stocks.

You have to separate the Procter and Gambles from the Bethlehem Steels, and the Digital Equipments from the Alicos. Unless it's a turn-around, there's no point in owning a utility and expecting it to do as well as Philip Morris. There's no point in treating a young company with the potential of a Wal-Mart like a stalwart, and selling for a 50 per-cent gain, when there's a good chance that your fast grower will give you a 1,000-percent gain. On the other hand, if Ralston Purina already has doubled and the fundamentals look unexciting, you're crazy to hold on to it with the same hope.

If you buy Bristol-Myers for a good price, it's reasonable to think you might put it away and forget about it for twenty years, but you wouldn't want to forget about Texas Air. Shaky companies in cyclical industries are not the ones you sleep on through recessions.

Putting stocks in categories is the first step in developing the story. Now at least you know what kind of story it's supposed to be. The next step is filling in the details that will help you guess how the story is going to turn out.

8

The Perfect Stock,
What a Deal!

Getting the story on a company is a lot easier if you understand the basic business. That's why I'd rather invest in panty hose than in communications satellites, or in motel chains than in fiber optics. The simpler it is, the better I like it. When somebody says, "Any idiot could run this joint," that's a plus as far as I'm concerned, because sooner or later any idiot probably is going to be running it.

If it's a choice between owning stock in a fine company with excellent management in a highly competitive and complex industry, or a humdrum company with mediocre management in a simpleminded industry with no competition, I'd take the latter. For one thing, it's easier to follow. During a lifetime of eating donuts or buying tires, I've developed a feel for the product line that I'll never have with laser beams or microprocessors.

"Any idiot can run this business" is one characteristic of the perfect company, the kind of stock I dream about. You never find the perfect company, but if you can imagine it, then you'll know how to recognize favorable attributes, the most important thirteen of which are as follows:

(1) It Sounds Dull—or, Even Better, Ridiculous
The perfect stock would be attached to the perfect company, and the perfect company has to be engaged in a perfectly simple business, and

the perfectly simple business ought to have a perfectly boring name. The more boring it is, the better. Automatic Data Processing is a good start.

But Automatic Data Processing isn't as boring as Bob Evans Farms. What could be duller than a stock named Bob Evans? It puts you to sleep just thinking about it, which is one reason it's been such a great prospect. But even Bob Evans Farms won't win the prize for the best name you could give to a stock, and neither will Shoney's or Crown, Cork, and Seal. None of these has a chance against Pep Boys—Manny, Moe, and Jack.

Pep Boys—Manny, Moe, and Jack is the most promising name I've ever heard. It's better than dull, it's ridiculous. Who wants to put money into a company that sounds like the Three Stooges? What Wall Street analyst or portfolio manager in his right mind would recommend a stock called Pep Boys—Manny, Moe, and Jack—unless of course the Street already realizes how profitable it is, and by then it's up tenfold already.

Blurting out that you own Pep Boys won't get you much of an audience at a cocktail party, but whisper "GeneSplice International" and everybody listens. Meanwhile, GeneSplice International is going nowhere but down, while Pep Boys—Manny, Moe, and Jack just keeps going higher.

If you discover an opportunity early enough, you probably get a few dollars off the price just for the dull or odd name, which is why I'm always on the lookout for the Pep Boys or the Bob Evanses, or the occasional Consolidated Rock. Too bad that wonderful aggregate company changed its name to Conrock and then the trendier Calmat. As long as it was Consolidated Rock, nobody paid attention to it.

(2) IT DOES SOMETHING DULL

I get even more excited when a company with a boring name also does something boring. Crown, Cork, and Seal makes cans and bottle caps. What could be duller than that? You won't see an interview with the CEO of Crown, Cork, and Seal in *Time* magazine alongside an interview with Lee Iacocca, but that's a plus. There's nothing boring about what's happened to the shares of Crown, Cork, and Seal.

I already mentioned Seven Oaks International, the company that processes the coupons that you hand in at the grocery store. There's another tale that's guaranteed to shut your eyes as the stock sneaks up from $4 to $33. Seven Oaks International and Crown, Cork, and Seal make IBM seem like a Las Vegas revue, and how about Agency Rent-A-

Car? That's the glamorous outfit that provides the car the insurance company lets you drive while yours is being repaired. Agency Rent-A-Car came public at $4 a share and Wall Street hardly noticed. What self-respecting tycoon would want to think about what people drive while their cars are in the shop? The Agency Rent-A-Car prospectus could have been marketed as an anesthetic, but the last time I looked, the stock was $16.

A company that does boring things is almost as good as a company that has a boring name, and both together is terrific. Both together is guaranteed to keep the oxymorons away until finally the good news compels them to buy in, thus sending the stock price even higher. If a company with terrific earnings and a strong balance sheet also does dull things, it gives you a lot of time to purchase the stock at a discount. Then when it becomes trendy and overpriced, you can sell your shares to the trend-followers.

(3) It Does Something Disagreeable

Better than boring alone is a stock that's boring and disgusting at the same time. Something that makes people shrug, retch, or turn away in disgust is ideal. Take Safety-Kleen. That's a name with promise to begin with—any company that uses a k where there ought to be a c is worth investigating. The fact that Safety-Kleen was once related to Chicago Rawhide is also favorable (see "It's a Spinoff" later in this chapter).

Safety-Kleen goes around to all the gas stations and provides them with a machine that washes greasy auto parts. This saves auto mechanics the time and trouble of scrubbing the parts by hand in a pail of gasoline, and gas stations gladly pay for the service. Periodically the Safety-Kleen people come around to remove the dirty sludge and oil from the machine, and they carry the sludge back to the refinery to be recycled. This goes on and on, and you'll never see a miniseries about it on network TV.

Safety-Kleen hasn't rested on the spoils of greasy auto parts. It has since branched out into restaurant grease traps and other sorts of messes. What analyst would want to write about this, and what portfolio manager would want to have Safety-Kleen on his buy list? There aren't many, which is precisely what's endearing about Safety-Kleen. Like Automatic Data Processing, this company has had an unbroken run of increased earnings. Profits have gone up every quarter, and so has the stock.

Or how about Envirodyne? This one was pointed out to me a few years ago by Thomas Sweeney, then Fidelity's forest products analyst and now the manager of Fidelity Capital Appreciation Fund. Envirodyne passes the odd name test: it sounds like something you could bounce off the ozone layer, when actually it has to do with lunch. One of its subsidiaries, Clear Shield, makes plastic forks and straws, the perfect business that any idiot could run, but in reality it has topflight management with a large personal stake in the company.

Envirodyne is number two in plastic cutlery and number three in plastic straws, and being the lowest-cost producer gives it a big advantage in the industry.

In 1985, Envirodyne started negotiating to buy Viskase, a leading producer of intestinal byproducts, particularly the casings surrounding hot dogs and sausages. They got Viskase from Union Carbide at a bargain price. Then in 1986 they bought Filmco, the leading producer of the PVC film that's used to wrap leftover food items. Plastic forks, hotdog casings, plastic wrap—pretty soon they'll take over the family picnic.

Largely as a result of these acquisitions, the earnings increased from 34 cents a share in 1985 to $2 a share in 1987—and should top $2.50 in 1988. The company has used its substantial cash flow to pay down its debt on the various acquisitions. I bought it for $3 a share in September, 1985. At the high in 1988 it sold for $36⅞.

(4) It's a Spinoff

Spinoffs of divisions or parts of companies into separate, freestanding entities—such as Safety-Kleen out of Chicago Rawhide or Toys "R" Us out of Interstate Department Stores—often result in astoundingly lucrative investments. Dart & Kraft, which merged years ago, eventually separated so that Kraft could become a pure food company again. Dart (which owns Tupperware) was spun off as Premark International and has been a great investment on its own. So has Kraft, which was bought out by Philip Morris in 1988.

Large parent companies do not want to spin off divisions and then see those spinoffs get into trouble, because that would bring embarrassing publicity that would reflect back on the parents. Therefore, the spinoffs normally have strong balance sheets and are well-prepared to succeed as independent entities. And once these companies are granted their independence, the new management, free to run its own show, can cut costs and take creative measures that improve the near-term and long-term earnings.

Here is a list of some recent spinoffs that have done well, and a couple that haven't done so well:

STRONG PERFORMERS

PARENT	SPINOFF	APPROX. FIRST TRADE	LOW	HIGH	OCTOBER 31, 1988
Teledyne	Argonaut[1]	$18	$15	$52⅛	$43¼
	Amer. Ecology	4	2¾	50¼	12¾
US Gypsum	AP Green	11	11	26	26¾
IU Intl.	Gotaas Larsen	6	2⅝	36¼	47¾
Masco Corp.	Masco Ind.	2	1½	18¾	11⅜
Kraft	Premark Intl.	19	17½	36¼	29⅞
Tandy	Intertan	10	10	31¼	35¼
Singer	SSMC	13	11½	31⅜	23
Natomas	Amer. President	16	13⅞	51	32⅜
Interlake	Acme Steel	8	7⅝	24½	23½
Transamer.	Imo Delaval	8	6¾	23	18½
Transunion	Intl. Shiphold.	2	2⅜	20	17
Gen. Mills	Kenner Parker	16	13⅞	51½	—[2]
Borg Warner	York Int.	14	13½	59¾	51⅝
Time Inc.	Temple Inland	34	20½	68½	50¾

WEAKER PERFORMERS

PARENT	SPINOFF	APPROX. FIRST TRADE	LOW	HIGH	OCTOBER 31, 1988
Penn Cent.	Sprague Tech.	$15	$ 7⅛	$20	$12⅛
John Blair	Advo Systems	6	4	12¾	3⅞
Datapoint	Intelogic Trace[3]	8	2½	18⅛	3¾
Coca-Cola	Coca-Cola Ent.	15½	10½	21¼	14½

[1] Both Argonaut and American Ecology were spun out of Teledyne, which is one of the great all-time stocks in its own right.
[2] Acquired by Tonka in Oct. 1987 for $49.50 a share
[3] Troubled company during spinoff

The literature sent to shareholders explaining the spinoff is usually hastily prepared, blasé, and understated, which makes it even better than the regular annual reports. Spinoff companies are often misunderstood and get little attention from Wall Street. Investors often are sent shares in the newly created company as a bonus or a dividend for owning the parent company, and institutions, especially, tend to dismiss these shares as pocket change or found money. These are favorable omens for the spinoff stocks.

This is a fertile area for the amateur shareholder, especially in the recent frenzy of mergers and acquisitions. Companies that are targets of hostile takeovers frequently fight off raiders by selling or spinning off divisions that then become publicly traded issues on their own. When a company is taken over, the parts are often sold off for cash, and they, too, become separate entities in which to invest. If you hear about a spinoff, or if you're sent a few fractions of shares in some newly created company, begin an immediate investigation into buying more. A month or two after the spinoff is completed, you can check to see if there is heavy insider buying among the new officers and directors. This will confirm that they, too, believe in the company's prospects.

The greatest spinoffs of all were the "Baby Bell" companies that were created in the breakup of ATT: Ameritech, Bell Atlantic, Bell South, Nynex, Pacific Telesis, Southwestern Bell, and US West. While the parent has been an uninspiring performer, the average gain from stock in the seven newly created companies was 114 percent from November, 1983, to October, 1988. Add in the dividends and the total return is more like 170 percent. This beats the market twice around, and it beats the majority of all known mutual funds, including the one run by yours truly.

Once liberated, the seven regional companies were able to increase earnings, cut costs, and enjoy higher profits. They got all the local and regional telephone business, the yellow pages, along with 50 cents for every $1 of long-distance business generated by ATT. It was a great niche. They had already gone through an earlier period of heavy spending on modern equipment, so they didn't have to dilute shareholders' equity by selling extra stock. And human nature being what it is, the seven Baby Bells set up a healthy competition amongst themselves, and also between themselves and their proud parent, Ma Bell. Ma, meanwhile, was losing its stranglehold on its highly profitable leased equipment business, and facing new competitors such as Sprint and MCI, and sustaining heavy losses in its computer operations.

Investors who owned the old ATT stock had eighteen months to decide what to do. They could sell ATT and be done with the whole complicated mess, they could keep ATT plus the shares and fractions of shares in the new Baby Bells that they received, or they could sell the parent and keep the Baby Bells. If they did their homework, they sold ATT, kept the Baby Bells, and added to their position with as many more shares as they could afford.

Pounds of material were sent out to the 2.96 million ATT shareholders explaining the Baby Bells' plans. The new companies laid out exactly what they were going to do. A million employees of ATT and countless suppliers could have seen what was going on. So much for the amateur's edge being restricted to a lucky few. For that matter, anyone who had a phone knew that there were big changes going on. I participated in the rally, but only in a modest way—I never dreamed that conservative companies such as these could do so well so quickly.

(5) THE INSTITUTIONS DON'T OWN IT, AND THE ANALYSTS DON'T FOLLOW IT

If you find a stock with little or no institutional ownership, you've found a potential winner. Find a company that no analyst has ever visited, or that no analyst would admit to knowing about, and you've got a double winner. When I talk to a company that tells me the last analyst showed up three years ago, I can hardly contain my enthusiasm. It frequently happens with banks, savings-and-loans, and insurance companies, since there are thousands of these and Wall Street only keeps up with fifty to one hundred.

I'm equally enthusiastic about once-popular stocks the professionals have abandoned, as many abandoned Chrysler at the bottom and Exxon at the bottom, just before both began to rebound.

Data on institutional ownership are available from the following sources: *Vicker's Institutional Holdings Guide, Nelson's Directory of Investment Research,* and the *Spectrum Surveys,* a publication of CDA Investment Technologies. Although these publications are not always easy to find, you can get similar information from the *Value Line Investment Survey* and from the S&P stock sheets, also called tear sheets. Both are routinely provided by regular stockbrokers.

(6) The Rumors Abound: It's Involved with Toxic Waste and/or the Mafia

It's hard to think of a more perfect industry than waste management. If there's anything that disturbs people more than animal casings, grease and dirty oil, it's sewage and toxic waste dumps. That's why I got very excited one day when the solid waste executives showed up in my office. They had come to town for a solid waste convention complete with booths and slides—imagine how attractive that must have been. Anyway, instead of the usual blue cotton button-down shirts that I see day after day, they were wearing polo shirts that said "Solid Waste." Who would put on shirts like that, unless it was the Solid Waste bowling team? These are the kind of executives you dream about.

As you already know if you were fortunate enough to have bought some, Waste Management, Inc. is up about a hundredfold.

Waste Management is a better prospect even than Safety-Kleen because it has two unthinkables going for it: toxic waste itself, and also the Mafia. Everyone who fantasizes that the Mafia runs all the Italian restaurants, the newsstands, the dry cleaners, the construction sites, and the olive presses also probably thinks that the Mafia controls the garbage business. This fantastic assertion was a great advantage to the earliest buyers of shares in Waste Management, which as usual were underpriced relative to the actual opportunity.

Maybe the rumors of the Mafia in waste management kept away the same investors who worried about the Mafia in hotel/casino management. Remember the dreaded casino stocks that are now on everybody's buy list? Respectable investors weren't supposed to touch them because the casinos allegedly were all Mafia. Then the earnings exploded and the profits exploded, and the Mafia faded into the background. When Holiday Inn and Hilton got into the casino business, it suddenly was all right to own casino stocks.

(7) There's Something Depressing about It

In this category my favorite all-time pick is Service Corporation International (SCI), which also has a boring name. I got this pick from George Vanderheiden, the onetime Fidelity electronics analyst who's done a great job running the Fidelity Destiny Fund.

Now, if there's anything Wall Street would rather ignore besides toxic waste, it's mortality. And SCI does burials.

For several years this Houston-based enterprise has been going around the country buying up local funeral homes from the mom-and-pop owners, just as Gannett did with the small-town newspapers. SCI has become a sort of McBurial. It has picked up the active funeral parlors that bury a dozen or more people a week, ignoring the smaller one- or two-burial parlors.

At last count the company owned 461 funeral parlors, 121 cemeteries, 76 flower shops, 21 funeral product-and-supply manufacturing centers, and 3 casket distribution centers, so they're vertically integrated. They broke into the big-time when they buried Howard Hughes.

They also pioneered the pre-need policy, a layaway plan that's been very popular. It enables you to pay off your funeral service and your casket right now while you can still afford it, so your family won't have to pay for it later. Even if the cost has tripled by the time you require a funeral service, you're locked in at the old prices. This is a great deal for the family of the deceased, and an even greater deal for the company.

SCI gets the money from its pre-need sales right away, and the cash just keeps on compounding. If they sell $50 million worth of these policies each year, it will add up to billions by the time they've had all the funerals. Lately they've gone beyond their own operations to offer the pre-need policies to other funeral homes. Over the past five years the sales of prearranged funerals have been climbing at 40 percent a year.

Once in a while a positive story is topped off by an extraordinary kicker, an unexpected valuable card that turns up. In SCI's case it happened when the company struck a very lucrative bargain with another company (American General) that wanted to buy the real estate under one of SCI's Houston locations. In return for the rights to this land, American General, which owned 20 percent of SCI's stock, gave all their stock back to SCI. Not only did SCI retrieve 20 percent of its shares at no cost, but it was allowed to continue to operate the funeral home at the old location for two years, until it could open a new home at a different site in Houston.

The best thing about this company is that it was shunned by most professional investors for years. Despite an incredible record, the SCI executives had to go out on cavalcades to beg people to listen to their story. That meant that amateurs in the know could buy stock in a proven winner with a record of solid growth in earnings, and at much lower prices than they'd have to pay for a hot stock in a popular industry. Here was the perfect opportunity—everything was working, you could see it happening, the earnings kept increasing, there was rapid growth with almost no debt—and Wall Street turned the other way.

Only in 1986 did SCI develop a big following among the institutions, who now own over 50 percent of the shares, and more analysts started covering the company. Predictably the stock was a twentybagger before SCI got Wall Street's full attention, but since then it has greatly underperformed the market. In addition to the burdens of high institutional ownership and broad coverage by brokers, the company has been hurt in the last few years by entering the casket business through two acquisitions that have not contributed to profits. Also, the price of buying quality funeral homes and cemeteries has risen sharply, and the growth in pre-need insurance has been less than expected.

(8) IT'S A NO-GROWTH INDUSTRY

Many people prefer to invest in a high-growth industry, where there's a lot of sound and fury. Not me. I prefer to invest in a low-growth industry like plastic knives and forks, but only if I can't find a no-growth industry like funerals. That's where the biggest winners are developed.

There's nothing thrilling about a thrilling high-growth industry, except watching the stocks go down. Carpets in the 1950s, electronics in the 1960s, computers in the 1980s, were all exciting high-growth industries, in which numerous major and minor companies unerringly failed to prosper for long. That's because for every single product in a hot industry, there are a thousand MIT graduates trying to figure out how to make it cheaper in Taiwan. As soon as a computer company designs the best word-processor in the world, ten other competitors are spending $100 million to design a better one, and it will be on the market in eight months. This doesn't happen with bottle caps, coupon-clipping services, oil-drum retrieval, or motel chains.

SCI was helped by the fact that there's almost no growth in the funeral industry. Growth in the burial business in this country limps along at one percent a year, too slow for the action-seekers who've gone into computers. But it's a steady business with as reliable a customer base as you could ever find.

In a no-growth industry, especially one that's boring and upsets people, there's no problem with competition. You don't have to protect your flanks from potential rivals because nobody else is going to be interested. This gives you the leeway to continue to grow, to gain market share, as SCI has done with burials. SCI already owns 5 percent of the nation's funeral homes, and there's nothing stopping them from owning 10 percent or 15 percent. The graduating class of Wharton isn't going to want to challenge SCI, and you can't tell your friends in the investment banking firms that you've decided to specialize in picking up dirty oil from the gas stations.

(9) IT'S GOT A NICHE

I'd much rather own a local rock pit than own Twentieth Century-Fox, because a movie company competes with other movie companies, and the rock pit has a niche. Twentieth Century-Fox understood that when it bought up Pebble Beach, and the rock pit with it.

Certainly, owning a rock pit is safer than owning a jewelry business. If you're in the jewelry business, you're competing with other jewelers from across town, across the state, and even abroad, since vacationers can buy jewelry anywhere and bring it home. But if you've got the only gravel pit in Brooklyn, you've got a virtual monopoly, plus the added protection of the unpopularity of rock pits.

The insiders call this the "aggregate" business, but even the exalted name doesn't alter the fact that rocks, sand, and gravel are as close to inherently worthless as you can get. That's the paradox: mixed together, the stuff probably sells for $3 a ton. For the price of a glass of orange juice, you can purchase a half ton of aggregate, which, if you've got a truck, you can take home and dump on your lawn.

What makes a rock pit valuable is that nobody else can compete with it. The nearest rival owner from two towns over isn't going to haul his rocks into your territory because the trucking bills would eat up all his profit. No matter how good the rocks are in Chicago, no Chicago rock-pit owner can ever invade your territory in Brooklyn or Detroit. Due to the weight of rocks, aggregates are an exclusive franchise. You don't have to pay a dozen lawyers to protect it.

There's no way to overstate the value of exclusive franchises to a company or its shareholders. Inco is the world's great producer of nickel today, and it will be the world's great producer in fifty years. Once I was standing at the edge of the Bingham Pit copper mine in Utah, and looking down into that impressive cavern, it occurred to me that nobody in Japan or Korea can invent a Bingham pit.

Once you've got an exclusive franchise in anything, you can raise prices. In the case of rock pits you can raise prices to just below the point that the owner of the next rock pit might begin to think about competing with you. He's figuring his prices via the same method.

To top it off, you get big tax breaks from depreciating your earth movers and rock crushers, plus you get a mineral depletion allowance, the same as Exxon and Atlantic Richfield get for their own oil and gas deposits. I can't imagine anyone's going bankrupt over a rock pit. So if you can't run your own rock pit, the next best thing is buying shares in aggregate-producing companies such as Vulcan Materials, Calmat, Boston Sand & Gravel, Dravo, and Florida Rock. When larger companies such as Martin-Marietta, General Dynamics, or Ashland sell off various parts of their businesses, they always keep the rock pits.

I always look for niches. The perfect company would have to have one. Warren Buffett started out by acquiring a textile mill in New Bedford, Massachusetts, which he quickly realized was not a niche business. He did poorly in textiles but went on to make billions for his shareholders by investing in niches. He was one of the first to see the value in newspapers and TV stations that dominated major markets, beginning with the *Washington Post*. Thinking along the same lines, I bought as much stock as I could in Affiliated Publications, which owns the local *Boston Globe*. Since the *Globe* gets over 90 percent of the print ad revenues in Boston, how could the *Globe* lose?

The *Globe* has a niche, and the Times Mirror Company has several, including the *Los Angeles Times, Newsday,* the *Hartford Courant,* and the *Baltimore Sun*. Gannett owns 90 daily newspapers, and most of them are the only major dailies in town. Investors who discovered the advantages of exclusive newspaper and cable franchises in the early 1970s were rewarded with a number of tenbaggers as the cable stocks and media stocks got popular on Wall Street.

Any reporter, ad executive, or editor who worked at the *Washington Post* could have seen the profits and the earnings and understood the value of the niche. A newspaper company is a great business for a variety of reasons as well.

Drug companies and chemical companies have niches—products that no one else is allowed to make. It took years for SmithKline to get the patent for Tagamet. Once a patent is approved, all the rival companies with their billions in research dollars can't invade the territory. They have to invent a different drug, prove it is different, and then go through three years of clinical trials before the government will let them sell it. They have to prove that it doesn't kill rats, and most drugs, it seems, do kill rats.

Or perhaps rats aren't as healthy as they used to be. Come to think of it, I once made money on a rat stock—Charles River Breeding Labs. There's a business that turns people off.

Chemical companies have niches in pesticides and herbicides. It's not any easier to get a poison approved than it is to get a cure approved. Once you have a patent and the federal go-ahead on a pesticide or a herbicide, you've got a money machine. Monsanto has several today.

Brand names such as Robitussin or Tylenol, Coca-Cola or Marlboro, are almost as good as niches. It costs a fortune to develop public confidence in a soft drink or a cough medicine. The whole process takes years.

(10) PEOPLE HAVE TO KEEP BUYING IT

I'd rather invest in a company that makes drugs, soft drinks, razor blades, or cigarettes than in a company that makes toys. In the toy industry somebody can make a wonderful doll that every child has to have, but every child gets only one each. Eight months later that product is taken off the shelves to make room for the newest doll the children have to have—manufactured by somebody else.

Why take chances on fickle purchases when there's so much steady business around?

(11) IT'S A USER OF TECHNOLOGY

Instead of investing in computer companies that struggle to survive in an endless price war, why not invest in a company that benefits from the price war—such as Automatic Data Processing? As computers get cheaper, Automatic Data can do its job cheaper and thus increase its own profits. Or instead of investing in a company that makes automatic scanners, why not invest in the supermarkets that install the scanners? If a scanner helps a supermarket company cut costs just three percent, that alone might double the company's earnings.

(12) THE INSIDERS ARE BUYERS

There's no better tip-off to the probable success of a stock than that people in the company are putting their own money into it. In general, corporate insiders are net sellers, and they normally sell 2.3 shares to every one share that they buy. After the 1,000-point drop from August to October, 1987, it was reassuring to discover that there were four shares bought to every one share sold by insiders across the board. At least they hadn't lost their faith.

When insiders are buying like crazy, you can be certain that, at a minimum, the company will not go bankrupt in the next six months. When insiders are buying, I'd bet there aren't three companies in history that have gone bankrupt near term.

Long term, there's another important benefit. When management owns stock, then rewarding the shareholders becomes a first priority, whereas when management simply collects a paycheck, then increasing salaries becomes a first priority. Since bigger companies tend to pay bigger salaries to executives, there's a natural tendency for corporate wage-earners to expand the business at any cost, often to the detriment of shareholders. This happens less often when management is heavily invested in shares.

Although it's a nice gesture for the CEO or the corporate president with the million-dollar salary to buy a few thousand shares of the company stock, it's more significant when employees at the lower echelons add to their positions. If you see someone with a $45,000 annual salary buying $10,000 worth of stock, you can be sure it's a meaningful vote of confidence. That's why I'd rather find seven vice presidents buying 1,000 shares apiece than the president buying 5,000.

If the stock price drops after the insiders have bought, so that you have a chance to buy it cheaper than they did, so much the better for you.

It's simple to keep track of insider purchases. Every time an officer or a director buys or sells shares, he or she has to declare it on Form 4 and send the form to the Securities and Exchange Commission advising them of the fact. Several newsletter services, including *Vicker's Weekly Insider Report* and *The Insiders,* keep track of these filings. *Barron's, The Wall Street Journal,* and *Investor's Daily* also carry the information. Many local business newspapers report on insider trading on local companies—I know the *Boston Business Journal* has such a column. Your broker may also be able to provide the information, or you may find that your local library subscribes to the newsletters. There's also a tabulation of insider buying and selling in the *Value Line* publication.

(Insider selling usually means nothing, and it's silly to react to it. If a stock had gone from $3 to $12 and nine officers were selling, I'd take notice, particularly if they were selling a majority of their shares. But in normal situations insider selling is not an automatic sign of trouble within a company. There are many reasons that officers might sell. They may need the money to pay their children's tuition or to buy a new house or to satisfy a debt. They may have decided to diversify into other stocks. But there's only one reason that insiders buy: They think the stock price is undervalued and will eventually go up.)

(13) THE COMPANY IS BUYING BACK SHARES

Buying back shares is the simplest and best way a company can reward its investors. If a company has faith in its own future, then why shouldn't it invest in itself, just as the shareholders do? The announcement of massive share buybacks by company after company broke on October 20, 1987 the fall of many stocks, and stabilized the market at the height of its panic. Long term, these buybacks can't help but reward investors.

When stock is bought in by the company, it is taken out of circulation, therefore shrinking the number of outstanding shares. This can have a magical effect on earnings per share, which in turn has a magical effect on the stock price. If a company buys back half its shares and its overall earnings stay the same, the earnings per share have just doubled. Few companies could get that kind of result by cutting costs or selling more widgets.

Exxon has been buying in shares because it's cheaper than drilling for oil. It might cost Exxon $6 a barrel to find new oil, but if each of its shares represents $3 a barrel in oil assets, then retiring shares has the same effect as discovering $3 oil on the floor of the New York Stock Exchange.

This sensible practice was almost unheard of until quite recently. Back in the 1960s, International Dairy Queen was one of the pioneers in share buybacks, but there were few others who followed suit. At the delightful Crown, Cork, and Seal they've bought back shares every year for the last twenty. They never pay a dividend, and they never make unprofitable acquisitions, but by shrinking shares they've gotten the maximum impact from the earnings. If this keeps up, someday there will be a thousand shares of Crown, Cork, and Seal—worth $10 million apiece.

At Teledyne, chairman Henry E. Singleton periodically offers to buy in the stock at a much higher price than is bid on the stock exchange. When Teledyne was selling for $5, he might have paid $7, and when the stock was at $10, then he was paying $14, and so on. All along he's given shareholders a chance to get out at a fancy premium. This practical demonstration of Teledyne's belief in itself is more convincing than the adjectives in the annual report.

The common alternatives to buying back shares are (1) raising the dividend, (2) developing new products, (3) starting new operations, and (4) making acquisitions. Gillette tried to do all four, with emphasis on the final three. Gillette has a spectacularly profitable razor business, which it gradually reduced in relative size as it acquired less profitable operations. If the company had regularly bought back its shares and raised its dividend instead of diverting its capital to cosmetics, toiletries, ballpoint pens, cigarette lighters, curlers, blenders, office products, toothbrushes, hair care, digital watches, and lots of other diversions, the stock might well be worth over $100 instead of the current $35. In the last five years, Gillette has gotten back on track by eliminating losing operations and emphasizing its core shaving business, where it dominates the market.

The reverse of buying back shares is adding more shares, also called diluting. International Harvester, now Navistar, sold millions of additional shares to raise cash to help it survive a financial crisis brought about by the collapse of the farm-equipment business (see chart). Chrysler, remember, did just the opposite—buying back stock and stock warrants and shrinking the number of outstanding shares as the business improved (see chart). Navistar is once again a profitable company, but because of the extraordinary dilution, the earnings have a minimal impact, and shareholders have yet to benefit from the recovery to any significant degree.

THE GREATEST COMPANY OF ALL

If I could dream up a single glorious enterprise that combines all of the worst elements of Waste Management, Pep Boys, Safety-Kleen, rock pits, and bottle caps, it would have to be Cajun Cleansers. Cajun Cleansers is engaged in the boring business of removing mildew stains from furniture, rare books, and draperies that are victims of subtropical humidity. It's a recent spinoff from Louisiana BayouFeedback.

Its headquarters are located in the bayous of Louisiana, and to get

★ NAVISTAR INTERNATIONAL CORP. (NAV)

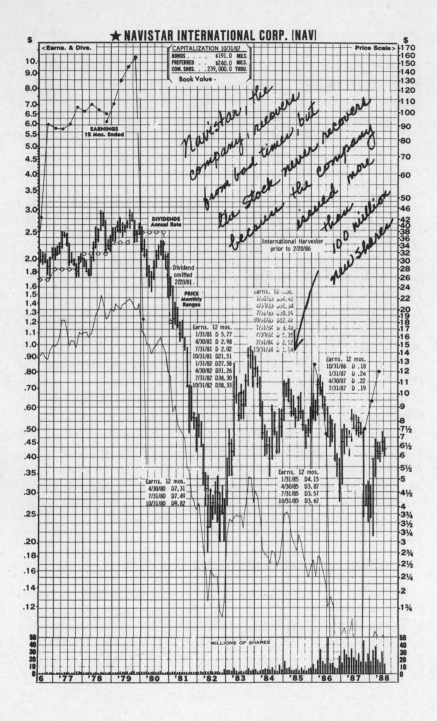

<Earns. & Divs.

Price Scale>

CAPITALIZATION 10/31/87
BONDS . . . . $191.0 MILS.
PREFERRED . . $240.0 MILS.
COM. SHRS. . . 239,000.0 THOU.

Book Value -

EARNINGS
12 Mos. Ended

DIVIDENDS
Annual Rate

International Harvester
prior to 2/20/86

Dividend
omitted
2/20/81.

PRICE
Monthly
Ranges

Navistar, the company, recovers from bad times, but the stock never recovers because the company issued more than 100 million new shares

Earns. 12 mos.
1/31/83 D54.45
4/5/83 D31.34
7/31/83 D30.59
10/31/83 D12.44
1/31/84 D 3.43
2/31/84 D 5.35
7/31/84 D 2.12
10/31/84 D 1.14

Earns. 12 mos.
1/31/81 D 5.77
4/30/81 D 2.98
7/31/81 D 2.02
10/31/81 D21.51
1/31/82 D27.58
4/30/82 D31.26
7/31/82 D38.30
10/31/82 D38.33

Earns. 12 mos.
10/31/86 D .18
1/31/87 D .24
4/30/87 D .22
7/31/87 D .19

Earns. 12 mos.
4/30/80 D7.31
7/31/80 D7.49
10/31/80 D9.82

Earns. 12 mos.
1/31/85 D4.15
4/30/85 D3.87
7/31/85 D3.57
10/31/85 D3.67

MILLIONS OF SHARES

6 '77 '78 '79 '80 '81 '82 '83 '84 '85 '86 '87 '88

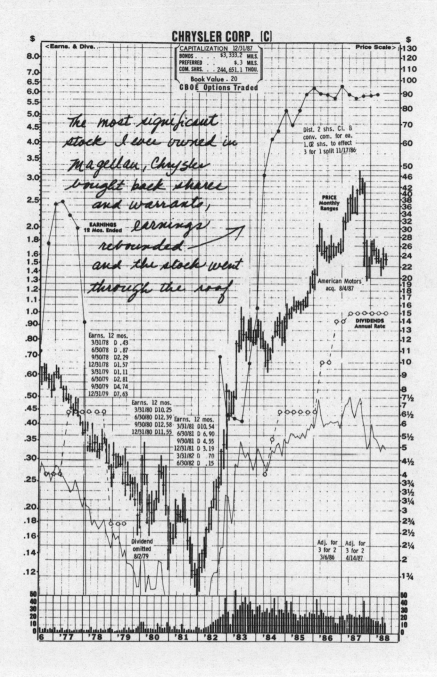

CHRYSLER CORP. (C)

CAPITALIZATION 12/31/87
BONDS . . . . $3,333.2 MILS.
PREFERRED . . $.3 MILS.
COM. SHRS. . 244,651.1 THOU.
Book Value - 20
CBOE Options Traded

The most significant stock I ever owned in Magellan, Chrysler bought back shares and warrants, earnings rebounded and the stock went through the roof

Dist. 2 shs. Cl. B
conv. com. for ea.
1.02 shs. to effect
3 for 1 split 11/17/86

PRICE
Monthly
Ranges

American Motors
acq. 8/4/87

EARNINGS
12 Mos. Ended

DIVIDENDS
Annual Rate

Earns. 12 mos.
3/31/78 D .43
6/30/78 D .87
9/30/78 D2.29
12/31/78 D1.57
3/31/79 D1.11
6/30/79 D2.81
9/30/79 D4.74
12/31/79 D7.63

Earns. 12 mos.
3/31/80 D10.25
6/30/80 D12.39
9/30/80 D12.58
12/31/80 D11.55

Earns. 12 mos.
3/31/81 D10.54
6/30/81 D 6.90
9/30/81 D 4.55
12/31/81 D 3.19
3/31/82 D .70
6/30/82 D .15

Dividend
omitted
8/2/79

Adj. for
3 for 2
3/6/86

Adj. for
3 for 2
4/14/87

'6 '77 '78 '79 '80 '81 '82 '83 '84 '85 '86 '87 '88

there you have to change planes twice, then hire a pickup truck to take you from the airport. Not one analyst from New York or Boston ever visited Cajun Cleansers, nor has any institution bought a solitary share.

Mention Cajun Cleansers at a cocktail party and soon you'll be talking to yourself. It sounds ridiculous to everyone within earshot.

While expanding quickly through the bayous and the Ozarks, Cajun Cleansers has had incredible sales. These sales will soon accelerate because the company just received a patent on a new gel that removes all sorts of stains from clothes, furniture, carpets, bathroom tiles, and even aluminum siding. The patent gives Cajun the niche it's been looking for.

The company is also planning to offer lifetime prestain insurance to millions of Americans, who can pay in advance for a guaranteed removal of all the future stain accidents they ever cause. A fortune in off-balance-sheet revenue will soon be pouring in.

No popular magazines except the ones that think Elvis is alive have mentioned Cajun and its new patent. The stock opened at $8 in a public offering seven years ago and soon rose to $10. At that price the important corporate directors bought as many shares as they could afford.

I hear about Cajun from a distant relative who swears it's the only way to get mildew off leather jackets left too long in dank closets. I do some research and discover that Cajun has had a 20 percent growth rate in earnings for the past four years, it's never had a down quarter, there's no debt on the balance sheet, and it did well in the last recession. I visit the company and find out that any trained crustacean could oversee the making of the gel.

The day before I decide to buy Cajun Cleansers, the noted economist Henry Kaufman has predicted that interest rates are going up, and then the head of the Federal Reserve slips on the lane at a bowling alley and injures his back, both of which combine to send the market down 15 percent, and Cajun Cleansers with it. I get in at $7.50, which is $2.50 less than the directors paid.

That's the situation at Cajun Cleansers. Don't pinch me. I'm dreaming.

9

Stocks I'd Avoid

If I could avoid a single stock, it would be the hottest stock in the hottest industry, the one that gets the most favorable publicity, the one that every investor hears about in the car pool or on the commuter train—and succumbing to the social pressure, often buys.

Hot stocks can go up fast, usually out of sight of any of the known landmarks of value, but since there's nothing but hope and thin air to support them, they fall just as quickly. If you aren't clever at selling hot stocks (and the fact that you've bought them is a clue that you won't be), you'll soon see your profits turn into losses, because when the price falls, it's not going to fall slowly, nor is it likely to stop at the level where you jumped on.

Look at the chart for Home Shopping Network, a recent hot stock in the hot teleshop industry, which in 16 months went from $3 to $47 back to $3½ (adjusted for splits). That was terrific for the people who said good-bye at $47, but what about the people who said hello at $47, when the stock was at its hottest? Where were the earnings, the profits, the future prospects? This investment had all the underlying security of a roulette spin.

The balance sheet was deteriorating rapidly (the company was taking on debt to buy television stations), there were problems with the

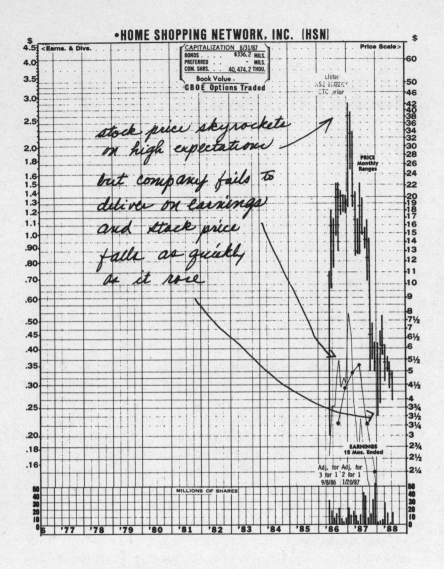

stock price skyrockets on high expectations but company fails to deliver on earnings and stock price falls as quickly as it rose

telephones, and competitors had begun to appear. How many zirconium necklaces can people wear?

I already mentioned the various hot industries where sizzle led to fizzle. Mobile homes, digital watches, and health maintenance organizations were all hot industries where fervent expectations put a fog on the arithmetic. Just when the analysts predict double-digit growth rates forever, the industry goes into a decline.

If you had to live off the profits from investing in the hottest stocks in each successive hot industry, soon you'd be on welfare.

There couldn't have been a hotter industry than carpets. As I was growing up, every housewife in America wanted wall-to-wall carpeting. Somebody invented a new tufting process that drastically reduced the amount of fiber that went into a rug, and somebody else automated the looms, and the prices dropped from $28 a yard to $4 a yard. The newly affordable rugs were laid down in schools, offices, airports, and in millions of tract houses in all the nation's suburbs.

Wood floors were once cheaper than carpets, but now carpets were cheaper, so the upper classes switched from carpets to wood floors and the masses switched from wood floors to carpets. Carpet sales rose dramatically, and the five or six major producers were earning more money than they knew how to spend, and growing at an astonishing pace. That's when the analysts started telling the stockbrokers that the carpet boom would last forever, and the brokers told their clients, and the clients bought the carpet stocks. At the same time, the five or six major producers were joined by two hundred new competitors, and they all fought for customers by dropping their prices, and nobody made another dime in the carpet business.

High growth and hot industries attract a very smart crowd that wants to get into the business. Entrepreneurs and venture capitalists stay awake nights trying to figure out how to get into the act as quickly as possible. If you have a can't-fail idea but no way of protecting it with a patent or a niche, as soon as you succeed, you'll be warding off the imitators. In business, imitation is the sincerest form of battery.

Remember what happened to disk drives? The experts said that this exciting industry would grow at 52 percent a year—and they were right, it did. But with thirty or thirty-five rival companies scrambling on the action, there were no profits.

Remember oil services? All you had to say was "oil" on a prospectus and people bought the stocks, even if the closest they ever got to oil services was having the gashop check under the hood.

In 1981, I attended a dinner at an energy conference in Colorado where Tom Brown was the featured speaker. Tom Brown was the principal owner and CEO of Tom Brown, Inc., a popular oil-service company that was selling for $50 a share at the time. Mr. Brown mentioned that an acquaintance of his had bragged about having shorted the stock (betting on it to go down), after which Mr. Brown made the following psychological observation: "You must hate money to be shorting my stock. You'll lose your car and your house and have to go naked to the Christmas party." Mr. Brown got a laugh out of repeating this to us, but in the four years that followed the stock did fall from $50 to $1. The acquaintance who shorted the stock must have been delighted with the fortune he made. If anyone had to go naked to the Christmas party, it would have been the regular shareholders in the long position. They would have avoided this fate by ignoring the hottest stock in this hot industry, or at least by having done some homework. There was nothing to Tom Brown, Inc., but a bunch of useless rigs, some dubious oil and gas acreage, some impressive debts, and a bad balance sheet.

There's never been a hotter stock than Xerox in the 1960s. Copying was a fabulous industry, and Xerox had control of the entire process. "To xerox" became a verb, which should have been a positive development. Many analysts thought so. They assumed that Xerox would keep growing to infinity when the stock was selling for $170 a share in 1972. But then the Japanese got into it, IBM got into it, and Eastman Kodak got into it. Soon there were twenty firms that made nice dry copies, as opposed to the original wet ones. Xerox got frightened and bought some unrelated businesses it didn't know how to run, and the stock lost 84 percent of its value. Several competitors didn't fare much better.

Copying has been a respectable industry for two decades and there's never been a slowdown in demand, yet the copy machine companies can't make a decent living.

Contrast the sorry stock performance of Xerox to that of Philip Morris, a company that sells cigarettes—a negative-growth industry in the U.S. Over the past fifteen years Xerox dropped from $160 to $60, while Philip Morris rose from $14 to $90. Year after year Philip Morris increases its earnings by expanding its market share abroad, by raising prices, and by cutting costs. Because of its brand names—Marlboro, Virginia Slims, Benson & Hedges, Merit, etc.—Philip Morris has found its niche. Negative-growth industries do not attract flocks of competitors.

BEWARE THE NEXT SOMETHING

Another stock I'd avoid is a stock in a company that's been touted as the next IBM, the next McDonald's, the next Intel, or the next Disney, etc. In my experience the next of something almost never is—on Broadway, the best-seller list, the National Basketball Association, or Wall Street. How many times have you heard that some player is supposed to be the next Willie Mays, or that some novel is supposed to be the next *Moby Dick,* only to find that the first is cut from the team, and the second is quietly remaindered? In stocks there's a similar curse.

In fact, when people tout a stock as the next of something, it often marks the end of prosperity not only for the imitator but also for the original to which it is being compared. When other computer companies were called the "next IBM," you could have guessed that IBM would go through some terrible times, and it has. Today most computer companies are trying not to become the next IBM, which may mean better times ahead for that beleaguered firm.

After Circuit City Stores (formerly Wards) became a successful electronics retailer, there was a string of nexts, including First Family, Good Guys, Highland Superstores, Crazy Eddie, and Fretters. Circuit City is up fourfold since 1984, when it was listed on the New York Stock Exchange, somehow avoiding the IBM curse, while all of the nexts have lost between 59 and 96 percent of their original value.

The next Toys "R" Us was Child World, which also stumbled; and the next Price Club was the Warehouse Club, which fared no better.

AVOID DIWORSEIFICATIONS

Instead of buying back shares or raising dividends, profitable companies often prefer to blow the money on foolish acquisitions. The dedicated diworseifier seeks out merchandise that is (1) overpriced, and (2) completely beyond his or her realm of understanding. This ensures that losses will be maximized.

Every second decade the corporations seem to alternate between rampant diworseification (when billions are spent on exciting acquisitions) and rampant restructuring (when those no-longer-exciting acquisitions are sold off for less than the original purchase price). The same thing happens to people and their sailboats.

These frequent episodes of acquiring and then regretting, only to divest and acquire and regret once again, could be applauded as a form of transfer payment from the shareholders of the large and cash-rich corporation to the shareholders of the smaller entity being taken over, since the large corporations so often overpay. The why of all this I've never understood, except perhaps that corporate management finds it more exciting to take over smaller companies, however expensive, than to buy back shares or mail dividend checks, which requires no imagination.

Perhaps psychologists should analyze this. Some corporations, like some individuals, just can't stand prosperity.

From an investor's point of view, the only two good things about diworseification are owning shares in the company that's being acquired, or in finding turnaround opportunities among the victims of diworseification that have decided to restructure.

There are so many examples of diworseification I hardly know where to begin. Mobil Oil once diworseified by buying Marcor Inc. One of Marcor's businesses was a retailer in an unfamiliar business that plagued Mobil for years. Marcor's other main business was Container Corporation, which Mobil later sold at a very low price. Mobil blew more millions by paying too much for Superior Oil.

Since the 1980 peak in oil prices, Mobil stock has risen only 10 percent, while Exxon has doubled. Beyond a couple of unfortunate and relatively small acquisitions such as Reliance Electric, plus an ill-fated venture-capital subsidiary, Exxon resisted diworseification and stuck to its own business. Its excess cash went to buying back its own stock. The shareholders of Exxon have done much better than the shareholders of Mobil, although new management is turning Mobil around. It sold Montgomery Ward in 1988.

The follies of Gillette I've already described. That company not only bought the medicine chest, it diworseified into digital watches and then announced a write-off of the whole fiasco. It's the only time in my memory that a major company explained how it got out of a losing business before anybody realized it had gotten into the business in the first place. Gillette, too, has made major reforms and has lately mended its ways.

General Mills owned Chinese restaurants, Italian restaurants, steak houses, Parker Brothers toys, Izod shirts, coins, stamps, travel companies, Eddie Bauer retail outlets, and Footjoy products, many acquired in the 1960s.

The 1960s was the greatest decade for diworseification since the Roman Empire diworseified all over Europe and northern Africa. It's hard to find a respectable company that didn't diworseify in the 1960s, when the best and the brightest believed they could manage one business as well as the next.

Allied Chemical bought everything but the kitchen sink, and probably somewhere in there it actually took over a company that made kitchen sinks. Times Mirror diworseified, and so did Merck, but both have wised up and returned to their publishing and their drugs.

U.S. Industries made 300 acquisitions in a single year. They should have called themselves one-a-day. Beatrice Foods expanded from edibles into inedibles, and after that anything was possible.

This great acquisitive era ended in the market collapse of 1973–74, when Wall Street finally realized that the best and the brightest were not as ingenious as expected, and even the most charming of corporate directors could not turn all those toads they bought into princes.

That's not to say it's always foolish to make acquisitions. It's a very good strategy in situations where the basic business is terrible. We would never have heard of Warren Buffett or his Berkshire Hathaway if Buffett had stuck to textiles. The same might be said of the Tisches, who started out with a chain of movie theaters (Loew's) and used the proceeds to buy a tobacco company (Lorillard), which in turn helped them acquire an insurance company (CNA), which led to their taking a huge position in CBS. The trick is that you have to know how to make the right acquisitions and then manage them successfully.

Consider the story of Melville and Genesco, two shoe manufacturers—one that successfully diversified and one that diworseified (see charts). Thirty years ago Melville was manufacturing men's shoes almost exclusively for its own family of shoe stores, Thom McAn. Sales grew as the company began to lease shoe departments in other stores, most notably the chain of K mart stores. When K mart began its great expansion in 1962, Melville's profits exploded. After years of experience in discount shoe retailing, the company launched into a series of acquisitions, always establishing the success of one before proceeding with another: they purchased CVS, a discount drugstore operation, in 1969; Marshall's, a discount apparel chain, in 1976; and Kay-Bee Toys in 1981. During the same period, Melville reduced the number of its shoe manufacturing plants from twenty-two in 1965 to just one in 1982. Slowly, but efficiently, a shoe manufacturer had transformed itself into a diversified retailer.

Unlike Melville, Genesco went off in a frenzy. Starting in 1956, it acquired Bonwit Teller, Henri Bendel, Tiffany, and Kress (variety stores), then got into security consulting, men's and women's jewelry, knitting

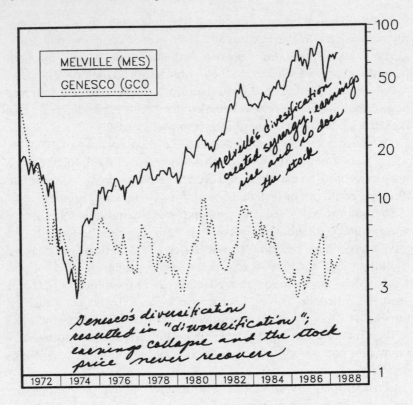

MELVILLE (MES)
GENESCO (GCO)

Melville's diversification created synergy; earnings rise and so does the stock

Genesco's diversification resulted in "diworseification"; earnings collapse and the stock price never recovers

100
50
20
10
3
1

1972 | 1974 | 1976 | 1978 | 1980 | 1982 | 1984 | 1986 | 1988

materials, textiles, blue jeans, and numerous other forms of retailing and wholesaling—while still trying to manufacture shoes. In the seventeen-year period between 1956 and 1973, Genesco made 150 acquisitions. These purchases greatly increased the company's sales, so Genesco got bigger on paper, but its fundamentals were deteriorating.

The difference in Melville's and Genesco's strategies ultimately showed up in the earnings and stock performances of the two companies. Both stocks suffered during the 1973–74 bear market. But Melville's earnings were growing steadily and its stock rebounded; it had become a thirtybagger by 1987. As for Genesco, its financial position continued to deteriorate after 1974, and the stock has never come back.

Why did Melville succeed while Genesco failed? The answer has a lot to do with a concept called synergy. "Synergy" is a fancy name for the two-plus-two-equals-five theory of putting together related businesses and making the whole thing work.

The synergy theory suggests, for example, that since Marriott already operates hotels and restaurants, it made sense for them to acquire the Big Boy restaurant chain, and also to acquire the subsidiary that provides meal service to prisons and colleges. (College students will tell you there's a lot of synergy between prison food and college food.) But what would Marriott know about auto parts or video games?

In practice, sometimes acquisitions produce synergy, and sometimes they don't. Gillette, the leading manufacturer of razor blades, got some synergy when it acquired the Foamy shaving cream line. However, that didn't extend to shampoo, lotion, and all the other toiletry items that Gillette brought under its control. Buffett's Berkshire Hathaway has bought everything from candy stores to furniture stores to newspapers, with spectacular results. Then again, Buffett's company is devoted to acquisitions.

If a company must acquire something, I'd prefer it to be a related business, but acquisitions in general make me nervous. There's a strong tendency for companies that are flush with cash and feeling powerful to overpay for acquisitions, expect too much from them, and then mismanage them. I'd rather see a vigorous buyback of shares, which is the purest synergy of all.

BEWARE THE WHISPER STOCK

I get calls all the time from people who recommend solid companies for Magellan, and then, usually after they've lowered their voices as if to confide something personal, they add: "There's this great stock I want to tell you about. It's too small for your fund, but you ought to look at it for your own account. It's a fascinating idea, and it could be a big winner."

These are the longshots, also known as whisper stocks, and the whiz-bang stories. They probably reach your neighborhood about the same time they reach mine: the company that sells papaya juice derivative as a cure for slipped-disc pain (Smith Labs); jungle remedies in general; high-tech stuff; monoclonal antibodies extracted from cows (Bioresponse); various miracle additives; and energy breakthroughs that violate the laws of physics. Often the whisper companies are on the brink of solving the latest national problem: the oil shortage, drug addiction, AIDS. The solution is either (a) very imaginative, or (b) impressively complicated.

My favorite is KMS Industries, which, according to the 1980–82 annual reports, was engaged in "amorphous silicon photovoltaics," in 1984 was emphasizing the "video multiplexer" and "optical pins," by 1985 had settled on "material processing using chemically driven spherical implosions," and by 1986 was hard at work on the "inertial confinement fusion program," "laser-initiated shock compression," and "visual immunodiagnostic assays." The stock fell from $40 to $2½ during this period. Only an eight-for-one reverse split kept it from becoming a penny stock. Smith Labs fell from a high of $25 to $1.

I visited Bioresponse at its headquarters in San Francisco, after Bioresponse had first come to see me in Boston. There in an upper-floor office in a rather shabby section of San Francisco (this should be seen as a good sign) were the executives on one side of the hall, and the cows on the other. As I talked to the president and the accountant, technicians in lab coats were busily removing lymph from the animals. This was a low-cost alternative to removing lymph from mice, which was the usual procedure. Two cows could make all the insulin for the entire country, and one gram of cow lymph could support a million diagnostic tests.

Bioresponse was being closely followed by several brokerage firms, and Dean Witter, Montgomery Securities, Furman Selz, and J.C. Bradford had recommended it. I bought the stock in a secondary offering at $9¼ in February, 1983. It reached a high of $16, but now it's a goner. Fortunately I sold at only a small loss.

Whisper stocks have a hypnotic effect, and usually the stories have emotional appeal. This is where the sizzle is so delectable that you forget to notice there's no steak. If you or I regularly invested in these stocks, we both would need part-time jobs to offset the losses. They may go up before they come down, but as a long-term proposition I've lost money on every single one I've ever bought. Some examples:

—Worlds of Wonder; Pizza Time Theater (Chuck E. Cheese bought the farm); One Potato, Two (symbol SPUD); National Health Care ($14 to 50 cents); Sun World Airways ($8 to 50 cents); Alhambra Mines (too bad they never found a decent mine); MGF oil (a penny stock today); American Surgery Centers (do they need patients!); Asbetec Industries (now selling for ⅛); American Solar King (find it on the pink sheets of forgotten stocks); Televideo (fell off the bus); Priam (I should have stayed away from disk drives); Vector Graphics Microcomputers (I should have stayed away from microcomputers); GD Ritzys (fast food, but no McDonald's); Integrated Circuits; Comdial Corp; and Bowmar.

What all these longshots had in common besides the fact that you lost money on them was that the great story had no substance. That's the essence of a whisper stock.

The stockpicker is relieved of the burden of checking earnings and so forth because usually there are no earnings. Understanding the p/e ratio is no problem because there is no p/e ratio. But there's no shortage of microscopes, Ph.D.'s, high hopes, and cash from the stock sale.

What I try to remind myself (and obviously I'm not always successful) is that if the prospects are so phenomenal, then this will be a fine investment next year and the year after that. Why not put off buying the stock until later, when the company has established a record? Wait for the earnings. You can get tenbaggers in companies that have already proven themselves. When in doubt, tune in later.

Often with the exciting longshots the pressure builds to buy at the initial public offering (IPO) or else you're too late. This is rarely true, although there are some cases where the early buying surge brings fantastic profits in a single day. On October 4, 1980, Genentech came public at $35 and on the same afternoon traded as high as $89 before backing off to $71¼. Magellan was allocated a small number of shares (you can't always get shares in hot public offerings). I did better with Apple Computer, which I sold on the first day for a 20 percent gain, because I was able to buy as many shares as I wanted. That was because a day before the offering, the Commonwealth of Massachusetts ruled that only sophisticated buyers could purchase Apple because the company was too speculative for the general public. I didn't buy Apple again until after it collapsed and became a turnaround.

IPOs of brand-new enterprises are very risky because there's so little to go on. Although I've bought some that have done well over time (Federal Express was my first and it's gone up twenty-five-fold), I'd say three out of four have been long-term disappointments.

I've done better with IPOs of companies that have been spun out of other companies, or in related situations where the new entity actually has a track record. Toys "R" Us was one of those, and so was Agency Rent-A-Car and Safety-Kleen. These were established businesses already, and you could research them the same way you research Ford or Coca-Cola.

BEWARE THE MIDDLEMAN

The company that sells 25 to 50 percent of its wares to a single customer is in a precarious situation. SCI Systems (not to be confused with the funeral-home firm) is a well-managed company and a major supplier of computer parts to IBM, but you never know when IBM will decide that it can make its own parts, or that it can do without the parts, and then cancel the SCI contract. If the loss of one customer would be catastrophic to a supplier, I'd be wary of investing in the supplier. Disk-drive companies such as Tandon were always on the brink of disaster because they were too dependent on a few clients.

Short of cancellation, the big customer has incredible leverage in extracting price cuts and other concessions that will reduce the supplier's profits. It's rare that a great investment could result from such an arrangement.

BEWARE THE STOCK WITH THE EXCITING NAME

It's too bad that Xerox didn't have a name like David's Dry Copies, because then more people would have been skeptical of it. As often as a dull name in a good company keeps early buyers away, a flashy name in a mediocre company attracts investors and gives them a false sense of security. As long as it has "advanced," "leading," "micro," or something with an x in it, or it's a mystifying acronym, people will fall in love with it. UAL changed its name to Allegis hoping to appeal to modern trendy thinkers. It's a good thing that Crown, Cork, and Seal left its name alone. If they'd listened to the corporate-image consultants, they would have changed it to CroCorSea, which would have guaranteed a big institutional following from the start.

10

Earnings, Earnings, Earnings

Let's say you noticed Sensormatic, the company that invented the clever tag and buzzer system for foiling shoplifters, and whose stock rose from $2 to $42 as the business expanded between 1979 and 1983. Your broker tells you it's a small company and a fast grower. Or perhaps you've reviewed your portfolio and you've found two stalwarts and three cyclicals. What possible assurance do you have that Sensormatic, or any of the stocks you own already, will go up in price? And if you're buying, how much should you pay?

What you're asking here is what makes a company valuable, and why it will be more valuable tomorrow than it is today. There are many theories, but to me, it always comes down to earnings and assets. Especially earnings. Sometimes it takes years for the stock price to catch up to a company's value, and the down periods last so long that investors begin to doubt that will ever happen. But value always wins out—or at least in enough cases that it's worthwhile to believe it.

Analyzing a company's stock on the basis of earnings and assets is no different from analyzing a local laundromat, drugstore, or apartment building that you might want to buy. *Although it's easy to for-*

get sometimes, a share of stock is not a lottery ticket. It's part ownership of a business.

Here's another way of thinking about earnings and assets. If you were a stock, your earnings and assets would determine how much an investor would be willing to pay for a percentage of your action. Evaluating yourself as you might evaluate General Motors is an instructive exercise, and it helps you get the hang of this phase of the investigation.

The assets would include all your real estate, cars, furniture, clothes, rugs, boats, tools, jewelry, golf clubs, and everything else that would go in a giant garage sale, if you decided to liquidate yourself and go out of business. Of course you'd have to subtract all outstanding mortgages, liens, car loans, other loans from banks, relatives, or neighbors, unpaid bills, IOUs, poker debts, and so forth. The result would be your positive bottom line, or book value, or net economic worth as a tangible asset. (Or if the result is negative, then you're a human candidate for Chapter 11.)

As long as you're not liquidated and sold off to the creditors, you also represent the other kind of value: the capacity to earn income. Over your working life you may bring home either thousands, hundreds of thousands, or millions of dollars, depending on how much they pay you and how hard you work. Here again, there are huge differences in cumulative results.

Now that you're thinking about it, you might want to put yourself in one of the six categories of stocks we've already gone over. This could be a halfway decent party game:

People who work in secure jobs that pay low salaries and modest raises are slow growers, the human equivalents of the electric utilities such as American Electric Power. Librarians, schoolteachers, and policemen are slow growers.

People who command good salaries and get predictable raises, such as the middle-level managers of corporations, are stalwarts: the Coca-Colas and Ralston Purinas of the work force.

Farmers, hotel and resort employees, jai alai players, summer-camp operators, and Christmas tree sales-lot operators who make all their money in short bursts and then try to budget it through long, unprofitable stretches are cyclicals. Writers and actors may also be cyclicals, but the possibility of sudden increases in fortune makes them potential fast growers.

Ne'er-do-wells, trust-fund men and women, squires, bon vivants, and others, who live off family fortunes but contribute nothing from their own labor are asset plays, the gold-mining stocks and railroads of our analogy. The issue with asset plays is always what will be left after all the debts are run up, and the creditors at the liquor store and the travel agency paid off.

Guttersnipes, drifters, down-and-outers, bankrupts, workers who've been laid off, and others in the unemployment lines are all potential turnarounds, as long as there's any energy and enterprise left in them.

Actors, inventors, real estate developers, small businessmen, athletes, musicians, and criminals are all potential fast growers. In this group there's a higher failure rate than there is among stalwarts, but if and when a fast grower succeeds, he or she may boost income tenfold, twentyfold, or even a hundredfold overnight, making him or her the human equivalent of Taco Bell or Stop & Shop.

When you buy a stock in a fast-growing company, you're really betting on its chances to earn more money in the future. Consider the decision to invest in a young Dunkin' Donuts such as Harrison Ford, as opposed to a Coca-Cola type such as a corporate lawyer. Investing in the Coca-Cola type seems a lot more sensible while Harrison Ford is working as an itinerant carpenter in Los Angeles, but look what happens to earnings when Mr. Ford makes a hit movie such as *Star Wars*.

The storefront lawyer isn't likely to become a tenbagger overnight unless he wins a big divorce case, but the guy who scrapes barnacles off boats and writes novels might be the next Hemingway. (Read the books before you invest!) That's why investors seek out promising fast growers and bid the stocks up, even when the companies are earning nothing at present—or when the earnings are paltry as compared to the price per share.

You can see the importance of earnings on any chart that has an earnings line running alongside the stock price. Books of stock charts are available from most brokerage firms, and it's instructive to flip through them. On chart after chart the two lines will move in tandem, or if the stock price strays away from the earnings line, sooner or later it will come back to the earnings.

People may wonder what the Japanese are doing and what the Koreans are doing, but ultimately the earnings will decide the fate of a stock. People may bet on the hourly wiggles in the market, but it's the earnings that waggle the wiggles, long term. Now and then you'll find an exception, but if you examine the charts of stocks you own, you'll likely see the relationship I'm describing.

During the last decade we've seen recessions and inflation, oil prices going up and oil prices going down, and all along, these stocks have followed earnings. Look at the chart of Dow Chemical. When earnings are up the stock is up. That's what happened during the period from 1971 to 1975 and again from 1985 through 1988. In between, from 1975 through 1985, earnings were erratic and so was the stock price.

Look at Avon, a stock that jumped from $3 in 1958 to $140 in 1972 as earnings continued to rise. Optimism abounded, and the stock price became inflated relative to earnings. Then, in 1973, the fantasy ended. The stock price collapsed because earnings collapsed, and you could have seen it coming. *Forbes* magazine warned us all in a cover article ten months before the collapse began.

And how about Masco Corporation, which developed the single-handle ball faucet, and as a result enjoyed thirty consecutive years of up earnings through war and peace, inflation and recession, with the earnings rising 800-fold and the stock rising 1,300-fold between 1958 and 1987? It's probably the greatest stock in the history of capitalism. What would you expect from a company that started out with the wonderfully ridiculous name of Masco Screw Products? As long as the earnings continued to increase, there was nothing to stop it.

Look at Shoney's, a restaurant chain that has had 116 consecutive quarters (twenty-nine years) of higher revenues—a record few companies could match. Sure enough, the stock price has steadily moved up. In those few spots where the price got ahead of the earnings, it promptly fell back to reality, as you can see in the chart.

The chart for Marriott, another great growth stock, tells the same story. And look at The Limited. When earnings stumbled in the late seventies, so did the stock. When earnings then soared, the stock soared as well. But when the stock got way ahead of earnings, as it did in 1983 and again in 1987, the result was a short-term disaster. The same was true for countless other stocks in the October, 1987 market decline.

(A quick way to tell if a stock is overpriced is to compare the price line to the earnings line. If you bought familiar growth companies—such as Shoney's, The Limited, or Marriott—when the stock price fell

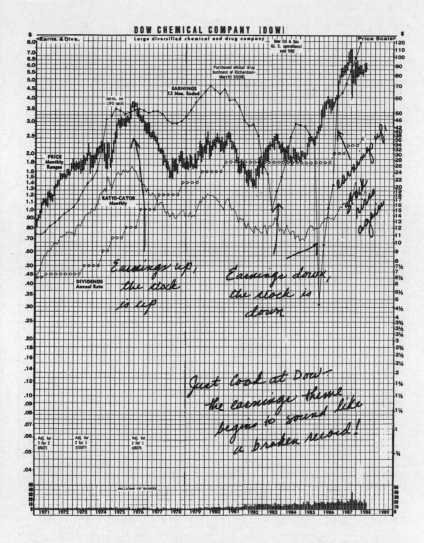

DOW CHEMICAL COMPANY [DOW]

Large diversified chemical and drug company

Earnings up, the stock is up

Earnings down, the stock is down

Just look at Dow— the earnings theme begins to sound like a broken record!

well below the earnings line, and sold them when the stock price rose dramatically above it, the chances are you'd do pretty well. [It sure would have worked with Avon!] I'm not necessarily advocating this practice, but I can think of worse strategies.)

THE FAMOUS P/E RATIO

Any serious discussion of earnings involves the price/earnings ratio—also known as the p/e ratio, the price-earnings multiple, or sim-

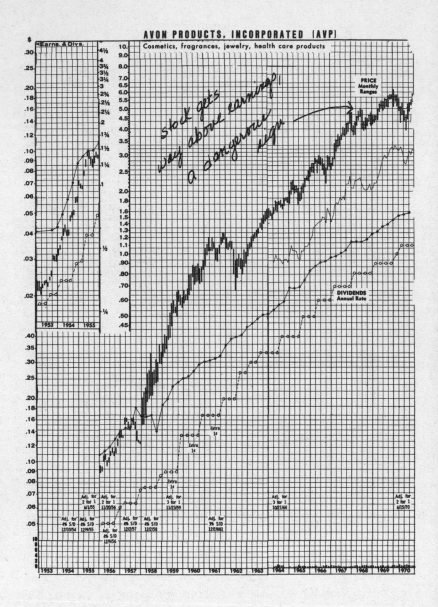

AVON PRODUCTS, INCORPORATED (AVP)

Cosmetics, fragrances, jewelry, health care products

Stock gets way above earnings — a dangerous sign

PRICE
Monthly Ranges

DIVIDENDS
Annual Rate

ply, the multiple. This ratio is a numerical shorthand for the relationship between the stock price and the earnings of the company. The p/e ratio for each stock is listed in the daily stock tables of most major newspapers, as shown here.

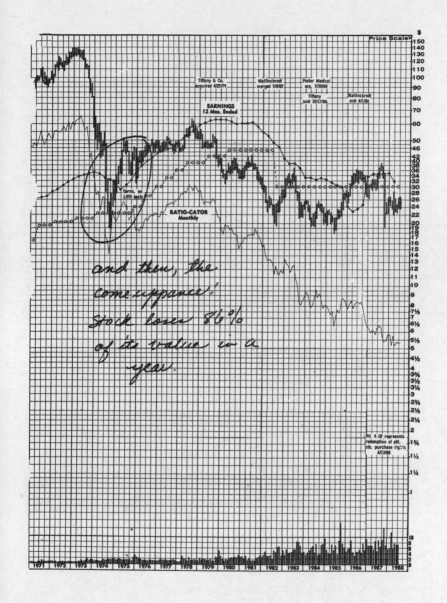

and then, the
come-uppance!
Stock loses 86%
of its value in a
year.

THE WALL STREET JOURNAL TUESDAY, SEPTEMBER 13, 1988   73

| 52 Weeks | | | | | Yld | P-E | Sales | | | | Net |
High	Low	Stock	Div.	%	Ratio	100s	High	Low	Close	Chg.
43¼	21⅝	K mart	1.32	3.8	10	4696	35⅛	34½	35	+⅜

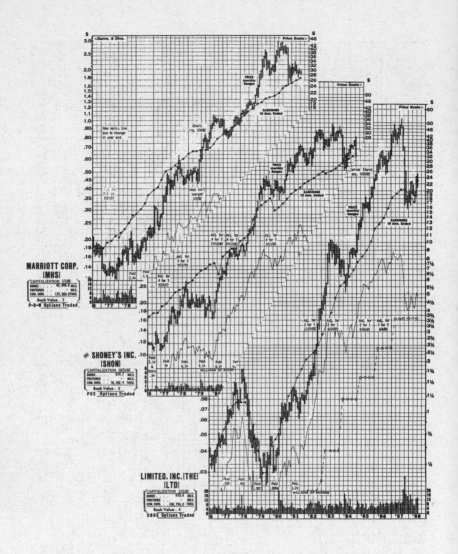

Like the earnings line, the p/e ratio is often a useful measure of whether any stock is overpriced, fairly priced, or underpriced relative to a company's money-making potential.

(In a few cases the p/e ratio listed in the newspaper may be abnormally high, often because a company has written off some long-term losses against the current short-term earnings, thus "punishing" those earnings. If the p/e seems out of line, you can ask your broker to provide you with an explanation.)

In today's *Wall Street Journal,* for instance, I see that K mart has a p/e ratio of 10. This was derived by taking the current price of the stock ($35 a share) and dividing it by the company's earnings for the prior 12 months or fiscal year (in this case, $3.50 a share). The $35 divided by the $3.50 results in the p/e of 10.

The p/e ratio can be thought of as the number of years it will take the company to earn back the amount of your initial investment— assuming, of course, that the company's earnings stay constant. Let's say you buy 100 shares of K mart for $3,500. Current earnings are $3.50 per share, so your 100 shares will earn $350 in one year, and the original investment of $3,500 will be earned back in ten years. However, you don't have to go through this exercise because the p/e ratio of 10 tells you it's ten years.

If you buy shares in a company selling at two times earnings (a p/e of 2), you will earn back your initial investment in two years, but in a company selling at 40 times earnings (a p/e of 40) it would take forty years to accomplish the same thing. Cher might be a great-grandmother by then. With all the low p/e opportunities around, why then would anybody buy a stock with a high p/e? Because they're looking for Harrison Ford at the lumber yard. Corporate earnings do not stay constant any more than human earnings do.

The fact that some stocks have p/e's of 40 and others have p/e's of 3 tells you that investors are willing to take substantial gambles on the improved future earnings of some companies, while they're quite skeptical about the future of others. Look in the newspaper and you'll be amazed at the range of p/e's that you see.

You'll also find that the p/e levels tend to be lowest for the slow growers and highest for the fast growers, with the cyclicals vacillating in between. That's as it should be, if you follow the logic of the discussion above. An average p/e for a utility (7 to 9 these days) will be lower than the average p/e for a stalwart (10 to 14 these days), and that in turn will be lower than the average p/e of a fast grower (14–20). Some bargain hunters believe in buying any and all stocks with low p/e's, but that strategy makes no sense to me. We shouldn't compare apples to oranges. What's a bargain p/e for a Dow Chemical isn't necessarily the same as a bargain p/e for a Wal-Mart.

MORE ON THE P/E

A full discussion of p/e ratios of various industries and different types of companies would take an entire book that nobody would want to read. It's silly to get bogged down in p/e's, but you don't want to ignore them. Once again, your broker may be your best source for p/e analysis. You might begin by asking whether the p/e ratios of various stocks you own are low, high, or average, relative to the industry norms. Sometimes you'll hear things like "this company is selling at a discount to the industry"—meaning that its p/e is at a bargain level.

A broker can also give you the historical record of a company's p/e—and the same information can be found on the S&P reports also available from the brokerage firm. Before you buy a stock, you might want to track its p/e ratio back through several years to get a sense of its normal levels. (New companies, of course, haven't been around long enough to have such records.)

If you buy Coca-Cola, for instance, it's useful to know whether what you're paying for the earnings is in line with what others have paid for the earnings in the past. The p/e ratio can tell you that.

(The *Value Line Investment Survey,* available in most large libraries and also from most brokers, is another good source for p/e histories. In fact, *Value Line* is a good source for all the pertinent data that amateur investors need to know. It's the next best thing to having your own private securities analyst.)

If you remember nothing else about p/e ratios, remember to avoid stocks with excessively high ones. You'll save yourself a lot of grief and a lot of money if you do. With few exceptions, an extremely high p/e ratio is a handicap to a stock, in the same way that extra weight in the saddle is a handicap to a racehorse.

A company with a high p/e must have incredible earnings growth to justify the high price that's been put on the stock. In 1972, McDonald's was the same great company it had always been, but the stock was bid up to $75 a share, which gave it a p/e of 50. There was no way that McDonald's could live up to those expectations, and the stock price fell from $75 to $25, sending the p/e back to a more realistic 13. There wasn't anything wrong with McDonald's. It was simply overpriced at $75 in 1972.

And if McDonald's was overpriced, look at what happened to Ross Perot's company, Electronic Data Systems (EDS), a hot stock in the late 1960s. I couldn't believe it when I saw a brokerage report on the company. This company had a p/e of 500! It would take five centuries to make back your investment in EDS if the earnings stayed constant. Not only that, but the analyst who wrote the report was suggesting that the p/e was conservative, because EDS ought to have a p/e of 1,000.

If you had invested in a company with a p/e of 1,000 when King Arthur roamed England, and the earnings stayed constant, you'd just be breaking even today.

I wish I had saved this report and had it framed for my office wall, to put alongside one that was sent to me from another brokerage firm that read: "Due to the recent bankruptcy, we're removing this stock from our buy list."

In the years that followed, EDS the company performed very well. The earnings and sales grew dramatically, and everything it did was a whopping success. EDS the stock is another story. The price declined from $40 to $3 in 1974, not because there was anything amiss at head-quarters, but because the stock was the most overpriced of any I've ever seen before or since. You often hear about companies whose future performance is "discounted" in the stock price. If that's the case, then EDS investors were discounting the Hereafter. More on EDS later.

When Avon Products sold for $140 a share, it had an extremely high p/e ratio of 64—though nowhere near as extreme as EDS's. The important thing here is that Avon was a huge company. It's a miracle for even a small company to expand enough to justify a p/e of 64, but for a company the size of Avon, which already had over a billion in sales, it would have had to sell megabillions worth of cosmetics and lotions. In fact, somebody calculated that for Avon to justify a 64 p/e it would have to earn more than the steel industry, the oil industry, and the State of California combined. That was the best-case scenario. But how many lotions and bottles of cologne can you sell? As it was, Avon's earnings didn't grow at all. They declined, and the stock price promptly plummeted to $18⅝ in 1974.

The same thing happened at Polaroid. This was another solid company, with 32 years of prosperity behind it, but it lost 89 percent of its value in 18 months. The stock sold for $143 in 1973 and dropped to $14⅛ in 1974, only to bounce up to $60 in 1978 and then stumble once again, back to $19 in 1981. At the market high in 1973, Polaroid's p/e was 50. It got that high because investors expected an incredible growth spurt from the new SX-70 camera, but the camera and the film were overpriced, there were operating problems, and people lost interest in it.

Again, the expectations were so unrealistic that even if the SX-70 had succeeded, Polaroid would probably have had to sell four of them to every family in America to earn enough money to justify the high p/e. The camera as a rousing success wouldn't have done much for the stock. As it was, the camera was only a moderate success, so it was bad news all around.

THE P/E OF THE MARKET

Company p/e ratios do not exist in a vacuum. The stock market as a whole has its own collective p/e ratio, which is a good indicator of whether the market at large is overvalued or undervalued. I know I've already advised you to ignore the market, but when you find that a few stocks are selling at inflated prices relative to earnings, it's likely that most stocks are selling at inflated prices relative to earnings. That's what happened before the big drop in 1973–74, and once again (although not to the same extent) before the big drop of 1987.

During the five years of the latest bull market, from 1982 to 1987, you could see the market's overall p/e ratio creep gradually higher, from about 8 to 16. This meant that investors in 1987 were willing to pay twice what they paid in 1982 for the same corporate earnings—which should have been a warning that most stocks were overvalued.

Interest rates have a large effect on the prevailing p/e ratios, since investors pay more for stocks when interest rates are low and bonds are less attractive. But interest rates aside, the incredible optimism that develops in bull markets can drive p/e ratios to ridiculous levels, as it did in the cases of EDS, Avon, and Polaroid. In that period, the fast growers commanded p/e ratios that belonged somewhere in Wonderland, the slow growers were commanding p/e ratios normally reserved for fast growers, and the p/e of the market itself hit a peak of 20 in 1971.

Any student of the p/e ratio could have seen that this was lunacy, and I wish one of them had told me. In 1973–74 the market had its most brutal correction since the 1930s.

FUTURE EARNINGS

Future earnings—there's the rub. How do you predict those? The best you can get from current earnings is an educated guess whether a stock is fairly priced. If you do this much, you'll never buy a Polaroid or an Avon at a 40 p/e, nor will you overpay for Bristol-Myers, Coca-Cola, or McDonald's. However, what you'd really like to know is what's going to happen to earnings in the next month, the next year, or the next decade.

Earnings, after all, are supposed to grow, and every stock price carries with it a built-in growth assumption.

Battalions of analysts and statisticians are launched against the questions of future growth and future earnings, and you can pick up the nearest financial magazine to see for yourself how often they get the wrong answer (the word most frequently seen with "earnings" is "surprise"). I'm not about to suggest that you can begin to predict earnings, or growth in earnings, successfully on your own.

Once you got into this game seriously, you'd be boggled by the examples of stocks that go down even though the earnings are up, because professional analysts and their institutional clients expected the earnings to be higher, or stocks that go up even though earnings are down, because that same cheering section expected the earnings to be lower. These are short-term anomalies, but nonetheless frustrating to the shareholder who notices them.

If you can't predict future earnings, at least you can find out *how* a company plans to increase its earnings. Then you can check periodically to see if the plans are working out.

There are five basic ways a company can increase earnings*: reduce costs; raise prices; expand into new markets; sell more of its product in the old markets; or revitalize, close, or otherwise dispose of a losing operation. These are the factors to investigate as you develop the story. If you have an edge, this is where it's going to be most helpful.

---

* Some people confuse dividends with the earnings we've been discussing in this chapter. A company's earnings is what it makes every year after all expenses and taxes are taken out. A dividend is what it pays out to stockholders on a regular basis as their share of the profits. A company may have terrific earnings and yet pay no dividend at all.

11

The Two-Minute Drill

Already you've found out whether you're dealing with a slow grower, a stalwart, a fast grower, a turnaround, an asset play, or a cyclical. The p/e ratio has given you a rough idea of whether the stock, as currently priced, is undervalued or overvalued relative to its immediate prospects. The next step is to learn as much as possible about what the company is doing to bring about the added prosperity, the growth spurt, or whatever happy event is expected to occur. This is known as the "story."

With the possible exception of the asset play (where you can sit back and wait for the value of the real estate or the oil reserves or the TV stations to be recognized by others), something dynamic has to happen to keep the earnings moving along. The more certain you are about what that something is, the better you'll be able to follow the script.

The analyst's reports on the company you get from your broker, and the short essays in the *Value Line* give you the professional version of the story, but if you've got an edge in the company or in the industry, you'll be able to develop your own script in useful detail.

Before buying a stock, I like to be able to give a two-minute monologue that covers the reasons I'm interested in it, what has to happen for the company to succeed, and the pitfalls that stand in its path. The two-minute monologue can be muttered under your breath or repeated out loud to colleagues who happen to be standing within earshot. Once you're able to tell the story of a stock to your family, your friends, or the dog (and I don't mean "a guy on the bus says Caesars World is a takeover"), and so that even a child could understand it, then you have a proper grasp of the situation.

Here are some of the topics that might be addressed in the monologue:

If it's a slow-growing company you're thinking about, then presumably you're in it for the dividend, (Why else own this kind of stock?) Therefore, the important elements of the script would be: "This company has increased earnings every year for the last ten, it offers an attractive yield; it's never reduced or suspended a dividend, and in fact it's raised the dividend during good times and bad, including the last three recessions. It's a telephone utility, and the new cellular operations may add a substantial kicker to the growth rate."

If it's a cyclical company you're thinking about, then your script revolves around business conditions, inventories, and prices. "There has been a three-year business slump in the auto industry, but this year things have turned around. I know that because car sales are up across the board for the first time in recent memory. I notice that GM's new models are selling well, and in the last eighteen months the company has closed five inefficient plants, cut twenty percent off labor costs, and earnings are about to turn sharply higher."

If it's an asset play, then what are the assets, how much are they worth? "The stock sells for $8, but the videocassette division alone is worth $4 a share and the real estate is worth $7. That's a bargain in itself, and I'm getting the rest of the company for a minus $3. Insiders are buying, and the company has steady earnings, and there's no debt to speak of."

If it's a turnaround, then has the company gone about improving its fortunes, and is the plan working so far? "General Mills has made great progress in curing its diworseification. It's gone from eleven basic businesses to two. By selling off Eddie Bauer, Talbot's, Kenner, and Parker Brothers and getting top dollar for these excellent companies, General Mills has returned to doing what it does best: restaurants and packaged foods. The company has been buying back millions of its shares. The seafood subsidiary, Gortons, has grown from 7 percent of the seafood market to 25 percent. They are coming out with low-cal yogurt, no-cholesterol Bisquick, and microwave brownies. Earnings are up sharply."

If it's a stalwart, then the key issues are the p/e ratio, whether the stock already has had a dramatic run-up in price in recent months, and what, if anything, is happening to accelerate the growth rate. You might say to yourself: "Coca-Cola is selling at the low end of its p/e range. The stock hasn't gone anywhere for two years. The company has improved itself in several ways. It sold half its interest in Columbia Pictures to the public. Diet drinks have sped up the growth rate dramatically. Last year the Japanese drank 36 percent more Cokes than they did the year before, and the Spanish upped their consumption by 26 percent. That's phenomenal progress. Foreign sales are excellent in general. Through a separate stock offering, Coca-Cola Enterprises, the company has bought out many of its independent regional distributors. Now the company has better control over distribution and domestic sales. Because of these factors, Coca-Cola may do better than people think."

If it is a fast grower, then where and how can it continue to grow fast? "La Quinta is a motel chain that started out in Texas. It was very profitable there. The company successfully duplicated its successful formula in Arkansas and Louisiana. Last year it added 20 percent more motel units than the year before. Earnings have increased every quarter. The company plans rapid future expansion. The debt is not excessive. Motels are a low-growth industry, and very competitive, but La Quinta has found something of a niche. It has a long way to go before it has saturated the market."

Those are some basic themes for the story, and you can fill in as much detail as you want. The more you know the better. I often devote several hours to developing a script, though that's not always necessary. Let me give you two examples, one a situation that I checked out properly, and the other where there was something I forgot to ask. The first was La Quinta, which has been a fifteenbagger, and the second was Bildner's, a fifteenbagger in reverse.

CHECKING OUT LA QUINTA

At one point I'd decided the motel industry was due for a cyclical turnaround. I'd already invested in United Inns, the largest franchiser of Holiday Inns, and I was keeping my ears open for other opportunities. During a telephone interview with a vice president at United Inns, I asked which company was Holiday Inn's most successful competitor.

Asking about the competition is one of my favorite techniques for finding promising new stocks. Muckamucks speak negatively about the competition ninety-five percent of the time, and it doesn't mean much. But when an executive of one company admits he's impressed by another company, you can bet that company is doing something right. Nothing could be more bullish than begrudging admiration from a rival.

"La Quinta Motor Inns," the vice president of United Inns enthused. "They're doing a great job. They're killing us in Houston and in Dallas." He sounded very impressed, and so was I.

That's the first I'd ever heard of La Quinta, but as soon as I got off the phone with this exciting new tip, I got back on the phone with Walter Biegler at La Quinta headquarters in San Antonio to find out what the story was. Mr. Biegler told me that in two days he'd be coming to Boston for a business conference at Harvard, at which time he'd be glad to tell me the story in person.

Between the United Inns man's dropping the hint and five minutes later the La Quinta man's mentioning that he just happened to be traveling to Boston, the whole thing sounded like a set-up job to sucker me into buying millions of shares. But as soon as I heard Biegler's presentation, I knew it wasn't a set-up job, and the best way to have gotten suckered would have been not to have bought this wonderful stock.

The concept was simple. La Quinta offered rooms of Holiday Inn quality, but at a lower price. The room was the same size as a Holiday Inn room, the bed was just as firm (there are bed consultants to the motel industry who figure these things out), the bathrooms were just as nice, the pool was just as nice, yet the rates were 30 percent less. How was that possible? I wanted to know. Biegler went on to explain.

La Quinta had eliminated the wedding area, the conference rooms, the large reception area, the kitchen area, and the restaurant—all excess space that contributed nothing to the profits but added substantially to the costs. La Quinta's idea was to install a Denny's or some similar 24-hour place next door to every one of its motels. La Quinta didn't even have to own the Denny's. Somebody else could worry about the food. Holiday Inn isn't famous for its cuisine, so it's not as if La Quinta was giving up a major selling point. Right here, La Quinta avoided a big capital investment and sidestepped some big trouble. It turns out that most hotels and motels lose money on their restaurants, and the restaurants cause 95 percent of the complaints.

I always try to learn something new from every investment conversation I have. From Mr. Biegler I learned that hotel and motel customers routinely pay one one-thousandth of the value of a room for each night's lodging. If the Plaza Hotel in New York is worth $400,000 a room, you're probably going to pay $400 a night to stay there, and if the No-Tell Motel is built for $20,000 a room, then you'll be paying $20 a night. Because it cost 30 percent less to build a La Quinta than it did to build a Holiday Inn, I could see how La Quinta could rent out rooms at a 30-percent discount and still make the same profit as a Holiday Inn.

Where was the niche? I wanted to know. There were hundreds of motel rooms at every fork in the road already. Mr. Biegler said they had a specific target: the small businessman who didn't care for the budget motel, and if he had the choice, he'd rather pay less for the equivalent luxury of a Holiday Inn. La Quinta was there to provide the equivalent luxury, and at locations that were often more convenient to traveling businessmen.

Holiday Inn, which wanted to be all things to all travelers, frequently built its units just off the access ramps of major turnpikes. La Quinta built its units near the business districts, government offices, hospitals, and industrial complexes where its customers were most likely to do business. And because these were business travelers and not vacationers, a higher percentage of them booked their rooms in advance, giving La Quinta the advantage of a steadier and more predictable clientele.

Nobody else had captured this part of the market, the middle ground between the Hilton hotels above and the budget inn below. Also, there was no way that some newer competitor could sneak up on La Quinta without Wall Street's knowing about it. That's one reason I prefer hotel and restaurant stocks to technology stocks—the minute you invest in an exciting new technology, a more exciting and newer technology is brought out of somebody else's lab. But the prototypes of would-be hotel and restaurant chains have to show up someplace—you simply can't build 100 of them overnight, and if they are in a different part of the country, they wouldn't affect you anyway.

What about the costs? When small and new companies undertake expensive projects like hotel construction, the burden of debt can weigh them down for years. Biegler reassured me on this point as well. He said that La Quinta had kept costs low by building 120-room inns instead of 250-room inns, by supervising the construction in-house, and by following a cookie-cutter blueprint. Furthermore, a 120-room operation could be managed by a live-in retired couple, which saved on overhead. And most impressive, La Quinta had struck a deal with major insurance companies who were providing all the financing at favorable terms, in exchange for a small share in the profits.

As partners in La Quinta's success or failure, insurance companies weren't likely to make loan demands that would drive the company into bankruptcy if a shortfall ever occurred. In fact, this access to insurance-company money is what enabled La Quinta to grow rapidly in a capital-intensive business without incurring the dreaded bank debt (see Chapter 13).

Soon enough, I was satisfied that Biegler and his employers had thought of everything. La Quinta was a great story, and not one of those would-be, could-be, might-be, soon-to-be tales. If they aren't already doing it, then don't invest in it.

La Quinta had already been operating for four or five years at the time Biegler visited my office. The original La Quinta had been duplicated several times and in several different locations. The company was growing at an astounding 50 percent a year, and the stock was selling at ten times earnings, which made it an incredible bargain. I knew how many new units La Quinta was proposing to build, so I could keep track of progress in the future.

To top it all off, I was delighted to discover that only three brokerage firms covered La Quinta in 1978, and that less than 20 percent of the stock was held by the big institutions. The only thing wrong with La Quinta that I could see was it wasn't boring enough.

I followed up on this conversation by spending three nights in three different La Quintas while I was on the road talking to other companies. I bounced on the beds, stuck my toe into the shallow end of the swimming pools (I never learned to swim), tugged at the curtains, squeezed the towels, and satisfied myself that La Quinta was the equal of Holiday Inn.

The La Quinta story checked out in every detail, and even then I almost talked myself out of buying any shares. That the stock had doubled in the previous year wasn't bothersome—the p/e ratio relative to the growth rate still made it a bargain. What bothered me was that one

of the important insiders had sold his shares at half the price I was star-
ing at in the newspaper. (I found out later that this insider, a member
of the founding family of La Quinta, was simply diversifying his portfolio.)

Fortunately I reminded myself that insider selling is a terrible reason
to dislike a stock, and then I bought as much La Quinta as possible for
Magellan fund. I made elevenfold on it over a ten-year period before it
suffered a downturn due to declining fortunes in the energy-producing
states. Recently the company has become an exciting combination of
asset play and turnaround.

BILDNER'S, ALAS

The mistake I didn't make with La Quinta I made with J. Bildner and
Sons. My having invested in Bildner's is a perfect example of what happens when you get so caught up in the euphoria of an enterprise that
you ask all the questions except a most important one, and that turns
out to be the fatal flaw.

Bildner's is a specialty food store located right across the street from
my office on Devonshire in Boston. There was also a Bildner's out in
the town where I live—although it's gone now. Among other things,
Bildner's sells gourmet sandwiches and prepared hot foods, a sort of
happy compromise between a convenience store and a three-star
restaurant. I'm well-acquainted with their sandwiches, since I've been
eating them for lunch for several years. That was my edge on Bildner's:
I had firsthand information that they had the best bread and the best
sandwiches in Boston.

The story was that Bildner's was planning to expand into other cities
and was going public to raise the money. It sounded good to me. The
company had carved out a perfect niche—the millions of white-collar
types who had no tolerance for microwave sandwiches in plastic wrappers, and yet who also refused to cook.

Bildner's takeout already was the salvation of working couples who
were too tired to set up the Cuisinart and yet who wanted to serve
something that looked as if it could have been prepared in a Cuisinart
for dinner. Before they went home to the suburbs, they could stop at
Bildner's and buy the kind of designer meal they would have cooked
themselves, if they were still cooking: something with French beans,
béarnaise sauce, and/or almonds.

I'd fully researched the operation by wandering into the store across the street. One of the original Bildner's, it was clean, efficient, and full of satisfied customers, a regular yuppie 7-Eleven. I also discovered it was a fabulous money-maker. When I heard that Bildner's was planning to sell stock and use the proceeds to open more stores, I was understandably excited.

From the prospectus of the stock offering, I learned that the company was not going to burden itself with excessive bank debt. This was a plus. It was going to lease space for its new stores, as opposed to buying the real estate. This, too, was a plus. Without further investigation I bought Bildner's at the initial offering price of $13 in September, 1986.

Soon after this sale of stock, Bildner's opened two new outlets in a couple of Boston department stores, and these flopped. Then it opened three new outlets in the center of Manhattan, and these got killed by the delis. It expanded into more distant cities, including Atlanta. By quickly spending more than the proceeds from the public offering, Bildner's had overextended itself financially. One or two mistakes at a time might not have been so damaging, but instead of moving cautiously, Bildner's suffered multiple and simultaneous failures. The company no doubt learned from these mistakes, and Jim Bildner was a bright, hardworking, and dedicated man, but after the money ran out, there was no second chance. It's too bad, because I thought Bildner's could have been the next Taco Bell. (Did I really say the "next Taco Bell"? That probably doomed it from the start.)

The stock eventually bottomed out at $1/8, and the management retreated to its original stores, including the one across the street. Bildner's optimistic new goal was to avoid bankruptcy, but recently it's bought The Chapter. I gradually unloaded my shares at losses ranging from 50 percent to 95 percent.

I continue to eat sandwiches from Bildner's, and every time I take a bite of one it reminds me of what I did wrong. I didn't wait to see if this good idea from the neighborhood would actually succeed someplace else. Successful cloning is what turns a local taco joint into a Taco Bell or a local clothing store into The Limited, but there's no point buying the stock until the company has proven that the cloning works.

If the prototype's in Texas, you're smart to hold off buying until the company shows it can make money in Illinois or in Maine. That's what I forgot to ask Bildner's: Does the idea work elsewhere? I should have worried about a shortage of skilled store managers, its limited financial resources, and its ability to survive those initial mistakes.

It's never too late not to invest in an unproven enterprise. If I'd waited to buy Bildner's until later, I wouldn't have bought it at all. I should also have sold sooner. It was clear from the two department-store flops and the New York flops that Bildner's had a problem, and it was time to fold the hand right then, before the cards got worse. I must have been asleep at the table.

Great sandwiches, though.

12
Getting the Facts

Although there are various drawbacks to being a fund manager, there's the advantage that companies will talk to us—several times a week if we'd like. It's amazing how popular you feel when enough people want you to buy a million shares of their stock. I get to travel from coast to coast, visiting one opportunity after another. Chairmen, presidents, vice presidents, and analysts fill me in on capital spending, expansion plans, cost-cutting programs, and anything else that's relevant to future results. Fellow portfolio managers pass along what they've heard. And if I can't visit the company, the company will come to me.

On the other hand, I can't imagine anything that's useful to know that the amateur investor can't find out. All the pertinent facts are just waiting to be picked up. It didn't use to be that way, but it is now. These days, companies are required to tell nearly all in their prospectuses, their quarterlies, and their annual reports. Industry trade associations report on the general industry outlook in their publications. (Companies are also happy to send you the company newsletter. Sometimes you can find useful information in these chatty highlights.)

Rumors, I know, are still more exciting than public information, which is why a snippet of conversation overheard in a restaurant—

"Goodyear is on the move"—carries more weight than Goodyear's own literature. It's the old oracle rule at work: the more mysterious the source, the more persuasive the advice. Investors continually put their ears to the walls when it's the handwriting that tells everything. Perhaps if they stamped the annual and quarterly reports "classified" or mailed them out in plain brown wrappers, more recipients would browse through them.

What you can't get from the annual report you can get by asking your broker, by calling the company, by visiting the company, or by doing some grassroots research, also known as kicking the tires.

GETTING THE MOST OUT OF A BROKER

If you buy and sell stocks through a full-service brokerage firm instead of a discount house, you're probably paying an extra 30 cents a share in commissions. That's not a lot, but it ought to be worth something besides a Christmas card and the firm's latest ideas. Remember, it only takes a broker about four seconds to fill out a buy or sell order, and another fifteen seconds to walk it to the order desk. Sometimes this job is handled by a courier or a runner.

Why is it that people who wouldn't dream of paying for gas at the full-service pump without getting the oil checked and the windows washed demand nothing from the full-service broker? Well, maybe they call him or her a couple of times a week to ask "How are my stocks doing?" or "How good is this market?"—but figuring the up-to-the-minute value of a portfolio doesn't count as investment research. I realize the broker may also serve as a parental figure, market forecaster, and human tranquilizer during unfavorable price swings. None of this actually helps you pick good companies.

Even as far back as the early nineteenth century, the poet Shelley found stockbrokers (or at least one of them) eager to lend a helping hand to their clients. "Is it not odd that the only generous person I ever knew, who had money to be generous with, should be a stockbroker?" Today's brokers may be less likely to send large, unsolicited donations to their clients, but as information gatherers they can be the stockpicker's best friend. They can provide the S&P reports and the investment newsletters, the annuals, quarterlies and prospectuses and proxy statements, the *Value Line* survey and the research from the firm's analysts. Let them get the data on p/e ratios and growth rates, on insider buying and ownership by institutions. They'll be happy to do it, once they realize that you're serious.

If you use the broker as an advisor (a foolhardy practice generally, but sometimes worthwhile), then ask the broker to give you the two-minute speech on the recommended stocks. You'll probably have to prompt the broker with some of the questions I've listed before, and a typical dialogue that now goes—

BROKER: "We're recommending Zayre. It's a special situation."

YOU: "Do you really think it's good?"

BROKER: "We really think it's good."

YOU: "Great. I'll buy it."

—would be transformed into something like this:

BROKER: "We're recommending La Quinta Motor Inns. It just made our buy list."

YOU: "How would you classify this stock? Cyclical, slow grower, faster grower, or what?"

BROKER: "Definitely a fast grower."

YOU: "How fast? What's the recent growth in earnings?"

BROKER: "Offhand, I don't know. I can check into it."

YOU: "I'd appreciate that. And while you're at it, could you get me the p/e ratio relative to historic levels."

BROKER: "Sure."

YOU: "What is it about La Quinta that makes it a good buy now? Where is the market? Are the existing La Quintas making a profit? Where's the expansion coming from? What's the debt situation? How will they finance growth without selling lots of new shares and diluting the earnings? Are insiders buying?"

BROKER: "I think a lot of that will be covered in our analyst's report."

YOU: "Send me a copy. I'll read it and get back to you. Meanwhile, I'd also like a chart of the stock price versus the earnings for the last five years. I want to know about dividends, if any, and whether they've always been paid. While you are at it, find out what percentage of the shares is owned by institutions. Also, how long has your firm's analyst been covering this stock?"

BROKER: "Is that all?"

YOU: "I'll let you know after I read the report. Then maybe I'll call the company. . . ."

BROKER: "Don't delay too long. It's a great time to buy."

YOU: "Right now in October? You know what Mark Twain says: 'October is one of the peculiarly dangerous months to speculate in stocks. The others are July, January, September, April, November, May, March, June, December, August, and February.' "

CALLING THE COMPANY

Professionals call companies all the time, yet amateurs never think of it. If you have specific questions, the investor relations office is a good place to get the answers. That's one more thing the broker can do: get you the phone number. Many companies would welcome a chance to exchange views with the owner of 100 shares from Topeka. If it's a small outfit, you may find yourself talking to the president.

In the unlikely event that investor relations gives you the cold shoulder, you can tell them that you own 20,000 shares and are trying to decide whether to double your position. Then casually mention that your shares are held in "street name." That ought to warm things up. Actually I'm not recommending this, but fibbing is something that some people would think of, and the odds of your being caught in it here are nil. The company has to take your word for the 20,000 shares, because shares held in street name are lumped together by the brokerage firms and stored in an undifferentiated mass.

Before you call the company, it's advisable to prepare your questions, and you needn't lead off with "Why is the stock going down?" Asking why the stock is going down immediately brands you as a neophyte and undeserving of serious response. In most cases a company has no idea why the stock is going down.

Earnings are a good topic, but for some reason it's not regarded as proper etiquette to ask the company "How much are you going to make?" any more than it's proper etiquette for strangers to ask you your annual salary. The accepted form of the question is subtle and indirect:

"What are the Wall Street estimates of your company's earnings for the upcoming year?"

As you already know by now, future earnings are hard to predict. Even the analysts vary widely in their predictions, and companies themselves can't be sure how much they'll earn. The people at Procter and Gamble have a pretty good idea, since that company makes 82 different products in 100 different brands and sells them in 107 different countries, so everything tends to even out. But the people at Reynolds Metals couldn't possibly tell you, because it all depends on aluminum prices. If you ask Phelps Dodge what it will earn next year, Phelps Dodge will turn around and ask you what the price of copper is going to be.

What you really want from investor relations is the company's reaction to whatever script you've been trying to develop. Does it make sense? Is it working? If you wonder if the drug Tagamet will have a significant effect on SmithKline's fortunes, the company can tell you that—and they can also give you the latest figures for Tagamet sales.

Is there really a two-month backlog on orders for Goodyear tires, and have tire prices really gone up as you've concluded from local evidence? How many new Taco Bells are being built this year? How much market share has Budweiser added? Are the Bethlehem Steel plants running at full capacity? What's the company's estimate of the market value of its cable TV properties? If your story line is well-defined, you'll know what points to check.

Better that you lead off with a question that shows you've done some research on your own, such as: "I see in the last annual report that you reduced debt by $500 million. What are the plans for further debt reduction?" This will get you a more serious answer than if you ask: "What are you guys doing about debt?"

Even if you have no script, you can learn something by asking two general questions: "What are the positives this year?" and "What are the negatives?" Maybe they'll tell you about the plant in Georgia that lost $10 million last year but has now been closed down, or about the unproductive division that's being sold off for cash. Maybe some new product has come along to speed up the growth rate. Back in 1987, investor relations at Sterling Drug could have told you if the recent medical news about aspirin had boosted sales.

On the negative side, you'll learn there's been an increase in labor costs, that demand for a major product has slipped, that there's a new competitor in the business, or that the falling (or rising) dollar is going to reduce profits. If it's a clothing manufacturer you're addressing, maybe you'll discover that this year's line isn't selling and that inventories have piled up.

At the end, you can sum up the conversation: three negatives, four positives. In most cases you'll hear something that confirms what you suspected—especially if you understand the business. But once in a while you'll learn something unexpected—that things are either better or worse than they appear. The unexpected can be very profitable if you're buying or selling stocks.

In the course of my research I find something out of the ordinary in about one out of every ten calls. If I'm calling depressed companies, then in nine cases the details will confirm that the companies ought to be depressed, but in the tenth case, there'll be some new cause for optimism that isn't generally perceived. The same ratio holds, but in reverse, for the companies that are supposedly in great shape. If I make 100 calls, I find 10 surprising situations, or if I make 1,000 calls, then 100.

Don't worry. If you don't own 1,000 companies, you don't have to make 1,000 calls.

CAN YOU BELIEVE IT?

For the most part, companies are honest and forthright in their conversations with investors. They all realize that the truth is going to come out sooner rather than later in the next quarterly report, so there's nothing to be gained by covering things up the way they sometimes do in Washington. In all my years of listening to thousands of corporate representatives tell their side of the story—as terrible as business might have gotten—I can only remember a few instances when I was misled deliberately.

So when you call investor relations, you can have full confidence that the facts you'll be hearing are correct. The adjectives, though, will vary widely. Different kinds of companies have different ways of describing the same scene.

Take textiles. Textile companies have been around since the nineteenth century. JP Stevens got started in 1899, West Point-Pepperell in 1866—these are the corporate equivalents of the Daughters of the American Revolution. When you've been through six wars, ten booms, fifteen busts, and thirty recessions, you tend not to get excited by any-thing new. You're also strong enough to admit readily to adversity.

The investor relations people in textiles have picked up enough of this old-guard attitude that they manage to sound unenthusiastic when business is terrific, and absolutely downcast when business is good. And if business is poor, you'd think by the spirit of the interviews that the executives were hanging themselves by their percale sheets out the windows of their offices.

Let's say you call up and inquire about the wool-worsted business. "Mediocre," they say. Then you ask about polyester-blend shirts, and they answer, "Not so hot." "How's denims?" you wonder. "Ah, it's been better." But when they give you the actual numbers, you realize that the company is doing great.

That's just how it is in textiles, and in mature industries in general. ***When looking at the same sky, people in mature industries see clouds where people in immature industries see pie.***

Take apparel companies, which make the finished products from textiles. These companies have a tenuous existence and are forever disappearing from financial life. For the number of times they've de-clared Chapter 11, you'd think it was an amendment to the Constitu-tion. Yet you'll never hear the word "mediocre" from an apparel person, even when sales are disastrous. The worst you'd ever hear from an apparel person during a retailers' Black Plague would be that things were "basically okay." And when things are basically okay, you'll hear that the situation is "fantastic," "unbelievable," "fabulous," and "out of this world."

The technology people and the software people are equally Pollyan-naish. You can almost assume that the more tenuous the enterprise, the more optimistic the rhetoric is going to be. From what I hear from the software people, you'd think that there's never been a down year in the history of software. Of course, why shouldn't they be upbeat? With so many competitors in software, you have to sound upbeat. If you ap-pear to lack confidence, some other sweet-talker will win all the con-tracts.

But there's no reason for the investor to waste time deciphering the corporate vocabulary. It's simpler to ignore all the adjectives.

VISITING HEADQUARTERS

One of the greatest joys of being a shareholder is visiting the head-quarters of the companies you own. If it's in the neighborhood, then getting an appointment is a cinch. They're delighted to give tours to the owners of 20,000 shares. If it's someplace across the country, maybe you can sneak in a visit on your summer vacation. "Gee whiz, kids, just sixty-three miles from here is the main office of Pacific Gas and Electric. Mind if I stop in for a peek at the balance sheet while you guys sit on the grass in the visitor's parking lot?" Okay, okay. Forget I suggested it.

When I visit a headquarters, what I'm really after is a feel for the place. The facts and figures can be gotten on the phone. I got positive feelings when I saw that Taco Bell's headquarters was stuck behind a bowling alley. When I saw those executives operating out of that grim little bunker, I was thrilled. Obviously they weren't wasting money on landscaping the office.

(The first thing I ask, by the way, is: "When is the last time a fund manager or an analyst visited here?" If the answer is "two years ago, I think," then I'm ecstatic. That was the case at Meridian Bank—22 years of up earnings, a great record of raising dividends, and they'd forgotten what an analyst looked like.)

Seek out the headquarters with the hope that if it's not stuck behind a bowling alley, then it will be located in some seedy neighborhood where financial analysts wouldn't want to be seen. The summer intern I sent to visit Pep Boys—Manny, Moe, and Jack reported that the Philadelphia cab drivers didn't want to take him there. I was as impressed with that as almost anything else he found out.

At Crown, Cork, and Seal, I noticed that the president's office had a scenic view of the can lines, the floors were faded linoleum, and the office furniture was shabbier than stuff I sat on in the Army. Now there's a company with the right priorities—and you know what's happened to the stock? It's gone up 280-fold in the last thirty years. Rich earnings and a cheap headquarters is a great combination.

So what do you make of Uniroyal, perched on a Connecticut hillside like all the fancy prep schools? I guessed it was a bad sign, and sure enough, the company went downhill. Other bad signs include fine antique furniture, trompe l'oeil drapes, and polished-walnut walls. I've seen it happen in many an office: when they bring the rubber trees indoors, it's time to fear for the earnings.

INVESTOR RELATIONS IN PERSON

Visiting headquarters also gives you a chance to meet one or more of the front-office representatives. Another way to meet one is to attend the annual meetings, not so much for the formal sessions, but for the informal gatherings. Depending on how serious you want to get about this, the annual meeting is your best chance to develop useful contacts.

It doesn't always happen this way, but occasionally I sense something about a corporate representative that gives me a feeling about the company's prospects. When I went to see Tandon, a company I dismissed in the first place on account of its being in the hot floppy-disk industry, I had an interesting encounter with the investor relations man. He was as polite, well-scrubbed, and well-spoken as any other investor relations person. However, when I looked him up in the Tandon proxy statement (among other things, proxy statements tell you how many shares are owned by the various corporate officers and directors, and how much those people are paid), I discovered that between his Tandon stock options and direct stock purchases, this man, who had not been with the company very long, was worth about $20 million.

Somehow, that this average person was so well-off thanks to Tandon seemed too good to be true. The stock already had gone up eightfold into high p/e euphoria. Thinking about this for a minute, I realized that if Tandon doubled again, the investor relations man would be worth $40 million. For me to make money in the stock, he would have to get twice as rich as he was already, and already he was many times richer than I figured he should be. The whole setup just wasn't realistic. There were other reasons I declined to invest, but the interview was the kicker. The stock dropped from $35¼ to $1⅜, adjusted for splits.

I had identical reservations about the founder and principal shareholder in Televideo, whom I'd met at a group luncheon in Boston. Already he owned $100 million worth of shares in a company with a high p/e ratio, and in the very competitive computer peripherals industry. I thought to myself: If I make money in Televideo, this guy is going to be worth $200 million. That didn't seem realistic, either. I declined to invest, and that stock went from $40½ in 1983 to $1 in 1987.

I could never prove this scientifically, but if you can't imagine how a company representative could ever get that rich, chances are you're right.

KICKING THE TIRES

From the time Carolyn discovered L'eggs in the supermarket, and I discovered Taco Bell via the burrito, I've continued to believe that wandering through stores and tasting things is a fundamental investment strategy. It's certainly no substitute for asking key questions, as the Bildner's case proves. But when you're developing a story, it's reassuring to be able to check out the practical end of it.

I'd already heard about Toys "R" Us from my friend Peter deRoetth, but one trip to the nearest local outlet convinced me that this company knew how to sell toys. If you asked customers if they liked the place, they all seemed to say that they planned to come back.

Before I bought La Quinta, I spent those three nights in their motor inns. Before I bought Pic 'N' Save, I stopped in at one of their stores in California and was impressed with the bargains. Pic 'N' Save's strategy was to take discontinued products out of the regular distribution channels and offer them at fire-sale prices.

I could have gotten that information from investor relations, but it wasn't the same as seeing the brand-name cologne for 79 cents a bottle, and the customers oohing and aahing over it. A financial analyst might have told me about the millions of dollars' worth of Lassie Dog Food that Pic 'N' Save bought from Campbell's Soup after Campbell's got out of the dog-food business, and that Pic 'N' Save promptly resold for a huge profit. But watching the people line up with their carts full of dog food, you could see proof that the strategy was working.

When I visited a Pep Boys outlet at a new location in California, a salesman there almost sold me a set of tires. I only wanted to look the place over, but he was so enthusiastic that I almost had four new tires shipped home with me on the airplane. He could have been an aberration, but I figured with personnel like that, Pep Boys could sell anything. Sure enough, they have.

After Apple computer fell apart and the stock dropped from $60 to $15, I wondered if the company would ever recover from its difficulties, and whether I should consider it as a turnaround. Apple's new Lisa, its entry into the lucrative business market, had been a total failure. But when my wife told me that she and the children needed a second Apple for the house, and when the Fidelity systems manager told me that Fidelity was buying 60 new Macintoshes for the office, then I just learned that (a) Apple still was popular in the home market, and

(b) it was making new inroads in the business market. I bought a million shares and I haven't regretted it.

My faith in Chrysler was considerably strengthened after my conversation with Lee Iacocca, who made a very bullish case for an auto industry revival, for Chrysler's successful cost-cutting, and for its improved lineup of cars. Outside the headquarters I noticed that the executive parking lot was half empty, another sign of progress. But my real enthusiasm developed in visiting a showroom and getting in and out of new Lasers, New Yorkers, and LeBaron convertibles.

Over the years Chrysler had developed the reputation as the old fogy's car, but from what I saw, it was obvious they were putting more pizzazz into the recent models—especially the convertible. (That one they made by cutting the tops off the regular LeBaron hardtops.)

Somehow I overlooked the minivan, which soon became the most successful vehicle Chrysler ever made, and the L'eggs of the 1980s. But at least I could sense that the company was doing something right. Lately Chrysler has stretched the minivan and added a bigger engine, which is what the customers wanted, and Chrysler minivans alone now represent three percent of the cars and trucks sold in the U.S. I may buy one for myself as soon as my eleven-year-old AMC Concord totally rusts out.

It's amazing how much analysis of the auto industry you can do in the parking lots of ski lodges, shopping centers, bowling alleys, or churches. Every time I see a Chrysler minivan or a Ford Taurus (Ford is still one of my biggest holdings) parked with a driver in it, I saunter over and ask "How do you like it?" and "How long have you owned it?" and "Would you recommend it?" So far, the answers are one hundred percent positive, which bodes well for Ford and Chrysler. Carolyn, meanwhile, is busy inside the stores, doing analysis on The Limited, Pier 1 Imports, and McDonald's new salads.

The more homogeneous the country gets, the more likely that what's popular in one shopping center will also be popular in all the other shopping centers. Think of all the brand names and products whose success or failure you've correctly predicted.

Why then didn't I buy OshKosh B'Gosh when our children have grown up in those wonderful OshKosh bib overalls? Why did I talk myself out of investing in Reebok because one of my wife's friends complained that the shoes hurt her feet? Imagine missing a fivebagger because the neighbor gave a pair of sneakers a bad review. Nothing is ever easy in this business.

READING THE REPORTS

It's no surprise why so many annual reports end up in the garbage can. The text on the glossy pages is the understandable part, and that's generally useless, and the numbers in the back are incomprehensible, and that's supposed to be important. But there's a way to get something out of an annual report in a few minutes, which is all the time I spend with one.

Consider the 1987 annual report of Ford. It has a nice cover shot of the back end of a Lincoln Continental, photographed by Tom Wojnowski, and inside there's a flattering tribute to Henry Ford II and a photograph of him standing in front of a portrait of his grandfather, Henry I. There's a friendly message to stockholders, a treatise on corporate culture, and mention of the fact that Ford sponsored an exhibition of the works of Beatrix Potter, creator of Peter Rabbit.

I flip past all that and turn directly to the Consolidated Balance Sheet printed on the cheaper paper on page 27 of the report (see charts). (That's a rule with annuals and perhaps with publications in general— the cheaper the paper the more valuable the information.) The balance sheet lists the assets and then the liabilities. That's critical to me.

In the top column marked Current Assets, I notice that the company has $5.672 billion in cash and cash items, plus $4.424 billion in marketable securities. Adding these two items together, I get the company's current overall-cash position, which I round off to $10.1 billion. Comparing the 1987 cash to the 1986 cash in the right-hand column, I see that Ford is socking away more and more cash. This is a sure sign of prosperity.

Then I go to the other half of the balance sheet, down to the entry that says "long-term debt." Here I see that the 1987 long-term debt is $1.75 billion, considerably reduced from last year's long-term debt. Debt reduction is another sign of prosperity. When cash increases relative to debt, it's an improving balance sheet. When it's the other way around, it's a deteriorating balance sheet.

Subtracting the long-term debt from the cash, I arrive at $8.35 billion, Ford's "net cash" position. The cash and cash assets alone exceed the debt by $8.35 billion. When cash exceeds debt it's very favorable. No matter what happens, Ford isn't about to go out of business.

(You may have noticed Ford's short-term debt of $1.8 billion. I ignore short-term debt in my calculations. The purists can fret all they

Consolidated Balance Sheet
December 31, 1987 and 1986 (in millions)
Ford Motor Company and Consolidated Subsidiaries

Assets	1987	1986
Current Assets		
Cash and cash items	$ 5,672.9	$ 3,459.4
Marketable securities, at cost and accrued interest (approximates market)	4,424.1	5,093.7
Receivables (including $1,554.9 and $733.3 from unconsolidated subsidiaries)	4,401.6	3,487.8
Inventories (Note 1)	6,321.3	5,792.6
Other current assets (Note 4)	1,161.6	624.5
Total current assets	21,981.5	18,458.0
Equity in Net Assets of Unconsolidated Subsidiaries and Affiliates (Note 6)	7,573.9	5,088.4
Property		
Land, plant, and equipment, at cost (Note 7)	25,079.4	22,991.8
Less accumulated depreciation	14,567.4	13,187.2
Net land, plant, and equipment	10,512.0	9,804.6
Unamortized special tools	3,521.5	3,396.1
Net property	14,033.5	13,200.7
Other Assets (Note 10)	1,366.8	1,185.9
Total Assets	$44,955.7	$37,933.0

Liabilities and Stockholders' Equity		
Current Liabilities		
Accounts payable		
Trade	$ 6,564.0	$ 5,752.3
Other	2,624.1	2,546.1
Total accounts payable	9,188.1	8,298.4
Income taxes	647.6	737.5
Short-term debt	1,803.3	1,230.1
Long-term debt payable within one year	79.4	73.9
Accrued liabilities (Note 8)	6,075.0	5,285.7
Total current liabilities	17,793.4	15,625.6
Long-Term Debt (Note 9)	1,751.9	2,137.1
Other Liabilities (Note 8)	4,426.5	3,877.0
Deferred Income Taxes (Note 4)	2,354.7	1,328.1
Minority Interests in Net Assets of Consolidated Subsidiaries	136.5	105.7
Guarantees and Commitments (Note 14)	—	—
Stockholders' Equity		
Capital Stock (Notes 10 and 11)		
Preferred Stock, par value $1.00 a share	—	—
Common Stock, par value $1.00 and $2.00 a share, respectively (469.8 and 249.1 shares issued)	469.8	498.2
Class B Stock, par value $1.00 and $2.00 a share, respectively (37.7 and 19.3 shares issued)	37.7	38.6
Capital in excess of par value of stock	595.1	605.5
Foreign-currency translation adjustments (Note 1)	672.6	(450.0)
Earnings retained for use in business	16,717.5	14,167.2
Total stockholders' equity	18,492.7	14,859.5
Total Liabilities and Stockholders' Equity	$44,955.7	$37,933.0
Memo: Stockholders' Equity a Share*	$36.44	$27.68

The accompanying notes are part of the financial statements.

* Adjusted to reflect the two-for-one stock split that was effective December 10, 1987.

want about this, but why complicate matters unnecessarily? I simply assume that the company's other assets [inventories and so forth] are valuable enough to cover the short-term debt, and I leave it at that.)

As often as not, it turns out that long-term debt exceeds cash, the

10-Year Financial Summary
(dollar amounts in millions)
Ford Motor Company and Consolidated Subsidiaries

Summary of Operations	1987	1986	1985	1984	1983	1982	1981	1980	1979	1978
Sales	$71,643.4	62,715.8	52,774.4	52,366.4	44,454.6	37,067.2	38,247.1	37,085.5	45,513.7	42,784.1
Total costs	65,442.2	58,659.3	50,044.7	48,944.2	42,650.9	37,550.8	39,502.9	39,363.8	42,596.7	40,425.6
Operating income (loss)	6,201.2	4,056.5	2,729.7	3,422.2	1,803.7	(483.6)	(1,255.8)	(2,278.3)	917.0	2,358.5
Interest income	866.0	678.8	749.1	917.5	569.2	562.7	624.6	543.1	693.0	456.0
Interest expense	440.6	482.9	446.6	536.0	567.2	745.5	674.7	432.5	246.8	194.8
Equity in net income of unconsolidated subsidiaries and affiliates	753.4	816.9	598.1	479.1	360.6	258.5	167.8	187.0	146.2	159.0
Income (loss) before income taxes	7,380.0	5,069.3	3,630.3	4,282.8	2,166.3	(407.9)	(1,138.1)	(1,980.7)	1,509.4	2,778.7
Provision (credit) for income taxes	2,726.0	1,774.2	1,103.1	1,328.9	27.02	256.6	(68.3)	(435.4)	330.1	1,175.0
Minority interests	28.8	10.0	11.8	47.1	29.2	(6.7)	(9.7)	(2.0)	10.0	14.8
Net income (loss)	4,625.2	3,285.1	2,515.4	2,906.8	1,866.9	(657.8)	(1,060.1)	(1,543.3)	1,169.3	1,588.9
Cash dividends	805.0	591.2	442.7	369.1	90.9	—	144.4	312.7	467.6	416.6
Retained income (loss)	$ 3,820.2	2,693.9	2,072.7	2,537.7	1,776.0	(657.8)	(1,204.5)	(1,856.0)	701.7	1,172.3
After-tax return on sales	6.5%	5.3%	4.8%	5.6%	4.3%	*	*	*	2.7%	3.7%
Stockholders' equity at year-end	$18,492.7	14,859.5	12,268.6	9,837.7	7,545.3	6,077.5	7,362.2	8,567.5	10,420.7	9,686.3
Assets at year-end	$44,955.7	37,933.0	31,603.6	27,485.6	23,868.9	21,961.7	23,021.4	24,347.6	23,524.6	22,101.4
Long-term debt at year-end	$ 1,751.9	2,137.1	2,157.2	2,110.9	2,712.9	2,353.3	2,709.7	2,058.8	1,274.6	1,144.5
Average number of shares of capital stock outstanding (in millions)	511.0	533.1	553.6	552.4	544.2	541.8	541.2	541.2	539.8	535.6
Net income (loss) a share (in dollars)	$ 9.05	6.16	4.54	5.26	3.43	(1.21)	(1.96)	(2.85)	2.17	2.97
Net income assuming full dilution	$ 8.92	6.05	4.40	4.97	3.21	—	—	—	2.03	2.76
Cash dividends	$ 1.58	1.11	0.80	0.67	0.17	0	0.27	0.58	0.87	0.78
Stockholders' equity at year-end	$ 36.44	27.68	21.97	17.62	13.74	11.20	13.57	15.79	19.21	17.95
Common Stock price range (NYSE)	$ 56³/₈	31³/₄	19³/₄	17¹/₈	15¹/₂	9¹/₈	5³/₄	8	10¹/₈	11¹/₈
	$ 28¹/₂	18	13³/₈	11	7⁷/₈	3³/₄	3¹/₂	4	6¹/₂	8⁵/₈
Facility and Tooling Data										
Capital expenditures for facilities (excluding special tools)	$ 2,268.7	2,068.0	2,319.8	2,292.1	1,358.6	1,605.8	1,257.4	1,583.8	2,152.3	1,571.5
Depreciation	$ 1,814.2	1,666.4	1,444.4	1,328.6	1,262.8	1,200.8	1,168.7	1,057.2	895.9	735.5
Expenditures for special tools	$ 1,343.3	1,284.6	1,417.3	1,223.1	974.4	1,361.6	970.0	1,184.7	1,288.0	970.2
Amortization of special tools	$ 1,353.2	1,293.2	948.4	979.2	1,029.3	955.6	1,010.7	912.1	708.5	578.2
Employee Data—Worldwide[1]										
Payroll	$11,669.6	11,289.7	10,175.1	10,018.1	9,284.0	9,020.7	9,536.0	9,663.4	10,293.8	9,884.0
Total labor costs	$16,567.1	15,610.4	14,033.4	13,802.9	12,558.3	11,957.0	12,428.5	12,598.1	13,386.3	12,631.7
Average number of employees	350,320	382,274	369,314	389,917	386,342	385,487	411,202	432.987	500,464	512,088
Employee Data—U.S. Operations[1]										
Payroll	$ 7,761.6	7,703.6	7,212.9	6,875.3	6,024.6	5,489.3	5,641.3	5,370.0	6,368.4	6,674.2
Average number of employees	180,838	181,476	172,165	178,758	168,507	161,129	176,146	185,116	244,297	261,132
Average hourly labor costs[2]										
Earnings	$ 16.50	16.12	15.70	15.06	13.93	13.38	12.75	11.45	10.35	9.73
Benefits	$ 12.38	11.01	10.75	9.40	8.54	9.79	8.93	8.54	5.59	4.36
Total	$ 28.88	27.13	26.45	24.46	22.47	23.17	21.68	19.99	15.94	14.09

Share data have been adjusted to reflect stock dividends and stock splits.
* 1982, 1981, and 1980 results were a loss.
[1] Includes unconsolidated finance, insurance, and land subsidiaries.
[2] Per hour worked (in dollars). Excludes data for subsidiary companies.

cash has been shrinking and debt has been growing, and the company is in weak financial shape. Weak or strong is what you want to know in this short exercise.

Next, I move on to the 10-Year Financial Summary, located on page 38, to get a look at the ten-year picture. I discover that there are 511 million shares outstanding. I can also see that the number has been reduced in each of the past two years. This means that Ford has been buying back its own shares, another positive step.

Dividing the $8.35 billion in cash and cash assets by the 511 million shares outstanding, I conclude that there's $16.30 in net cash to go along with every share of Ford. Why this is important will be apparent in the next chapter.

After that, I turn to . . . already this is getting complicated. If you don't want to proceed with this exercise, and you'd rather read about Henry Ford, then ask your broker whether Ford is buying back shares, whether cash exceeds long-term debt, and how much cash there is per share!

Let's be realistic. I'm not about to lead you on a wild-goose chase through the trails of the accounts. There are important numbers that will help you follow companies, and if you get them from the annual reports, fine. If you don't get them from the annual reports, you can get them from S&P reports, from your broker, or from *Value Line*.

Value Line is easier to read than a balance sheet, so if you've never looked at any of this, start there. It tells you about cash and debt, summarizes the long-term record so you can see what happened during the last recession, whether earnings are on the upswing, whether dividends have always been paid, etc. Finally, it rates companies for financial strength on a simple scale of 1 to 5, giving you a rough idea of a company's ability to withstand adversity. (There's also a rating system for the "timeliness" of stocks, but I don't pay attention to that.)

I'm putting aside the annual report for now. Let's instead consider the important numbers one by one on their own and not struggle further with finding them here.

13

Some Famous Numbers

Here, and not in any particular order of importance, are the various numbers worth noticing:

PERCENT OF SALES

When I'm interested in a company because of a particular product—such as L'eggs, Pampers, Bufferin, or Lexan plastic—the first thing I want to know is what that product means to the company in question. What percent of sales does it represent? L'eggs sent Hanes stock soaring because Hanes was a relatively small company. Pampers was more profitable than L'eggs, but it didn't mean as much to the huge Procter and Gamble.

Let's say you've gotten excited about Lexan plastic, and you find out that General Electric makes Lexan. Next, you discover from your broker (or from the annual report if you can follow it) that the plastics division is part of the materials division, and that entire division contributes only 6.8 percent to GE's total revenues. So what if Lexan is the next Pampers—it's not going to mean much to the shareholders of GE. You look at this and ask yourself who else makes Lexan, or you forget about Lexan.

THE PRICE/EARNINGS RATIO

We've gone on about this already, but here's a useful refinement: The p/e ratio of any company that's fairly priced will equal its growth rate. I'm talking about growth rate of earnings here. How do you find that out? Ask your broker what's the growth rate, as compared to the p/e ratio.

If the p/e of Coca-Cola is 15, you'd expect the company to be growing at about 15 percent a year, etc. But if the p/e ratio is less than the growth rate, you may have found yourself a bargain. A company, say, with a growth rate of 12 percent a year (also known as a "12-percent grower") and a p/e ratio of 6 is a very attractive prospect. On the other hand, a company with a growth rate of 6 percent a year and a p/e ratio of 12 is an unattractive prospect and headed for a comedown.

In general, a p/e ratio that's half the growth rate is very positive, and one that's twice the growth rate is very negative. We use this measure all the time in analyzing stocks for the mutual funds.

If your broker can't give you a company's growth rate, you can figure it out for yourself by taking the annual earnings from *Value Line* or an S&P report and calculating the percent increase in earnings from one year to the next. That way, you'll end up with another measure of whether a stock is or is not too pricey. As to the all-important future growth rate, your guess is as good as mine.

A slightly more complicated formula enables us to compare growth rates to earnings, while also taking the dividends into account. Find the long-term growth rate (say, Company X's is 12 percent), add the dividend yield (Company X pays 3 percent), and divide by the p/e ratio (Company X's is 10). 12 plus 3 divided by 10 is 1.5.

Less than a 1 is poor, and 1.5 is okay, but what you're really looking for is a 2 or better. A company with a 15 percent growth rate, a 3 percent dividend, and a p/e of 6 would have a fabulous 3.

THE CASH POSITION

We just went over Ford's $8.35 billion in cash net of long-term debt. When a company is sitting on billions in cash, it's definitely something you want to know about. Here's why:

Ford's stock had moved from $4 a share in 1982 to $38 a share in early 1988 (adjusted for splits). Along the way I'd bought my 5 million shares. At $38 a share I'd already made a huge profit in Ford, and the Wall Street chorus had been sounding off for almost two years about Ford's being overvalued. Numerous advisors said that this cyclical auto company had had its last hurrah and the next move was down. I almost cashed in the stock on several occasions.

But by glancing at the annual report I'd noticed that Ford had accumulated the $16.30 a share in cash beyond debt—as mentioned in the previous chapter. For every share of Ford I owned, there was this $16.30 bonus sitting there on paper like some delightful hidden rebate.

The $16.30 bonus changed everything. It meant that I was buying the auto company not for $38 a share, the stock price at the time, but for $21.70 a share ($38 minus the $16.30 in cash). Analysts were expecting Ford to earn $7 a share from its auto operations, which at the $38 price gave it a p/e of 5.4, but at the $21.70 price it had a p/e of 3.1.

A p/e of 3.1 is a tantalizing number, cycles or no cycles. Maybe I wouldn't have been impressed if Ford were a lousy company or if people were turned off by its latest cars. But Ford is a great company, and people loved the latest Ford cars and trucks.

The cash factor helped convince me to hold on to Ford, and it rose more than 40 percent after I made the decision not to sell.

I also knew (and you could have found out on page 5 of the annual report—still in the readable glossy section) that Ford's financial services group—Ford Credit, First Nationwide, U. S. Leasing, and others— earned $1.66 per share on their own in 1987. For Ford Credit, which alone contributed $1.33 per share, it was "its 13th consecutive year of earnings growth."

Assigning a hypothetical p/e ratio of 10 to the earnings of Ford's financial businesses (finance companies commonly have p/e ratios of 10) I estimated the value of these subsidiaries to be 10 times the $1.66, or $16.60 per share.

So with Ford selling for $38, you were getting the $16.30 in net cash and another $16.60 in the value of the finance companies, so the automobile business was costing you a grand total of $5.10 per share. And this same automobile business was expected to earn $7 a share. Was Ford a risky pick? At $5.10 per share it was an absolute steal, in spite of the fact that the stock was up almost tenfold already since 1982.

Boeing is another cash-rich stock. In early 1987 it sold in the low $40s, but with $27 in cash, you were buying the company for $15. I tuned in to Boeing with a small position in early 1988, then built it up to a major one—partly because of the cash and partly because Boeing had a record backlog of commercial orders yet to be filled.

Cash doesn't always make a difference, of course. More often than not, there isn't enough of it to worry about. Schlumberger has a lot of cash, but not an impressive amount per share. Bristol-Myers has $1.6 billion in cash and only $200 million in long-term debt, which produces an impressive ratio, but with 280 million shares outstanding, $1.4 billion net cash (after subtracting debt) works out to $5 per share. The $5 doesn't count for much with the stock selling for over $40. If the stock dropped to $15, it would be a big deal.

Nevertheless, it's always advisable to check the cash position (and the value of related businesses) as part of your research. You never know when you'll stumble across a Ford.

As long as we're on the subject, what is Ford going to do with all its cash? As cash piles up in a company, speculation about what will become of it can tug at the stock price. Ford's been raising the dividend and buying back shares at a furious pace, but it has still amassed excess billions over and above that. Some investors wonder if Ford will blow the money on a you-know-what, but so far, Ford has been prudent in its acquisitions.

Already Ford owns a credit company and a savings-and-loan, and it controls Hertz Rent A Car through a partnership. It made a low bid for Hughes Aerospace but lost out. TRW might create sensible synergy: it's a major worldwide producer of automotive parts and is in some of the same electronics markets. Furthermore, TRW could become the major supplier of airbags for cars. But if Ford buys Merrill Lynch or Lockheed (both were rumored), will it join the long list of diworseifiers?

THE DEBT FACTOR

How much does the company owe, and how much does it own? Debt versus equity. It's just the kind of thing a loan officer would want to know about you in deciding if you are a good credit risk.

A normal corporate balance sheet has two sides. On the left side are the assets (inventories, receivables, plant and equipment, etc.). The right side shows how the assets are financed. One quick way to determine the financial strength of a company is to compare the equity to the debt on the right side of the balance sheet.

This debt-to-equity ratio is easy to determine. Looking at Ford's balance sheet from the 1987 annual report, you see that the total stock-holder's equity is $18.492 billion. A few lines above that, you see that the long-term debt is $1.7 billion. (There's also short-term debt, but in these thumbnail evaluations I ignore that, as I've said. If there's enough cash—see line 2—to cover short-term debt, then you don't have to worry about short-term debt.)

A normal corporate balance sheet has 75 percent equity and 25 per-cent debt. Ford's equity-to-debt ratio is a whopping $18 billion to $1.7 billion, or 91 percent equity and less than 10 percent debt. That's a very strong balance sheet. An even stronger balance sheet might have 1 per-cent debt and 99 percent equity. A weak balance sheet, on the other hand, might have 80 percent debt and 20 percent equity.

Among turnarounds and troubled companies, I pay special attention to the debt factor. More than anything else, it's debt that determines which companies will survive and which will go bankrupt in a crisis. Young companies with heavy debts are always at risk.

Once I was looking at two depressed stocks in technology: GCA and Applied Materials. Both manufactured electronic capital equipment—machines to make computer chips. It's one of those highly technical fields that's best avoided, and these companies had proven it by falling off the ledge. In late 1985, GCA stock fell from $20 to $12, and Applied Materials did even worse, falling from $16 to $8.

The difference was that when GCA got into trouble, it had $114 mil-lion in debt, and almost all of it was bank debt. I'll explain this further on. It only had $3 million in cash, and its principal asset was $73 mil-lion of inventories—but in the electronics business, things change so fast that one year's $73-million inventory could be a $20-million inven-tory the next. Who knows what they could really get for it in a fire sale?

Applied Materials, on the other hand, had only $17 million in debt and $36 million in cash.

When the electronic-components business picked up, Applied Mate-rials rebounded from $8 to $36, but GCA wasn't around to enjoy the re-vival. One company went kaput and was bought out at about 10 cents a share, while the other went up more than fourfold. The debt burden was the difference.

It's the kind of debt, as much as the actual amount, that separates the winners from the losers in a crisis. There's bank debt and there's funded debt.

Bank debt (the worst kind, and the kind that GCA had) is due on demand. It doesn't have to come from a bank. It can also take the form of commercial paper, which is loaned from one company to another for short periods of time. The important thing is that it's due very soon, and sometimes even "due on call." That means that the lender can ask for his money back at the first sign of trouble. If the borrower can't pay back the money, it's off to Chapter 11. Creditors strip the company, and there's nothing left for the shareholders after they get through with it.

Funded debt (the best kind, from the shareholder's point of view) can never be called in no matter how bleak the situation, as long as the borrower continues to pay the interest. The principal may not be due for 15, 20, or 30 years. Funded debt usually takes the form of regular corporate bonds with long maturities. Corporate bonds may be upgraded or downgraded by the rating agencies depending on the financial health of the company, but whatever happens, the bondholders cannot demand immediate repayment of principal the way a bank can. Sometimes even the interest payments can be deferred. Funded debt gives companies time to wiggle out of trouble. (In one of the footnotes of a typical annual report, the company gives a breakdown of its long-term debt, the interest that is being paid, and the dates that the debt is due.)

I pay particular attention to the debt structure, as well as to the amount of the debt, when I'm evaluating a turnaround like Chrysler. Everyone knew that Chrysler had debt problems. In the famous bailout arrangement, the key element was that the government guaranteed a $1.4-billion loan in return for some stock options. Later the government sold these stock options and actually made a big profit on the deal, but at the time you couldn't have predicted that. What you could have realized, though, was that Chrysler's loan arrangement gave the company room to maneuver.

I also saw that Chrysler had $1 billion in cash, and that it had recently sold off its tank division to General Dynamics for another $336 million. True, Chrysler was losing a small amount of money at the time, but the cash and the structure of the loan from the government told you that the bankers weren't going to shut the place down for at least a year or two.

So if you believed the auto industry was coming back, as I did, and you knew that Chrysler had made major improvements and had become a low-cost producer in the industry, then you could have had some confidence in Chrysler's survival. It wasn't as risky as it looked from the newspapers.

Micron Technology is another company that was snatched from oblivion by the debt structure—and Fidelity had a major hand in it. This was a wonderful company from Idaho that staggered into our office on its last legs, a victim of the slowdown in the computer memory-chip industry and of the Japanese "dumping" of DRAM memory chips on the market. Micron sued, claiming that there was no way the Japanese could produce chips at lower cost than Micron, and therefore the Japanese were selling the merchandise at a loss to drive out the competition. Eventually Micron won the suit.

Meanwhile, all of the important domestic producers except Texas Industries and Micron got out of the business. Micron's survival was threatened by the bank debt it had built up, and its stock had fallen from $40 to $4. Its last hope was selling a large convertible debenture (a bond that can be converted into stock at the buyer's discretion). This would enable the company to raise enough cash to pay off the bank debt and ride out its short-term difficulties, since the principal on the convertible debenture wasn't due for several years.

Fidelity bought a large part of that debenture. When the memory-chip business turned around and Micron returned to profitability, the stock rose from $4 to $24, and Fidelity made a nice gain.

DIVIDENDS

"Do you know the only thing that gives me pleasure? It's to see my dividends coming in."

—*John D. Rockefeller, 1901*

Stocks that pay dividends are often favored over stocks that don't pay dividends by investors who desire the extra income. There's nothing wrong with that. A check in the mail always comes in handy, even for John D. Rockefeller. But the real issue, as I see it, is how the dividend, or the lack of a dividend, affects the value of a company and the price of its stock over time.

The basic conflict between corporate directors and shareholders over dividends is similar to the conflict between children and their parents over trust funds. The children prefer a quick distribution, and the parents prefer to control the money for the children's greater benefit.

One strong argument in favor of companies that pay dividends is that companies that don't pay dividends have a sorry history of blowing the money on a string of stupid diworseifications. I've seen this happen enough times to begin to believe in the bladder theory of corporate finance, as propounded by Hugh Liedtke of Pennzoil: The more cash that builds up in the treasury, the greater the pressure to piss it away. Liedtke's first claim to fame was building a small oil company, Pennzoil, into a strong competitor. His second claim to fame was beating Texaco (the Goliath) out of $3 billion in a court battle that everyone said Pennzoil (the David) would lose.

(The period of the late 1960s discussed earlier ought to be remembered as the Bladder Years. Still today, there is a propensity among corporate managers to piss away profits on ill-fated ventures—but much less than twenty years ago.)

Another argument in favor of dividend-paying stocks is that the presence of the dividend can keep the stock price from falling as far as it would if there were no dividend. In the wipeout of 1987, the high-dividend payers fared better than the nondividend payers and suffered less than half the decline of the general market. This is one reason I like to keep some stalwarts and even slow growers in my portfolio. When a stock sells for $20, a $2 per share dividend results in a 10 percent yield, but drop the stock price to $10, and suddenly you've got a 20 percent yield. If investors are sure that the high yield will hold up, they'll buy the stock just for that. This will put a floor under the stock price. Blue chips with long records of paying and raising dividends are the stocks people flock to in any sort of crisis.

Then again, the smaller companies that don't pay dividends are likely to grow much faster because of it. They're plowing the money into expansion. The reason that companies issue stock in the first place is so they can finance their expansion without having to burden themselves with debt from the bank. I'll take an aggressive grower over a stodgy old dividend-payer any day.

Electric utilities and telephone utilities are the major dividend-payers. In periods of slow growth they don't need to build plants or expand their equipment, and the cash piles up. In periods of fast growth the dividends are lures to attract the enormous amounts of capital that plant construction requires.

Consolidated Edison has discovered it can buy extra power from Canada, so why should it waste money on expensive new generators and all the expense of getting them approved and constructed? Be-

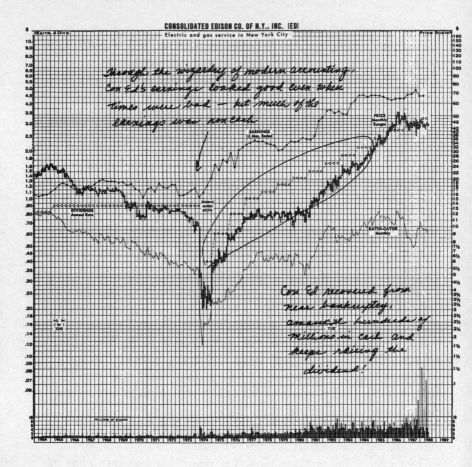

CONSOLIDATED EDISON CO. OF N.Y., INC. (ED)
Electric and gas service in New York City

Through the wizardry of modern accounting, Con Ed's earnings looked good even when times were bad — but much of the earnings was non-cash

Con Ed recovered from near bankruptcy, amassed hundreds of millions in cash and keeps raising the dividend!

cause it has no major expenses these days, Con Ed is amassing hundreds of millions in cash, buying back stock in above-average fashion, and continually raising the dividend.

General Public Utilities, now recovered from its Three Mile Island mishap, has reached the same stage of development that Con Ed did ten years ago (see chart). It, too, is now buying back stock and raising the dividend.

DOES IT PAY?

If you do plan to buy a stock for its dividend, find out if the company is going to be able to pay it during recessions and bad times. How about Fleet-Norstar, formerly Industrial National Bank, which has paid uninterrupted dividends since 1791?

If a slow grower omits a dividend, you're stuck with a difficult situation: a sluggish enterprise that has little going for it.

A company with a 20- or 30-year record of regularly raising the dividend is your best bet. Stocks such as Kellogg and Ralston Purina haven't reduced dividends—much less eliminated them—through the last three wars and eight recessions, so this is the kind you want to own if you believe in dividends. Heavily indebted companies like Southmark can never offer the same assurance as a Bristol-Myers, which has very little debt. (In fact, after Southmark recently suffered losses from its real estate operations, the stock price plummeted from $11 to $3 and the company suspended the dividend.) Cyclicals are not always reliable dividend-payers: Ford omitted its dividend back in 1982 and the stock price declined to under $4 per share (adjusted for splits)—a 25-year low. As long as Ford doesn't lose all its cash, nobody has to worry about their omitting dividends today.

BOOK VALUE

Book value gets a lot of attention these days—perhaps because it's such an easy number to find. You see it reported everywhere. Popular computer programs can tell you instantly how many stocks are selling for less than the stated book value. People invest in these on the theory that if the book value is $20 a share and the stock sells for $10, they're getting something for half price.

The flaw is that the stated book value often bears little relationship to the actual worth of the company. It often understates or overstates reality by a large margin. Penn Central had a book value of more than $60 a share when it went bankrupt!

At the end of 1976, Alan Wood Steel had a stated book value of $32 million, or $40 per share. In spite of that, the company filed for Chapter 11 bankruptcy six months later. The problem was that its new steel-making facility, worth perhaps $30 million on paper, was ineptly planned, and certain operational flaws rendered it practically useless. To pay off some of the debt, the steel-plate mill was sold to Lukens Corp. for somewhere around $5 million, and the rest of the plant was presumably sold for scrap.

A textile company may have a warehouse full of fabric that nobody wants, carried on the books at $4 a yard. In reality, they couldn't give the stuff away for 10 cents. There's another unwritten rule here: The closer you get to a finished product, the less predictable the resale value. You know how much cotton is worth, but who can be sure about an orange cotton shirt? You know what you can get for a bar of metal, but what is it worth as a floor lamp?

Look what happened a few years ago when Warren Buffett, the savviest of investors, decided to close down the New Bedford textile plant that was one of his earliest acquisitions. Management hoped to get something out of selling the loom machinery, which had a book value of $866,000. But at a public auction, looms that were purchased for $5,000 just a few years earlier were sold for $26 each—below the cost of having them hauled away. What was worth $866,000 in book value brought in only $163,000 in actual cash.

If textiles had been all there was to Buffett's company, Berkshire Hathaway, it would have been exactly the sort of situation that attracts the attention of the book-value sleuths. "Look at this balance sheet, Harry. The looms alone are worth $5 a share, and the stock is selling for $2. How can we miss?" They could miss, all right, because the stock would drop to 20 cents as soon as the looms were carted off to the nearest landfill.

Overvalued assets on the left side of the balance sheet are especially treacherous when there's a lot of debt on the right. Let's say that a company shows $400 million in assets and $300 million in debts, resulting in a positive book value of $100 million. You know the debt part is a real number. But if the $400 million in assets will bring only $200 million in a bankruptcy sale, then the actual book value is a negative $100 million. The company is less than worthless.

This is essentially what happened to the unlucky investors who bought stock in Radice, a Florida land-development company listed on the New York Stock Exchange, on the strength of its $50 a share in total assets, which must have looked pretty enticing with the stock at $10. But much of the value in Radice was illusory, the result of the strange rules of real estate accounting, in which the interest that's owed on the debt is counted as an "asset" until the project is completed and sold.

That's okay if the project succeeds, but Radice couldn't find any takers for some of its major development projects, and the creditors (banks) wanted their money back. The company was heavily indebted, and once the bankers called in their chits, the assets on the left side of the balance sheet disappeared while the liabilities remained. The stock price dropped to 75 cents. When the actual worth of a company is a minus $7 and enough people figure it out, it never helps the stock price. I ought to know. Magellan was a large shareholder.

When you buy a stock for its book value, you have to have a detailed understanding of what those values really are. At Penn Central, tunnels through mountains and useless rail cars counted as assets.

MORE HIDDEN ASSETS

Just as often as book value overstates true worth, it can understate true worth. This is where you get the greatest asset plays.

Companies that own natural resources—such as land, timber, oil, or precious metals—carry those assets on their book at a fraction of the true value. For instance, in 1987, Handy and Harman, a manufacturer of precious metals products, had a book value of $7.83 per share, including its rather large inventories of gold, silver, and platinum. But these inventories are carried on the books at the prices Handy and Harman originally paid for the metals—and that could have been thirty years ago. At today's prices ($6.40 an ounce for silver and $415 for gold) the metals are worth over $19 per share.

With Handy and Harman stock selling for around $17 per share, less than the value of the metals alone, is this a good asset play? Our friend Buffett thought so. He's held a large position in Handy and Harman for several years, but the stock hasn't gone anywhere, the company's earnings are spotty, and the diversification program hasn't been a rousing success, either. (You already know about diversification programs.)

Recently it was announced that Buffett is cutting back his interest in the company. So far, Handy and Harman looks like the only bad investment he's ever made, in spite of its hidden asset potential. But if gold and silver prices rise dramatically, so will this stock.

There are many kinds of hidden assets besides gold and silver. Brand names such as Coca-Cola or Robitussin have tremendous value that isn't reflected on the books. So do patented drugs, cable franchises, TV and radio stations—all are carried at original cost, then depreciated until they, too, disappear from the asset side of the balance sheet.

I've already mentioned Pebble Beach, a great hidden asset play in real estate. I could still kick myself for missing that stock. But real estate plays like that are all over the place; railroads are probably the best examples. Not only do Burlington Northern, Union Pacific, and Santa Fe Southern Pacific own vast amounts of land, as I mentioned before, but it's all carried on the books at a cost of next to nothing.

Santa Fe Southern Pacific is California's largest private landowner, with 1.3 million of the state's 100 million acres. Nationwide, it owns three million acres in fourteen states, an area four times the size of the state of Rhode Island. Another example is CSX, a southeastern railroad. In 1988, CSX sold an 80-mile right-of-way to the state of Florida. The land had a book value of almost zero, and the track was valued at $11 million. In the deal, CSX retained off-peak use of the track—so revenues were unaffected (freight ships during off-peak hours)—and the sale brought in $264 million after taxes. Talk about having your cake and eating it too!

Sometimes you'll find an oil company or a refiner that's kept inventory in the ground for forty years, and at the original cost of acquisition from the days of the Teddy Roosevelt administration. The oil alone is worth more than the current price of all the shares of stock. They could scrap the refinery, fire all the employees, and make a fortune for the shareholders in forty-five seconds by peddling the oil. It's no trouble to sell oil. It's not like selling dresses—nobody cares if it's this year's oil or last year's oil, or whether it's fuchsia or magenta.

A couple of years ago Channel 5 in Boston sold for something like $450 million—that was the fair market price. However, when that station was originally awarded its license, it probably paid $25,000 to file the proper papers, maybe $1 million for the tower, and another $1 or $2 million for the studio. The whole shebang was worth $2.5 million on paper to begin with, and the $2.5 million was depreciated. At the time it was sold, this enterprise probably had a book value that was 300 times too low.

Now that the station has changed owners, the new book value will be based on the $450-million sale price, so the anomaly will disappear. If you pay $450 million for a TV station worth $2.5 million on the books, the accounts call the extra $447.5 million "goodwill." Goodwill is carried on the new books as an asset, and eventually it, too, will be written off. This in turn will create another potential asset play.

The accounting methods for "goodwill" were changed after the 1960s, when many companies vastly overstated their assets. Now it's the other way around. For instance, Coca-Cola Enterprises, the new company that Coca-Cola created for its bottling operations, now carries

$2.7 billion worth of goodwill on its books. That $2.7 billion represents the amount that was paid for the bottling franchises above and beyond the cost of the plants, inventory, and equipment. It's the intangible value of the franchises.

Under the current rules of accounting, Coca-Cola Enterprises has to "write" this goodwill down to zero over the next four decades, while in reality the value of the franchises is rising by the year. By having to pay for goodwill, Coca-Cola Enterprises is punishing its own earnings. In 1987 the company reported 63 cents, but actually it earned another 50 cents that went to writing off the goodwill debt. Not only is Coca-Cola Enterprises doing considerably better than it would appear on paper, but every day the hidden asset is growing larger.

There's also hidden value in owning a drug that nobody else can make for seventeen years, and if the owner can improve the drug slightly, then he gets to keep the patent for another seventeen years. On the books, these wonderful drug patents may be worth zippo. When Monsanto bought Searle, it picked up NutraSweet. NutraSweet comes off patent in four years and will continue to be valuable even then, but Monsanto is writing the whole thing off against earnings. In four years NutraSweet will show up as a zero on Monsanto's balance sheet.

Just as in the case of Coca-Cola Enterprises, when Monsanto writes something off against earnings, the real earnings are understated. If the company actually makes $10 per share in profits, but has to devote $2 of that to "pay" to write things off such as NutraSweet, when it stops writing off NutraSweet the earnings will rise by $2 a share.

In addition, Monsanto is expensing all its research and development in the same fashion, and someday when the expenses stop and the new products come onto the market, the earnings will explode. If you understand this, you have a big edge.

There can be hidden assets in the subsidiary businesses owned wholly or in part by a large parent company. We've already gone over Ford's. Another was UAL, the diversified parent company of United Airlines before the brief period when it was called Allegis (not to be confused with ragweed and pollen). Fidelity's airline analyst Brad Lewis spotted this one. Within UAL, Hilton International was worth $1 billion, Hertz Rent A Car (later sold to a partnership headed by Ford) was worth $1.3 billion, Westin Hotels was worth $1.4 billion, and the travel reservation system another $1 billion more. After subtraction of debt and taxes, these assets together were worth more than the price of UAL's stock, so in essence the investor picked up one of the world's largest airlines for free. Fidelity backed up the truck on this one, and the stock was a twobagger for us.

There are hidden assets when one company owns shares of a separate company—as Raymond Industries did with Teleco Oilfield Services. People close to either situation realized that Raymond was selling for $12 a share, and each share represented $18 worth of Teleco. By buying Raymond you were getting Teleco for minus $6. Investors who did their homework bought Raymond and got Teleco for minus $6, and investors who didn't bought Teleco for $18. This sort of thing happens all the time.

For the past several years, if you were interested in DuPont, you got it cheaper by buying Seagram, which happens to own about 25 percent of DuPont's outstanding shares. Seagram became a DuPont play. Similarly, the stock in Beard Oil (now the Beard Company) was selling at $8, while each share included $12 worth of a company called USPCI. In this transaction, Beard and all its oil rigs and equipment was yours to keep for a minus $4.

Sometimes the best way to invest in a company is to find the foreign owner of it. I realize this is easier said than done, but if you have any access to European companies, you can stumble onto some unbelievable situations. European companies in general are not well-analyzed, and in many cases they're not analyzed at all. I discovered this on a fact-finding trip to Sweden, where Volvo and several other giants of Swedish industry were covered by one person who didn't even have a computer.

When Esselte Business Systems came public in the U.S., I bought the stock and kept up with the fundamentals, which were positive. George Noble, who manages Fidelity's Overseas Fund, suggested that I visit the parent company in Sweden. It was there that I discovered you could buy the parent company for less than the value of its U.S. subsidiary, plus pick up numerous other attractive businesses—not to mention real estate—as part of the deal. While the U.S. stock went up only slightly, the price of the parent company's stock doubled in two years.

If you followed the Food Lion Supermarkets story, you might have discovered that Del Haize of Belgium owned 25 percent of the stock, and the Food Lion holdings alone were worth a lot more than the price of a share of Del Haize. Again, when you bought Del Haize, you were getting valuable European operations for nothing. I purchased the European stock for Magellan and it rose from $30 to $120, while Food Lion gained a relatively unexciting 50 percent.

Back in the U.S., right now you can buy stock in various telephone companies and get a freebie on the cellular business. In every market they have awarded two cellular franchises. You've probably heard about the one that's given to a lucky person who wins the cellular lottery. Actually, he or she has to buy the franchise. The second franchise is given to the local phone company at no cost. It's going to be a great hidden asset to investors who've paid attention. As I'm writing this, you can buy a share in Pacific Telesis of California for $29 and get at least $9 a share worth of cellular value already. Or you can buy a $35 share of Contel and get $15 worth of cellular.

These stocks are selling at p/e ratios of less than 10, with dividend yields of more than 6 percent, and if you subtract the value of the cellular, the p/e's are even more attractive. You won't get tenbaggers out of these large telephone utilities, but you'll get a good yield and the possibility of 30–50 percent appreciation if everything goes right.

Finally, tax breaks turn out to be a wonderful hidden asset in turnaround companies. Because of its tax-loss carryforward, when Penn Central came out of bankruptcy it didn't have to pay any taxes on millions in profits from the new operations it was about to acquire. In those years the corporate tax rates were 50 percent, so Penn Central could buy a company and double its earnings overnight, simply by paying no tax. The Penn Central turnaround took the stock from $5 in 1979 to $29 in 1985.

Bethlehem Steel currently has $1 billion in operating-loss carryforwards, an extremely valuable asset if the company continues to recover. It means that the next $1 billion that Bethlehem earns in the U.S. will be tax-free.

CASH FLOW

Cash flow is the amount of money a company takes in as a result of doing business. All companies take in cash, but some have to spend more than others to get it. This is a critical difference that makes a Philip Morris such a wonderfully reliable investment, and a steel company such a shaky one.

Let's say Pig Iron, Inc. sells out its entire inventory of ingots and makes $100 million. That's good. Then again, Pig Iron, Inc. has to spend $80 million to keep the furnaces up-to-date. That's bad. The first year Pig Iron doesn't spend $80 million on furnace improvements, it loses business to more efficient competitors. In cases where you have to spend cash to make cash, you aren't going to get very far.

Philip Morris doesn't have this problem, and neither does Pep Boys or McDonald's. That's why I prefer to invest in companies that don't depend on capital spending. The cash that comes in doesn't have to struggle against the cash that goes out. It's simply easier for Philip Morris to earn money than it is for Pig Iron, Inc.

A lot of people use the cash flow numbers to evaluate stocks. For instance, a $20 stock with $2 per share in annual cash flow has a 10-to-1 ratio, which is standard. A ten percent return on cash corresponds nicely with the ten percent that one expects as a minimum reward for owning stocks long term. A $20 stock with a $4-per-share cash flow gives you a 20 percent return on cash, which is terrific. And if you find a $20 stock with a sustainable $10-per-share cash flow, mortgage your house and buy all the shares you can find.

There's no point getting bogged down in these calculations. But if cash flow is ever mentioned as a reason you're supposed to buy a stock, make sure that it's free cash flow that they're talking about. Free cash flow is what's left over after the normal capital spending is taken out. It's the cash you've taken in that you don't have to spend. Pig Iron, Inc. will have a lot less free cash flow than Philip Morris.

Occasionally I find a company that has modest earnings and yet is a great investment because of the free cash flow. Usually it's a company with a huge depreciation allowance for old equipment that doesn't need to be replaced in the immediate future. The company continues to enjoy the tax breaks (the depreciation on equipment is tax deductible) as it spends as little as possible to modernize and renovate.

Coastal Corporation is a good illustration of the virtues of free cash flow. By all the normal measures the company was fairly priced at $20 a share. Its earnings of $2.50 a share gave it a p/e of 8, which was standard for a gas producer and a diversified pipeline company at the time. But beneath this humdrum opportunity, something wonderful was going on. Coastal had borrowed $2.45 billion to acquire a major pipeline company, American Natural Resources. The beauty of the pipeline was that they didn't have to spend much to maintain it. A pipeline, after all, doesn't demand much attention. Mostly it just sits there. Maybe they'd dig down to patch a few holes, but otherwise they'd leave it alone in the ground. Meanwhile they'd depreciate it.

Coastal had $10–11 per share in total cash flow in a depressed gas environment, and $7 was left over after capital spending. That $7 a share was free cash flow. On the books this company could earn nothing for the next ten years, and shareholders would get the benefit of the $7-a-share annual influx, resulting in a $70 return on their $20 investment. This stock had great upside potential on cash flow alone.

Dedicated asset buyers look for this situation: a mundane company going nowhere, a lot of free cash flow, and owners who aren't trying to build up the business. It might be a leasing company with a bunch of railroad containers that have a 12-year life. All the company wants to do is contract the old container business and squeeze as much cash out of it as possible. In the upcoming decade, management will shrink the plant, phase out the containers, and pile up cash. From a $10 million operation, they might be able to generate $40 million this way. (It wouldn't work in the computer business, because the prices drop so fast that old inventory doesn't hold its value long enough for anybody to squeeze anything out of it.)

INVENTORIES

There's a detailed note on inventories in the section called "management's discussion of earnings" in the annual report. I always check to see if inventories are piling up. With a manufacturer or a retailer, an inventory buildup is usually a bad sign. When inventories grow faster than sales, it's a red flag.

There are two basic accounting methods to compute the value of inventories, LIFO and FIFO. As much as this sounds like a pair of poodles, LIFO actually stands for "last in, first out," and FIFO stands for "first in, and first out." If Handy and Harman bought some gold thirty years ago for $40 an ounce, and yesterday they bought some gold for $400 an ounce, and today they sell some gold for $450 an ounce, then what is the profit? Under LIFO, it's $50 ($450 minus $400), and under FIFO it's $410 ($450 minus $40).

I could go on about this, but I think we'd quickly reach a point of diminishing returns, if we haven't already. Two other popular accounting methods are GIGO (garbage in, garbage out), and FISH (first in, still here), which is what happens to a lot of inventories.

Whichever method is used, it's possible to compare this year's LIFO or FIFO value to last year's LIFO or FIFO value to determine whether or not there's been an increase or a decrease in the size of the inventory.

I once visited an aluminum company that had stockpiled so much unsold material that aluminum was stacked up to the ceiling inside the building, and outside it took up most of the employee parking lot. When workers have to park elsewhere so the inventory can be stored, it's a definite sign of excessive inventory buildup.

A company may brag that sales are up 10 percent, but if inventories are up 30 percent, you have to say to yourself: "Wait a second. Maybe they should have marked that stuff down and gotten rid of it. Since they didn't get rid of it, they might have a problem next year, and a bigger problem the year after that. The new stuff they make will compete with the old stuff, and inventories will pile up even higher until they're forced to cut prices, and that means less profit."

In an auto company an inventory buildup isn't so disturbing because a new car is always worth something, and the manufacturer doesn't have to drop the price very far to sell it. A $35,000 Jaguar isn't going to be marked down to $3,500. But a $300 purple miniskirt that's out of style might not sell for $3.

On the bright side, if a company has been depressed and the inventories are beginning to be depleted, it's the first evidence that things have turned around.

It's hard for amateurs and neophytes to have any feel for inventories and what they mean, but investors with an edge in a particular business will know how to figure this out. Whereas they didn't have to do so five years ago, companies must now publish balance sheets in their quarterly reports to shareholders, so that the inventory numbers can be regularly monitored.

PENSION PLANS

As more companies reward their employees with stock options and pension benefits, investors are well-advised to consider the consequences. Companies don't have to have pension plans, but if they do, the plans must comply with federal regulations. These plans are absolute obligations to pay—like bonds. (In profit-sharing plans there's no such obligation: no profits, no sharing.)

Even if a company goes bankrupt and ceases normal operations, it must continue to support the pension plan. Before I invest in a turn-around, I always check to make sure the company doesn't have an overwhelming pension obligation that it can't meet. I specifically look to see if pension fund assets exceed the vested benefit liabilities. USX shows pension plan assets of $8.5 billion and vested benefits of $7.3 billion, so that's not worrisome. Bethlehem Steel, on the other hand, reports pension assets of $2.3 billion and vested benefits of $3.8 billion, or a $1.5 billion deficit. This is a big negative if Bethlehem Steel gets into deeper financial trouble. It would mean that investors would put a lower value on the stock until the pension problem was cleared up.

This used to be a guessing game, but now the pension situation is laid out in the annual report.

GROWTH RATE

That "growth" is synonymous with "expansion" is one of the most popular misconceptions on Wall Street, leading people to overlook the really great growth companies such as Philip Morris. You wouldn't see it from the industry—cigarette consumption in the U.S. is growing at about a minus two percent a year. True, foreign smokers have taken up where the U.S. smokers left off. One out of four Germans now smokes Marlboros made by Philip Morris, and the company sends 747s full of Marlboros to Japan every week. But even the foreign sales can't account for Philip Morris's phenomenal success. The key to it is that Philip Morris can increase earnings by lowering costs and especially by raising prices. That's the only growth rate that really counts: earnings.

Philip Morris has lowered costs by installing more efficient cigarette-rolling machinery. Meanwhile, the industry raises prices every year. If the company's costs increase 4 percent, it can raise prices 6 percent, adding 2 percent to its profit margin. This may not seem like much, but if your profit margin is 10 percent (about what Philip Morris's is) a 2-percentage-point rise in the profit margin means a 20 percent gain in earnings.

(Procter and Gamble was able to "grow" its earnings in toilet paper by gradually changing the character of the paper, in effect adding ridges to the sheets, making them softer and slowly reducing the roll from 500 to 350 sheets. Then, they marketed the smaller roll as a "squeezable" improvement. This was the cleverest maneuver in the annals of short sheeting.)

If you find a business that can get away with raising prices year after year without losing customers (an addictive product such as cigarettes fills the bill), you've got a terrific investment.

You couldn't raise prices the way Philip Morris does in the apparel industry or the fast-food industry or else you'd soon be out of business. But Philip Morris gets progressively richer and richer and can't find enough things to do with the cash that piles up. The company doesn't have to invest in expensive blast furnaces, and it doesn't spend a lot to make a little. Moreover, the company's costs were greatly reduced after the government told cigarette companies they couldn't advertise on television! This is one time where there's so much loose money around that even diworseification hasn't hurt the shareholders.

Philip Morris bought Miller Brewing and got mediocre results, then duplicated the feat with General Foods. Seven-Up was another disappointment, and still Philip Morris stock shot straight up. On October 30, 1988, Philip Morris announced that it had signed a definitive agreement to purchase Kraft, the packaged foods company, for $13 billion. Despite the price tag of the acquisition (which amounted to over 20 times Kraft's 1988 earnings), the stock market took only 5% off Philip Morris's stock price, recognizing that the company's cash flow is so powerful it could pay off all the acquisition debt within five years. The big thing that may stop it is when the families of smoking victims start winning major lawsuit settlements.

This company has forty years of progressively better earnings and would sell at a p/e of 15 or higher if it weren't for the fear of lawsuits and the negative publicity about cigarette companies that keeps many investors away. It's this sort of emotionally charged situation that favors the bargain hunters, including me. The numbers couldn't be better. Today you can still buy this champion growth company at a p/e of 10, or half its growth rate.

One more thing about growth rate: all else being equal, a 20-percent grower selling at 20 times earnings (a p/e of 20) is a much better buy than a 10-percent grower selling at 10 times earnings (a p/e of 10). This may sound like an esoteric point, but it's important to understand what happens to the earnings of the faster growers that propels the stock price. Look at the widening gap in earnings between a 20-percent grower and a 10-percent grower that both start off with the same $1 a share in earnings:

BASE YEAR	COMPANY A (20% EARNINGS GROWTH) $1.00 A SHARE	COMPANY B (10% EARNINGS GROWTH) $1.00 A SHARE
Year 1	$1.20	$1.10
Year 2	$1.44	$1.21
Year 3	$1.73	$1.33
Year 4	$2.07	$1.46
Year 5	$2.49	$1.61
Year 7	$3.58	$1.95
Year 10	$6.19	$2.59

At the beginning of our exercise, Company A is selling for $20 a share (20 times earnings of $1), and by the end it sells for $123.80 (20 times earnings of $6.19). Company B starts out selling for $10 a share (10 times earnings of $1) and ends up selling for $26 (10 times earnings of $2.60).

Even if the p/e ratio of Company A is reduced from 20 to 15 because investors don't believe it can keep up its fast growth, the stock would still be selling for $92.85 at the end of the exercise. Either way, you'd rather own Company A than Company B.

If we had given Company A a 25 percent growth rate, tenth-year earnings would have been $9.31 per share: even with a conservative 15 p/e that's a stock price of $139. (Note that I didn't work out the earnings for a 30 percent growth rate or higher. That level of growth is very difficult to sustain for three years, much less ten.)

This in a nutshell is the key to the bigbaggers, and why stocks of 20-percent growers produce huge gains in the market, especially over a number of years. It's no accident that the Wal-Marts and The Limiteds can go up so much in a decade. It's all based on the arithmetic of compounded earnings.

THE BOTTOM LINE

Everywhere you turn these days you hear some reference to the "bottom line." "What's the bottom line?" is a common refrain in sports, business deals, and even courtship. So what is the real bottom line? It's the final number at the end of an income statement: profit after taxes.

Corporate profitability tends to be misunderstood by many in our society. In a survey I once saw, college students and other young adults were asked to guess the average profit margin on the corporate dollar. Most guessed 20–40 percent. In the last few decades the actual answer has been closer to 5 percent.

Profit before taxes, also known as the pretax profit margin, is a tool I use in analyzing companies. That's what's left of a company's annual sales dollar after all the costs, including depreciation and interest expenses, have been deducted. In 1987, Ford Motor had sales of $71.6 billion and earned $7.38 billion pretax, for a pretax profit margin of 10.3 percent. Retailers have lower profit margins than manufacturers—an outstanding supermarket and drugstore chain such as Albertson's still earns only 3.6 percent pretax. On the other hand, companies that make highly profitable drugs, such as Merck, routinely make 25 percent pretax or better.

There's not much to be gained in comparing pretax profit margins across industries, since the generic numbers vary so widely. Where it comes in handy is in comparing companies within the same industry. The company with the highest profit margin is by definition the lowest-cost operator, and the low-cost operator has a better chance of surviving if business conditions deteriorate.

Let's say that Company A earns 12 percent pretax and Company B earns only 2 percent. Suppose there's a business slowdown and both companies are forced to slash prices 10 percent to sell their merchandise. Sales drop by the same 10 percent. Company A is now earning 2 percent pretax and is still profitable, while Company B has fallen into the red with an 8 percent loss. It's headed for the endangered species list.

Without getting bogged down in the technicalities, pretax profit margin is one more factor to consider in evaluating a company's staying power in hard times.

This gets very tricky, because on the upswing, as business improves, the companies with the lowest profit margins are the biggest beneficiaries. Consider what happens to $100 in sales to our two companies in these two hypothetical situations:

COMPANY A

STATUS QUO	BUSINESS IMPROVES
$100 in sales	$110.00 in sales (prices up 10%)
$88 in costs	$92.40 in costs (up 5%)
$12 pretax profit	$17.60 pretax profit

COMPANY B

STATUS QUO	BUSINESS IMPROVES
$100 in sales	$110.00 in sales (up 10%)
$98 in costs	$102.90 in costs (up 5%)
$2 pretax profit	$7.10 pretax profit

In the recovery, Company A's profits have increased almost 50 percent, while Company B's profits have more than tripled. This explains why depressed enterprises on the edge of disaster can become very big winners on the rebound. It happens again and again in the auto, chemical, paper, airline, steel, electronics, and nonferrous metals industries. The same potential exists in such currently depressed industries as nursing homes, natural gas producers, and many retailers.

What you want, then, is a relatively high profit-margin in a long-term stock that you plan to hold through good times and bad, and a relatively low profit-margin in a successful turnaround.

14

Rechecking the Story

Every few months it's worthwhile to recheck the com-pany story. This may involve reading the latest *Value Line,* or the quarterly report, and inquiring about the earnings and whether the earnings are holding up as expected. It may involve checking the stores to see that the merchandise is still attractive, and that there's an aura of prosperity. Have any new cards turned over? With fast growers, especially, you have to ask yourself what will keep them growing.

There are three phases to a growth company's life: the start-up phase, during which it works out the kinks in the basic business; the rapid expansion phase, during which it moves into new markets; and the mature phase, also known as the saturation phase, when it begins to prepare for the fact that there's no easy way to continue to expand. Each of these phases may last several years. The first phase is the riskiest for the investor, because the success of the enterprise isn't yet established. The second phase is the safest, and also where the most money is made, because the company is growing simply by duplicating its successful formula. The third phase is the most problematic, because the company runs into its limitations. Other ways must be found to increase earnings.

As you periodically recheck the stock, you'll want to determine whether the company seems to be moving from one phase into another. If you look at Automatic Data Processing, the company that processes paychecks, you see that they haven't even begun to saturate the market, so Automatic Data Processing is still in phase two.

When Sensormatic was expanding its shoplifting detection system into store after store (the second phase), the stock went from $2 to $40, but eventually it reached the limit—no new stores to approach. The company was unable to think of new ways to maintain its momentum, and the stock fell from $42½ in 1983 to a low of $5⅝ in 1984. As you saw this time approaching, you needed to find out what the new plan was, and whether it had a realistic chance to succeed.

When Sears had reached every major metropolitan area, where else could it go? When The Limited had positioned itself in 670 of the 700 most popular malls in the country, then The Limited finally was.

At that point The Limited could only grow by luring more customers to its existing stores, and the story had begun to change. When The Limited bought Lerner and Lane Bryant, you got the feeling that the fast growth was over, and that the company didn't really know what to do with itself. In the second phase it would have invested all its money in its own expansion.

As soon as there's a Wendy's next door to every McDonald's, the only way Wendy's can grow is by winning over the McDonald's customers. Where can Anheuser-Busch grow if it already has captured 40 percent of the beer-drinking market? Even Spuds MacKenzie the party dog can't convince 100 percent of the nation to drink Bud, and at least a minority of brave souls is going to refuse to order Bud Light, even if they are zapped by lasers or abducted by aliens. Sooner or later Anheuser-Busch is going to slow down, and the stock price and the p/e multiple will both shrink accordingly.

Or perhaps Anheuser-Busch will think of new ways to grow, the same way McDonald's has. A decade ago investors began worrying that McDonald's incredible expansion was a thing of the past. Everywhere you looked, there seemed to be a McDonald's franchise, and sure enough the p/e ratio has been compressed from the 30 p/e of a fast grower down to the 12 p/e of a stalwart. But in spite of that vote of no confidence (the stock went sideways from '72 to '82), the earnings have been very strong. McDonald's has maintained its growth in imaginative ways.

First, they installed the drive-in windows, which now account for over one-third of the business. Then there was breakfast, which added a whole new dimension to sales, and at a time when the building would otherwise have been empty. Adding breakfast expanded restaurant sales by over 20 percent at very low cost. Then there were salads, and chicken, both of which added to earnings and also ended the company's dependence on the beef market. People assume that if beef prices go up, McDonald's will get clobbered—but they're talking about the old McDonald's.

As the construction of new franchises slows down, McDonald's has proven it can grow within its existing walls. It's also expanding rapidly in foreign countries, and it will be decades before there's a McDonald's on every street corner in England or in Germany. In spite of the lower p/e ratio, it's not all over for McDonald's.

If you bought just about any company in the cable industry, you would have seen a series of growth spurts: first, from the rural installations; second, from pay services such as HBO, Cinemax, the Disney channel, etc.; third, from the urban installations; fourth, from the royalties from programs such as Home Shopping Network (cable gets a cut for every item sold); and lately from the introduction of paid advertising, which has a huge future profit potential. The basic story gets better and better.

Texas Air is an example of a story that got worse, then better, then worse again in a matter of five years. I took a small position in the stock in mid-1983, only to watch the company's principal asset, Continental Air, deteriorate and file for Chapter 11. Texas Air stock fell from $12 to $4¾, and Continental stock, in which Texas Air held the majority position, fell to $3. I kept a close eye on the situation as a potential turnaround. Texas Air cut costs; Continental won back its customers and returned from the accountant's graveyard. On the strength of their improvement, I built up a large holding in both companies. By 1986 both stocks had tripled.

In February, 1986, Texas Air announced it had purchased a large share of Eastern Airlines—also viewed as a favorable development. In a single year Texas Air stock tripled once again to a high of $51½, making it a tenbagger since it solved its problems in 1983.

At this point my concern over the company's outlook unfortunately turned to complacency, and because the potential earning power of Eastern and Texas Air was so terrific, I forgot to pay attention to the near-term realities. When Texas Air bought out the remaining Continental shares, I was forced to cash in over half of my position in Continental stock and some bonds convertible to Continental stock. It was a stroke of fortune, and I made a tidy profit. But instead of selling my remaining Texas Air shares and making a happy exit from the whole situation, I actually bought *more* shares at $48¼ in February, 1987. Given Texas Air's mediocre balance sheet (total debt from all the various airlines was probably greater than that of several underdeveloped countries), and given that airlines are a precarious cyclical industry, why was I buying and not selling? I got blindsided because the stock price was going up. I fell for the latest, improved Texas Air story even when the fundamentals were falling apart.

The new, improved story was as follows: Texas Air was benefiting from a leaner operation and sharply reduced labor costs. In addition to its interest in Eastern, it had just bought Frontier Air and People's Express and planned to revive them in the same way it had revived Continental. The concept was great: acquire failed airlines, cut costs, and big profits would naturally follow.

What happened? Like Don Quixote, I was so enamored of the promise that I forgot to notice I was riding a nag. I focused on the predictions of $15 per share earnings for Texas Air in 1988, ignoring the warning signs that appeared every day in the newspaper: lost bags, botched schedules, delayed arrivals, angry customers, and disgruntled employees at Eastern.

An airline is a precarious business, the same as a restaurant. A few bad nights in a restaurant can ruin a fine reputation that took fifty years to develop. Eastern and Continental were having more than a few bad nights. The various parts didn't fit together smoothly. The grumblings at Eastern were symptoms of a bitter rift between management and the various unions over wages and benefits. The unions fought back hard.

Earnings at Texas Air started to deteriorate early in 1987. The idea was to cut $400 million out of Eastern's operating costs, but I should have reminded myself that it hadn't happened yet, and that there was a substantial likelihood that it would never occur. The existing labor contract didn't expire for several months, and meanwhile both sides were at loggerheads. Finally I came to my senses and started selling the stock at $17–18 a share. It fell to $9 by the end of 1987. I still own some shares, and I'm going to stay tuned.

Not only did I make a mistake by not cutting back on Texas Air in the summer of 1987, when the severe problems with Eastern became obvious and gave every evidence of persisting into 1988, but I should also have used this fundamental information to pick another winner: Delta Airlines. Delta was Eastern's main competitor and the greatest beneficiary of Eastern's operating problems and plans to reduce the size of Eastern on a permanent basis. I had a modest position in Delta, but I should have made it one of my top ten holdings. The stock went from $48 to $60 during the summer of 1987. In October, it fell to $35 and was only $37 at the end of the year. By mid-1988, it had risen sharply to $55. Thousands of people who flew Eastern and Delta could have seen the same things I saw and used their amateurs' edge.

15

The Final Checklist

All of this research I've been talking about takes a cou-
ple of hours, at most, for each stock. The more you know the better,
but it isn't imperative that you call the company. Nor do you have to
study the annual report with the concentration of a Dead Sea scroll
scholar. Some of the "famous numbers" apply only to specific categories of stocks and otherwise can be ignored altogether.

What follows is a summary of the things you'd like to learn about
stocks in each of the six categories:

STOCKS IN GENERAL

• The p/e ratio. Is it high or low for this particular company and for
similar companies in the same industry.

• The percentage of institutional ownership. The lower the better.

• Whether insiders are buying and whether the company itself is
buying back its own shares. Both are positive signs.

• The record of earnings growth to date and whether the earnings
are sporadic or consistent. (The only category where earnings may not
be important is in the asset play.)

• Whether the company has a strong balance sheet or a weak balance sheet (debt-to-equity ratio) and how it's rated for financial strength.

228 PETER LYNCH WITH JOHN ROTHCHILD

* The cash position. With $16 in net cash, I know Ford is unlikely to drop below $16 a share. That's the floor on the stock.

SLOW GROWERS

* Since you buy these for the dividends (why else would you own them?) you want to check to see if dividends have always been paid, and whether they are routinely raised.
* When possible, find out what percentage of the earnings are being paid out as dividends. If it's a low percentage, then the company has a cushion in hard times. It can earn less money and still retain the dividend. If it's a high percentage, then the dividend is riskier.

STALWARTS

* These are big companies that aren't likely to go out of business. The key issue is price, and the p/e ratio will tell you whether you are paying too much.
* Check for possible diworseifications that may reduce earnings in the future.
* Check the company's long-term growth rate, and whether it has kept up the same momentum in recent years.
* If you plan to hold the stock forever, see how the company has fared during previous recessions and market drops. (McDonald's did well in the 1977 break, and in the 1984 break it went sideways. In the big Sneeze of 1987, it got blown away with the rest. Overall it's been a good defensive stock. Bristol-Myers got clobbered in the 1973–74 break, primarily because it was so overpriced. It did well in 1982, 1984, and 1987. Kellogg has survived all the recent debacles, except for '73–'74, in relatively healthy fashion.)

CYCLICALS

* Keep a close watch on inventories, and the supply-demand relationship. Watch for new entrants into the market, which is usually a dangerous development.
* Anticipate a shrinking p/e multiple over time as business recovers and investors look ahead to the end of the cycle, when peak earnings are achieved.
* If you know your cyclical, you have an advantage in figuring out the cycles. (For instance, everyone knows there are cycles in the auto industry. Eventually there are going to be three or four up years to fol-

low three or four down years. There always are. Cars get older and they have to be replaced. People can put off replacing cars for a year or two longer than expected, but sooner or later they are back in the dealerships.

The worse the slump in the auto industry, the better the recovery. Sometimes I root for an extra year of bad sales, because I know it will bring a longer and more sustainable upside.

Lately we've had five years of good car sales, so I know we are in the middle, and perhaps somewhere close to the end, of a prosperous cycle. But it's much easier to predict an upturn in a cyclical industry than it is to predict a downturn.)

Fast Growers

- Investigate whether the product that's supposed to enrich the company is a major part of the company's business. It was with L'eggs, but not with Lexan.

- What the growth rate in earnings has been in recent years. (My favorites are the ones in the 20 to 25 percent range. I'm wary of companies that seem to be growing faster than 25 percent. Those 50 percenters usually are found in hot industries, and you know what that means.)

- That the company has duplicated its successes in more than one city or town, to prove that expansion will work.

- That the company still has room to grow. When I first visited Pic 'N' Save, they were established in southern California and were just beginning to talk about expanding into northern California. There were forty-nine other states to go. Sears, on the other hand, is everywhere.

- Whether the stock is selling at a p/e ratio at or near the growth rate.

- Whether the expansion is speeding up (three new motels last year and five new motels this year) or slowing down (five last year and three this year). For stocks of companies such as Sensormatic Electronics, whose sales are primarily "one-shot" deals—as opposed to razor blades, which customers have to keep on buying—a slowdown in growth can be devastating. Sensormatic's growth rate was spectacular in the late seventies and early eighties, but to increase earnings they had to sell more new systems each year than they had sold the year before. The revenue from the basic electronic surveillance system (the one-time purchase) far overshadowed whatever they got from selling those little white tags to their established customers. So, in 1983, when the rate of growth slowed, earnings didn't just slow, they dived. And so did the stock, from $42 to $6 in twelve months.

• That few institutions own the stock and only a handful of analysts have ever heard of it. With fast growers on the rise this is a big plus.

TURNAROUNDS

• Most important, can the company survive a raid by its creditors? How much cash does the company have? How much debt? (Apple Computer had $200 million in cash and no debt at the time of its crisis, so once again you knew it wasn't going out of business.)

What is the debt structure, and how long can it operate in the red while working out its problems without going bankrupt? (International Harvester—now Navistar—was a potential turnaround that has disappointed investors, because the company printed and sold millions of new shares to raise capital. This dilution resulted in the company's having turned around, but not the stock.)

• If it's bankrupt already, then what's left for the shareholders?

• How is the company supposed to be turning around? Has it rid itself of unprofitable divisions? This can make a big difference in earnings. For example, in 1980 Lockheed earned $8.04 per share from its defense business, but it lost $6.54 per share in its commercial aviation division because of its L-1011 TriStar passenger jet. The L-1011 was a great airplane, but it suffered from competition with McDonnell Douglas's DC10 in a relatively small market. And in the long-distance market, it was getting killed by the 747. These losses were persistent, and in December, 1981, the company announced that it would phase out the L-1011. This resulted in a large write-off in 1981 ($26 per share), but it was a one-time loss. In 1982, when Lockheed earned $10.78 per share from defense, there were no more losses to deal with. Earnings had gone from $1.50 to $10.78 per share in two years! You could have bought Lockheed for $15 at the time of the L-1011 announcement. Within four years it hit $60, for a fourbagger.

Texas Instruments was another classic turnaround. In October, 1983, the company announced it would leave the home-computer business (another hot industry with too many competitors). It had lost over $500 million from home computers in that year alone. Again, the decision made for big write-offs, but it meant that the company could concentrate on its strong semiconductor and defense-electronics businesses.

The day after the announcement, TI stock spurted from $101 to $124. And four months later it was $176.

Time also has sold off divisions and dramatically cut costs. It is one of my favorite recent turnarounds. Actually it's an asset play as well. The cable-TV part of the business is potentially worth $60 a share, so if the stock sells for $100, you're buying the rest of the company for $40.

- Is business coming back? (This is what's happening at Eastman Kodak, which has benefited from the new boom in film sales.)
- Are costs being cut? If so, what will the effect be? (Chrysler cut costs drastically by closing plants. It also began to farm out the making of a lot of the parts it used to make itself, saving hundreds of millions in the process. It went from being one of the highest-cost producers of automobiles to one of the lowest.

The turnaround in Apple Computer was harder to predict. However, if you'd been close to the company, you might have noticed the surge in sales, the cost-cutting, and the appeal of the new products, which all came at once.)

Asset Plays

- What's the value of the assets? Are there any hidden assets?
- How much debt is there to detract from these assets? (Creditors are first in line.)
- Is the company taking on new debt, making the assets less valuable?
- Is there a raider in the wings to help shareholders reap the benefits of the assets?

Here are some pointers from this section:

- Understand the nature of the companies you own and the specific reasons for holding the stock. ("It is really going up!" doesn't count.)
- By putting your stocks into categories you'll have a better idea of what to expect from them.
- Big companies have small moves, small companies have big moves.
- Consider the size of a company if you expect it to profit from a specific product.
- Look for small companies that are already profitable and have proven that their concept can be replicated.
- Be suspicious of companies with growth rates of 50 to 100 percent a year.
- Avoid hot stocks in hot industries.

- Distrust diversifications, which usually turn out to be diworseifications.
- Long shots almost never pay off.
- It's better to miss the first move in a stock and wait to see if a company's plans are working out.
- People get incredibly valuable fundamental information from their jobs that may not reach the professionals for months or even years.
- Separate all stock tips from the tipper, even if the tipper is very smart, very rich, and his or her last tip went up.
- Some stock tips, especially from an expert in the field, may turn out to be quite valuable. However, people in the paper industry normally give out tips on drug stocks, and people in the health care field never run out of tips on the coming takeovers in the paper industry.
- Invest in simple companies that appear dull, mundane, out of favor, and haven't caught the fancy of Wall Street.
- Moderately fast growers (20 to 25 percent) in nongrowth industries are ideal investments.
- Look for companies with niches.
- When purchasing depressed stocks in troubled companies, seek out the ones with the superior financial positions and avoid the ones with loads of bank debt.
- Companies that have no debt can't go bankrupt.
- Managerial ability may be important, but it's quite difficult to assess. Base your purchases on the company's prospects, not on the president's resume or speaking ability.
- A lot of money can be made when a troubled company turns around.
- Carefully consider the price-earnings ratio. If the stock is grossly overpriced, even if everything else goes right, you won't make any money.
- Find a story line to follow as a way of monitoring a company's progress.
- Look for companies that consistently buy back their own shares.
- Study the dividend record of a company over the years and also how its earnings have fared in past recessions.
- Look for companies with little or no institutional ownership.
- All else being equal, favor companies in which management has a significant personal investment over companies run by people that benefit only from their salaries.
- Insider buying is a positive sign, especially when several individuals are buying at once.
- Devote at least an hour a week to investment research. Adding up your dividends and figuring out your gains and losses doesn't count.

- Be patient. Watched stock never boils.
- Buying stocks based on stated book value alone is dangerous and illusory. It's real value that counts.
- When in doubt, tune in later.
- Invest at least as much time and effort in choosing a new stock as you would in choosing a new refrigerator.

Part III

THE LONG-TERM VIEW

In this section I add my two cents to important matters such as how to design a portfolio to maximize gain and minimize risk; when to buy and when to sell; what to do when the market collapses; some silly and dangerous misconceptions about why stocks go up and down; the pitfalls of gambling on options, futures, and the shorting of stocks; and finally what's new, old, exciting, and perturbing about companies and the stock market today.

16

Designing a Portfolio

I've heard people say they'd be satisfied with a 25 or 30 percent annual return from the stock market! Satisfied? At that rate they'd soon own half the country along with the Japanese and the Bass brothers. Even the tycoons of the twenties couldn't guarantee themselves 30 percent forever, and Wall Street was rigged in their favor.

In certain years you'll make your 30 percent, but there will be other years when you'll only make 2 percent, or perhaps you'll lose 20. That's just part of the scheme of things, and you have to accept it.

What's wrong with high expectations? If you expect to make 30 percent year after year, you're more likely to get frustrated at stocks for defying you, and your impatience may cause you to abandon your investments at precisely the wrong moment. Or worse, you may take unnecessary risks in the pursuit of illusory payoffs. It's only by sticking to a strategy through good years and bad that you'll maximize your long-term gains.

If 25 to 30 percent isn't a realistic return, then what is? Certainly you ought to do better in stocks than you'd do in bonds, so to make 4, 5, or 6 percent on your stocks over a long period of time is terrible. If you review your long-term record and find that your stocks have scarcely outperformed your savings account, then you know your technique is flawed.

By the way, when you are figuring out how you're doing in stocks, don't forget to include all the costs of subscriptions to newsletters, financial magazines, commissions, investment seminars, and long-distance calls to brokers.

Nine to ten percent a year is the generic long-term return for stocks, the historic market average. You can get ten percent, over time, by investing in a no-load mutual fund that buys all 500 stocks in the S&P 500 Index, thus duplicating the average automatically. That this return can be achieved without your having to do any homework or spending any extra money is a useful benchmark against which you can measure your own performance, and also the performance of the managed equity funds such as Magellan.

If professionals who are employed to pick stocks can't outdo the index funds that buy everything at large, then we aren't earning our keep. But give us a chance. First consider the kind of fund you've invested in. The best managers in the world won't do well with a gold-stock fund when gold prices are dropping. Nor is it fair to judge a fund for a single year's performance. But if after three to five years or so you find that you'd be just as well off if you'd invested in the S&P 500, then either buy the S&P 500 or look for a managed equity fund with a better record. For all the time and effort it takes to choose individual stocks, there ought to be some extra gain from it.

Given all these convenient alternatives, to be able to say that picking your own stocks is worth the effort, you ought to be getting a 12–15 percent return, compounded over time. That's after all the costs and commissions have been subtracted, and all dividends and other bonuses have been added.

Here's another place where the person who holds on to stocks is far ahead of the person who frequently trades in and out. It costs the small investor a lot of money to trade in and out. Trading is cheaper than it used to be, thanks to the discount commissions and also to a modification in the so-called odd-lot surcharge—the extra fee tacked on to transactions of less than 100 shares. (Now if you put in your odd-lot order before the market opens, your shares are pooled with those of other odd-lotters and you all avoid the surcharge.) Even so, it still costs between one and two percent for Houndstooth to buy or sell a stock.

So if Houndstooth turns over the portfolio once a year, he's lost as much as four percent to commissions. This means he's four percent in the hole before he starts. So to get his 12–15 percent after expenses, he's going to have to make 16–19 percent from picking stocks. And the more he trades, the harder it's going to be to outperform the index funds or any other funds. (The newer "families" of funds may charge you a 3–8½ percent fee to join, but that's the end of it, and from then on you can switch from stocks to bonds to money-market funds and back again without ever paying another commission.)

All these pitfalls notwithstanding, the individual investor who manages to make, say, 15 percent over ten years when the market average is 10 percent has done himself a considerable favor. If he started with $10,000, a 15 percent return will bring a $40,455 result, and a 10 percent return only $25,937.

HOW MANY STOCKS IS TOO MANY?

How do you design a portfolio to get that 12–15 percent return? How many stocks should you own? Right away I can tell you this: Don't own 1,400 stocks if you can help it, but that's my problem and not yours. You don't have to worry about the 5-percent rule and the 10-percent rule and the $9 billion to manage.

There's a long-standing debate between two factions of investment advisors, with the Gerald Loeb faction declaring, "Put all your eggs in one basket," and the Andrew Tobias faction retorting, "Don't put all your eggs in one basket. It may have a hole in it."

If the one basket I owned was Wal-Mart stock, I'd have been delighted to put all my eggs into it. On the other hand, I wouldn't have been too happy to risk everything on a basket of Continental Illinois. Even if I was handed five baskets—one apiece from Shoney's, The Limited, Pep Boys, Taco Bell, and Service Corporation International— I'd swear it was a fine idea to divide my eggs between them, but if this diversification included Avon Products or Johns-Manville, then I'd be yearning for a single, solid basket of Dunkin' Donuts. The point is not to rely on any fixed number of stocks but rather to investigate how good they are, on a case-by-case basis.

In my view it's best to own as many stocks as there are situations in which: (a) you've got an edge; and (b) you've uncovered an exciting prospect that passes all the tests of research. Maybe that's a single stock, or maybe it's a dozen stocks. Maybe you've decided to specialize in turnarounds or asset plays and you buy several of those; or perhaps you happen to know something special about a single turnaround or a single asset play. There's no use diversifying into unknown companies just for the sake of diversity. A foolish diversity is the hobgoblin of small investors.

That said, it isn't safe to own just one stock, because in spite of your best efforts, the one you choose might be the victim of unforeseen circumstances. In small portfolios I'd be comfortable owning between three and ten stocks. There are several possible benefits:

(1) If you are looking for tenbaggers, the more stocks you own the more likely that one of them will become a tenbagger. Among several fast growers that exhibit promising characteristics, the one that actually goes the furthest may be a surprise.

Stop & Shop was a big gainer that I never thought would give me more than a 30–40 percent profit. It was a mediocre company whose stock was declining, and I started buying it in 1979 partly because I liked the dividend yield. Then the story got better and better, both at the supermarkets and at the Bradlee's discount store division. The stock, which I started buying at $4, ended up at $44 when the company was taken private in 1988. Marriott is another example of a business whose stock market success I couldn't have predicted. I knew the company was a winner because I had stayed at its hotels countless times, but it never dawned on me how far the stock could go. I wish I had bought a few thousand shares instead of settling for a few thousand of those little bars of soap.

By the way, in spite of all the takeover rumors that fill the newspapers these days, I can't think of a single example of a company that I bought in expectation of a takeover that was actually taken over. Usually what happens is that some company I own for its fundamental virtues gets taken over—and that, too, is a complete surprise.

Since there's no way to anticipate when pleasant surprises of various kinds might occur, you increase your odds of benefiting from one by owning several stocks.

(2) The more stocks you own, the more flexibility you have to rotate funds between them. This is an important part of my strategy.

Some people ascribe my success to my having specialized in growth stocks. But that's only partly accurate. I never put more than 30–40 percent of my fund's assets into growth stocks. The rest I spread out among the other categories described in this book. Normally I keep about 10–20 percent or so in the stalwarts, another 10–20 percent or so in the cyclicals, and the rest in the turnarounds. Although I own 1,400 stocks in all, half of my fund's assets are invested in 100 stocks, and two-thirds in 200 stocks. One percent of the money is spread out among 500 secondary opportunities I'm monitoring periodically, with the possibility of tuning in later. I'm constantly looking for values in all areas, and if I find more opportunities in turnarounds than in fast-growth companies, then I'll end up owning a higher percentage of turnarounds. If something happens to one of the secondaries to bolster my confidence, then I'll promote it to a primary selection.

SPREADING IT AROUND

Spreading your money among several categories of stocks is another way to minimize downside risk, as discussed in Chapter 3. Assuming that you've done all the proper research and have bought companies that are fairly priced, then you've already minimized the risk to an important degree, but beyond that, it's worth considering the following:

Slow growers are low-risk, low-gain because they're not expected to do much and the stocks are usually priced accordingly. Stalwarts are low-risk, moderate gain. If you own Coca-Cola and everything goes right next year, you could make 50 percent; and if everything goes wrong, you could lose 20 percent. Asset plays are low-risk and high-gain if you're sure of the value of the assets. If you are wrong on an asset play, you probably won't lose much, and if you are right, you could make a double, a triple, or perhaps a fivebagger.

Cyclicals may be low-risk and high-gain or high-risk and low-gain, depending on how adept you are at anticipating cycles. If you are right, you can get your tenbaggers here, and if you are wrong, you can lose 80–90 percent.

Meanwhile, additional tenbaggers are likely to come from fast growers or from turnarounds—both high-risk, high-gain categories. The higher the potential upside, the greater the potential downside, and if a fast grower falters or the troubled old turnaround has a relapse, the downside can be losing all your money. At the time I bought Chrysler, if everything went right, I thought I could make 400 percent, and if everything went wrong, I could lose 100 percent. This is something you had to recognize going in. As it turned out, I was pleasantly surprised and made fifteenfold on it.

There's no pat way to quantify these risks and rewards, but in designing your portfolio you might throw in a couple of stalwarts just to moderate the thrills and chills of owning four fast growers and four turnarounds. Again, the key is knowledgeable buying. You don't want to buy an overvalued stalwart and thus add to the very risk you're trying to moderate. Remember that during several years in the 1970s, even the wonderful Bristol-Myers was a risky pick. The stock went nowhere because investors had bid it up to 30 times earnings and it was only a 15 percent grower. It took Bristol-Myers a decade of consistent growth to catch up to the inflated price. If you bought it at that price, which was twice its growth rate, you took unnecessary chances.

It's a real tragedy when you buy a stock that's overpriced, the company is a big success, and still you don't make any money. That's what happened with Electronic Data Systems, the stock that had the 500 p/e ratio in 1969. Earnings grew dramatically over the next 15 years, up about twentyfold. The stock price (adjusted for splits) fell from $40 all the way down to $3 in 1974 and then rebounded, and in 1984 the company was bought out by General Motors for $44, or about what the stock sold for ten years earlier.

Finally, your portfolio design may change as you get older. Younger investors with a lifetime of wage-earning ahead of them can afford to take more chances on tenbaggers than can older investors who must live off the income from their investments. Younger investors have more years in which they can experiment and make mistakes before they find the great stocks that make investing careers. The circumstances vary so widely from person to person that any further analysis of this point will have to come from you.

WATERING THE WEEDS

In the next chapter I'll explain what I know about when to sell a stock, but here I want to discuss selling as it relates to portfolio management. I'm constantly rechecking stocks and rechecking stories, adding and subtracting to my investments as things change. But I don't go into cash—except to have enough of it around to cover anticipated redemptions. Going into cash would be getting out of the market. My idea is to stay in the market forever, and to rotate stocks depending on the fundamental situations. I think if you decide that a certain amount you've invested in the stock market will always be invested in the stock market, you'll save yourself a lot of mistimed moves and general agony.

Some people automatically sell the "winners"—stocks that go up—and hold on to their "losers"—stocks that go down—which is about as sensible as pulling out the flowers and watering the weeds. Others automatically sell their losers and hold on to their winners, which doesn't work out much better. Both strategies fail because they're tied to the current movement of the stock price as an indicator of the company's fundamental value. (It wasn't that Taco Bell the company was in bad shape when the price was beaten down in 1972—only Taco Bell the stock. Taco Bell the company was doing well.) As we've seen, the current stock price tells us absolutely nothing about the future prospects of a company, and it occasionally moves in the opposite direction of the fundamentals.

A better strategy, it seems to me, is to rotate in and out of stocks depending on what has happened to the price as it relates to the story. For instance, if a stalwart has gone up 40 percent—which is all I expected to get out of it—and nothing wonderful has happened with the company to make me think there are pleasant surprises ahead, I sell the stock and replace it with another stalwart I find attractive that hasn't gone up. In the same situation, if you didn't want to sell all of it, you could sell some of it.

By successfully rotating in and out of several stalwarts for modest gains, you can get the same result as you would with a single big winner: six 30-percent moves compounded equals a fourbagger plus, and six 25-percent moves compounded is nearly a fourbagger.

The fast growers I keep as long as the earnings are growing and the expansion is continuing, and no impediments have come up. Every few months I check the story just as if I were hearing it for the first time. If between two fast growers I find that the price of one has increased 50 percent and the story begins to sound dubious, I'll rotate out of that one and add to my position in the second fast grower whose price has declined or stayed the same, and where the story is sounding better.

Ditto for cyclicals and turnarounds. Get out of situations in which the fundamentals are worse and the price has increased, and into situations in which the fundamentals are better and the price is down.

A price drop in a good stock is only a tragedy if you sell at that price and never buy more. To me, a price drop is an opportunity to load up on bargains from among your worst performers and your laggards that show promise.

If you can't convince yourself "When I'm down 25 percent, I'm

*a buyer" and banish forever the fatal thought "When I'm down
25 percent, I'm a seller," then you'll never make a decent profit in
stocks.*

For reasons that should by now be obvious, I've always detested
"stop orders," those automatic bailouts at a predetermined price, usually 10 percent below the price at which a stock is purchased. True,
when you put in a "stop order" you've limited your losses to 10 percent, but with the volatility in today's market, a stock almost always hits
the stop. It's uncanny how stop orders seem to guarantee that the stock
will drop 10 percent, the shares are sold, and instead of protecting
against a loss, the investor has turned losing into a foregone conclusion. You would have lost Taco Bell ten times over with stop orders!

Show me a portfolio with 10 percent stops, and I'll show you a portfolio that's destined to lose exactly that amount. When you put in a
stop, you're admitting that you're going to sell the stock for less than
it's worth today.

It's equally uncanny how stocks seem to shoot straight up after the
stop is hit, and the would-be cautious investor has been sold out.
There's simply no way to rely on stops as protection on the downside,
nor on artificial objectives as goals on the upside. If I'd believed in "Sell
when it's a double," I would never have benefited from a single big
winner, and I wouldn't have been given the opportunity to write a
book. Stick around to see what happens—as long as the original story
continues to make sense, or gets better—and you'll be amazed at the
results in several years.

17

The Best Time to Buy
and Sell

After all that's been said, I don't want to sound like a market timer and tell you that there's a certain best time to buy stocks. The best time to buy stocks will always be the day you've convinced yourself you've found solid merchandise at a good price—the same as at the department store. However, there are two particular periods when great bargains are likely to be found.

The first is during the peculiar annual ritual of end-of-the-year tax selling. It's no accident that the most severe drops have occurred between October and December. It's the holiday period, after all, and brokers need spending money like the rest of us, so there's extra incentive for them to call and ask what you might want to sell to get the tax loss. For some reason investors are delighted to get the tax loss, as if it's a wonderful opportunity or a gift of some kind—I can't think of another situation in which failure makes people so happy.

Institutional investors also like to jettison the losers at the end of the year so their portfolios are cleaned up for the upcoming evaluations. All this compound selling drives stock prices down, and especially in the lower priced issues, because once the $6-per-share threshold is reached, stocks do not count as collateral for people who buy on credit in margin accounts. Margin players sell their cheap stocks, and so do the

institutions, who cannot own them without violating one stricture or another. This selling begets more selling and drives perfectly good issues
to crazy levels.

If you have a list of companies that you'd like to own if only the
stock price were reduced, the end of the year is a likely time to find the
deals you've been waiting for.

The second is during the collapses, drops, burps, hiccups, and
freefalls that occur in the stock market every few years. If you can sum-
mon the courage and presence of mind to buy during these scary
episodes when your stomach says "sell," you'll find opportunities that
you wouldn't have thought you'd ever see again. Professionals are
often too busy or too constrained to act quickly in market breaks, but
look at the solid companies with excellent earnings growth that you
could have picked up in the latest ones:

GREAT COMPANIES THAT GAVE YOU
A SECOND CHANCE IN MARKET BREAKS

BREAK	HIGH	LOW	1987 HIGH
1972–74			
Genuine Parts	$15	$ 4	$ 44⅜
General Cinema	3½	30 cents	31¾
Teledyne	11	3	390
Abbott Labs	5	1⅞	67
Bristol-Myers	8	4	55
Cap Cities	34	9	450
Heinz	5¾	3	51¾
McDonald's	15	4	61⅛
Philip Morris	17½	8½	124½
Merck	17	7	74¼
1976–78 (not as bad)			
GE	15	11	66⅜
Marriott	3¾	1¾	44¾
1981–82			
Gannett	15	10	56
John Harland	6½	4	30¾
1983–84			
Browning-Ferris	12	6½	36
The Limited	10	5	53
Anheuser-Busch	12	9	40
NCR	34	22	87
Waste Management	16	7	48

THE 1987 BREAK

In the sell-off of October, 1987, you had a chance to buy many of the companies I've been mentioning throughout this book. The 1,000-point drop between summer and fall took everything with it, but in the real world all the companies listed below were healthy, profitable, and never missed a beat. Many of them recovered in quick fashion, and I took advantage whenever I could. I missed Dreyfus the first time around, but not this time (fool me once, shame on you; fool me twice, shame on me). Dreyfus was beaten down to $16 and the company had $15 in cash after debt, so what was the risk? In addition to the cash, Dreyfus actually profited from the crisis, as many investors switched out of stocks and into money-market funds that Dreyfus manages.

THE 1987 BREAK	1987 HIGH	1987 LOW	OCTOBER 1988
Wal-Mart	$41	$20	$31⅜
Dreyfus	45	16	25⅝
Albertson's	34	21	36⅛
Home Depot	28	12½	28⅜
Student Loan Marketing	88	62	83⅞
Toys "R" Us	42	22	38¼
Coca-Cola	53	28	43⅛
Pier 1	14	5	11¼
Inco	24	14	28⅝
Envirodyne	29¼	10⅞	26

WHEN TO SELL

Even the most thoughtful and steadfast investor is susceptible to the influence of skeptics who yell "Sell" before it's time to sell. I ought to know. I've been talked out of a few tenbaggers myself.

Soon after I started managing Magellan in May of 1977, I was attracted to Warner Communications. Warner was a promising turn-around from a conglomerate that had diworseified. Confident of the fundamentals, I invested three percent of my fund in Warner at $26.

A few days later I got a call from a technical analyst who follows Warner. I don't pay much attention to that science of wiggles, but just to be polite I asked him what he thought. Without hesitation he announced that the stock was "extremely extended." I've never forgotten those words. One of the biggest troubles with stock market advice is that good or bad it sticks in your brain. You can't get it out of there, and someday, sometime, you may find yourself reacting to it.

Six months or so had passed, and Warner had risen from $26 to $32. Already I was beginning to worry. "If Warner was extremely extended at $26," I argued to myself, "then it must be hyperextended at $32." I checked the fundamentals, and nothing there had changed enough to diminish my enthusiasm, so I held on. Then the stock hit $38. For no conscious reason I began a major sell program. I must have decided that whatever was extended at $26 and hyperextended at $32 has surely been stretched into three prefixes at $38.

Of course after I sold, the stock continued its ascent to $50, $60, $70, and over $180. Even after it suffered the consequences of the Atari fiasco, and the price declined by 60 percent in 1983–84, it was still twice my exit price of $38. I hope I've learned my lesson here.

Another time I made a premature exit from Toys "R" Us, that nifty fast grower that I've already bragged about. By 1978, when Toys "R" Us was liberated from Interstate Department Stores (a woeful dog) in that company's bankruptcy action (creditors were paid off in new Toys "R" Us shares), this was already a proven and profitable enterprise, expanding into one mall after another. It had passed the tests of success in one location, and then of duplication. I did my homework, visited the stores, and took a big position at an adjusted price of $1 per share. By 1985, when Toys "R" Us hit $25, it was a 25-bagger for some. Unfortunately, those some didn't include me, because I sold too soon. I sold too soon because somewhere along the line I'd read that a smart investor named Milton Petrie, one of the deans of retailing, had bought 20 percent of Toys "R" Us and that his buying was making the stock go up. The logical conclusion, I thought, was that when Petrie stopped buying, the stock would go down. Petrie stopped buying at $5.

I got in at $1 and out at $5 for a fivebagger, so how can I complain? We've all been taught the same adages: "Take profits when you can," and "A sure gain is always better than a possible loss." But when you've found the right stock and bought it, all the evidence tells you it's going higher, and everything is working in your direction, then it's a shame if you sell. A fivefold gain turns $10,000 into $50,000, but the next five folds turn $10,000 into $250,000. Investing in a 25-bagger is not a regular occurrence even among fund managers, and for the individual it may happen only once or twice in a lifetime. When you've got one, you might as well enjoy the full benefit. The clients of Peter deRoetth, who first told me about Toys "R" Us, did just that. He stuck with it all the way in his fund.

I managed to repeat the error with Flowers, a bakery company, and then again with Lance, a crackers company. Because somebody told me that these were takeover candidates, I kept waiting for them to be taken over and finally got bored and disposed of my shares. After I sold, you can imagine what happened. The lesson this time was that I shouldn't have cared if this profitable bakery company got taken over or not. In fact, I should have been delighted that it stayed independent.

I already reported that I almost didn't buy La Quinta because an important insider had been selling shares. Not buying because an insider has started selling can be as big a mistake as selling because an outsider (Petrie) has stopped buying. In the La Quinta case I ignored the nonsense, and I'm glad I did.

I'm sure there are other examples of my having been faked out that I've conveniently forgotten. It's normally harder to stick with a winning stock after the price goes up than it is to believe in it after the price goes down. These days if I feel there's a danger of being faked out, I try to review the reasons why I bought in the first place.

THE DRUMBEAT EFFECT

This is one instance where the amateur investor is just as vulnerable to folly as the professional. We have fellow experts whispering into our ears; you have friends, relatives, brokers, and assorted financial factotums from the media.

Maybe you've received the "Congratulations: Don't Be Greedy" announcement. That's when the broker calls to say: "Congratulations, you've doubled your money on ToggleSwitch, but let's not be greedy. Let's sell ToggleSwitch and try KinderMind." So you sell ToggleSwitch and it keeps going up, while KinderMind goes bankrupt, taking all of your profits with it. Meanwhile the broker gets a commission from both sides of the transaction, so every "Congratulations" message represents a double payday.

Beyond the broker, every single dumb idea you hear about stocks gets into your brain the same way that "Warner is overextended" got into mine. These days, dumb ideas are at a deafening roar.

Every time you turn on the television there's somebody declaring that bank stocks are in and airline stocks are out, that utilities have seen their best days and savings-and-loans are doomed. If you flip around the radio dial and happen to hear the offhand remark that an overheated Japanese economy will destroy the world, you'll remember that snippet the next time the market drops 10 percent, and maybe it will scare you into selling your Sony and your Honda, and even your Colgate-Palmolive, which isn't cyclical or Japanese.

When astrologers are interviewed alongside economists from Merrill Lynch, and both say contradictory things and yet sound equally convincing, no wonder we're all confused.

Lately we've had to contend with the drumbeat effect. A particularly ominous message is repeated over and over until it's impossible to get away from it. A couple of years ago there was a drumbeat around the M-1 money supply. When I was in the Army, M-1 was a rifle and I understood it. Suddenly M-1 was this critical digit on which the entire future of Wall Street depended, and I couldn't tell you what it was. Remember One Hour Martinizing? Nobody can tell you what that is, either, and millions of dry-cleaning patrons have never asked. Maybe M-1 actually stands for Martinizing One, and some guy on the Council of Economic Advisors used to run a dry-cleaning business. Anyway, for months there was something in the news about the M-1's growing too fast, and people worried that it would sink our economy and threaten the world. What better reason to sell stocks than that "the M-1 is rising"—even if you weren't sure what the M-1 was.

Then suddenly we heard nothing further about the dreaded rise in the M-1 money supply, and our attention was diverted to the discount rate that the Fed charges member banks. How many people know what this is? You can count me out once again. How many people know what the Fed does? William Miller, once Fed chairman, said that 23 percent of the U.S. population thought the Federal Reserve was an Indian reservation, 26 percent thought it was a wildlife preserve, and 51 percent thought it was a brand of whiskey.

Yet every Friday afternoon (it used to be Thursday afternoon until too many people jostled into the Fed building to get the number in advance of the Friday stock market opening) half the professional investing population was mesmerized by the news of the latest money supply figures, and stock prices were wafted up and down because of it. How many investors got faked out of good stocks because they heard that a higher money supply growth rate would sink the stock market?

More recently we've been warned (in no particular order) that a rise in oil prices is a terrible thing and a fall in oil prices is a terrible thing; that a strong dollar is a bad omen and a weak dollar is a bad omen; that a drop in the money supply is cause for alarm and an increase in the money supply is cause for alarm. A preoccupation with money supply figures has been supplanted with intense fears over budget and trade deficits, and thousands more must have been drummed out of their stocks because of each.

WHEN TO REALLY SELL

If the market can't tell you when to sell, then what can? No single formula could possibly apply. "Sell before the interest rates go up" or "sell before the next recession" would be advice worth following, if only we knew when these things would happen, but of course we don't, and so these mottos become platitudes as well.

Over the years I've learned to think about when to sell the same way I think about when to buy. I pay no attention to external economic conditions, except in the few obvious instances when I'm sure that a specific business will be affected in a specific way. When oil prices go down, it obviously has an effect on oil-service companies, but not on ethical drug companies. In 1986–87, I sold my Jaguar, Honda, Subaru, and Volvo holdings because I was convinced that the falling dollar would hurt the earnings of foreign automakers that sell a high percentage of their cars in the U.S. But in nine cases out of ten, I sell if company 380 has a better story than company 212, and especially when the latter story begins to sound unlikely.

As it turns out, if you know why you bought a stock in the first place, you'll automatically have a better idea of when to say good-bye to it. Let's review some of the sell signs, category by category.

WHEN TO SELL A SLOW GROWER

I can't really help you with this one, because I don't own many slow growers in the first place. The ones I do buy, I sell when there's been a 30–50 percent appreciation or when the fundamentals have deteriorated, even if the stock has declined in price. Here are some other signs:

- The company has lost market share for two consecutive years and is hiring another advertising agency.
- No new products are being developed, spending on research and development is curtailed, and the company appears to be resting on its laurels.
- Two recent acquisitions of unrelated businesses look like diworseifications, and the company announces it is looking for further acquisitions "at the leading edge of technology."
- The company has paid so much for its acquisitions that the balance sheet has deteriorated from no debt and millions in cash to no cash and millions in debt. There are no surplus funds to buy back stock, even if the price falls sharply.
- Even at a lower stock price the dividend yield will not be high enough to attract much interest from investors.

WHEN TO SELL A STALWART

These are the stocks that I frequently replace with others in the category. There's no point expecting a quick tenbagger in a stalwart, and if the stock price gets above the earnings line, or if the p/e strays too far beyond the normal range, you might think about selling it and waiting to buy it back later at a lower price—or buying something else, as I do.

Other sell signs:

- New products introduced in the last two years have had mixed results, and others still in the testing stage are a year away from the marketplace.
- The stock has a p/e of 15, while similar-quality companies in the industry have p/e's of 11–12.
- No officers or directors have bought shares in the last year.
- A major division that contributes 25 percent of earnings is vulnerable to an economic slump that's taking place (in housing starts, oil drilling, etc.).
- The company's growth rate has been slowing down, and though it's been maintaining profits by cutting costs, future cost-cutting opportunities are limited.

When to Sell a Cyclical

The best time to sell is toward the end of the cycle, but who knows when that is? Who even knows what cycles they're talking about? Sometimes the knowledgeable vanguard begins to sell cyclicals a year before there's a single sign of a company's decline. The stock price starts to fall for apparently no earthly reason.

To play this game successfully you have to understand the strange rules. That's what makes cyclicals so tricky. In the defense business, which behaves like a cyclical, the price of General Dynamics once fell 50 percent on higher earnings. Farsighted cycle-watchers were selling in advance to avoid the rush.

Other than at the end of the cycle, the best time to sell a cyclical is when something has actually started to go wrong. Costs have started to rise. Existing plants are operating at full capacity, and the company begins to spend money to add to capacity. Whatever inspired you to buy XYZ between the last bust and latest boom ought to clue you in that the latest boom is over.

One obvious sell signal is that inventories are building up and the company can't get rid of them, which means lower prices and lower profits down the road. I always pay attention to rising inventories. When the parking lot is full of ingots, it's certainly time to sell the cyclical. In fact, you may be a little late.

Falling commodity prices is another harbinger. Usually prices of oil, steel, etc., will turn down several months before the troubles show up in the earnings. Another useful sign is when the future price of a commodity is lower than the current, or spot, price. If you had enough of an edge to know when to buy the cyclical in the first place, then you'll notice the price changes.

Competition businesses are also a bad sign for cyclicals. The outsider will have to win customers by cutting prices, which forces everyone else to cut prices and leads to lower earnings for all the producers. As long as there's strong demand for nickel and nobody to challenge Inco, Inco will do fine, but as soon as demand slackens or rival nickel producers begin to sell nickel, Inco's got problems.

Other signs:

• Two key union contracts expire in the next twelve months, and labor leaders are asking for a full restoration of the wages and benefits they gave up in the last contract.

- Final demand for the product is slowing down.
- The company has doubled its capital spending budget to build a fancy new plant, as opposed to modernizing the old plants at low cost.
- The company has tried to cut costs but still can't compete with foreign producers.

WHEN TO SELL A FAST GROWER

Here, the trick is not to lose the potential tenbagger. On the other hand, if the company falls apart and the earnings shrink, then so will the p/e multiple that investors have bid up on the stock. This is a very expensive double whammy for the loyal shareholders.

The main thing to watch for is the end of the second phase of rapid growth, as explained earlier.

If The Gap has stopped building new stores, and the old stores are beginning to look shabby, and your children complain that The Gap doesn't carry acid-washed denim apparel, which is the current rage, then it's probably time to think about selling. If forty Wall Street analysts are giving the stock their highest recommendation, 60 percent of the shares are held by institutions, and three national magazines have fawned over the CEO, then it's definitely time to think about selling.

All the characteristics of the Stock You'd Avoid (see Chapter 9) are characteristics of the Stock You'd Want to Sell.

Unlike the cyclical where the p/e ratio gets smaller near the end, in a growth company the p/e usually gets bigger, and it may reach absurd and illogical dimensions. Remember Polaroid and Avon Products. P/e's of 50 for companies of their size? Any astute fourth-grader could have figured it was time to sell those. Was Avon going to sell a billion bottles of perfume? How could it, when every other housewife in America was an Avon representative?

You could have sold Holiday Inn when it hit 40 times earnings and been confident that the party was over there, and you were right. When you saw a Holiday Inn franchise every twenty miles along every major U.S. highway, and then you traveled to Gibraltar and saw a Holiday Inn at the base of the rock, it had to be time to worry. Where else could they expand? Mars?

Other signs:
- Same store sales are down 3 percent in the last quarter.
- New store results are disappointing.

- Two top executives and several key employees leave to join a rival firm.
- The company recently returned from a "dog and pony" show, telling an extremely positive story to institutional investors in twelve cities in two weeks.
- The stock is selling at a p/e of 30, while the most optimistic projections of earnings growth are 15–20 percent for the next two years.

WHEN TO SELL A TURNAROUND

The best time to sell a turnaround is after it's turned around. All the troubles are over and everybody knows it. The company has become the old self it was before it fell apart: growth company or cyclical or whatever. The shareholders aren't embarrassed to own it again. If the turnaround has been successful, you have to reclassify the stock.

Chrysler was a turnaround play at $2 a share, at $5, and even at $10 (adjusted for splits), but not at $48 in mid-1987. By then the debt was paid and the rot was cleaned out, and Chrysler was back to being a solid, cyclical auto company. The stock may go higher, but it's unlikely to see a tenfold rise. It has to be judged the same way that General Motors, Ford, or other prosperous companies are judged. If you like the autos, keep Chrysler. It's doing well in all divisions, and the acquisition of American Motors gives it some extra long-term potential, along with some extra short-term problems. But if you specialize in turnarounds, sell Chrysler and look for something else.

General Public Utilities was a turnaround at $4 a share, at $8, and at $12, but after the second nuclear unit was returned to service, and other utilities agreed to help pay the costs of the Three Mile Island cleanup, GPU became a quality electric utility again. Nobody thinks GPU is going out of business anymore. The stock, now at $38, may hit $45, but it certainly isn't going to hit $400.

Other signs:
- Debt, which has declined for five straight quarters, just rose by $25 million in the latest quarterly report.
- Inventories are rising at twice the rate of sales growth.
- The p/e is inflated relative to earnings prospects.
- The company's strongest division sells 50 percent of its output to one leading customer, and that leading customer is suffering from a slowdown in its own sales.

WHEN TO SELL AN ASSET PLAY

Lately, the best idea is to wait for the raider. If there are really hidden assets there, Saul Steinberg, the Hafts, or the Reichmanns will figure it out. As long as the company isn't going on a debt binge, thus reducing the value of the assets, then you'll want to hold on.

Alexander and Baldwin owns 96,000 acres of Hawaiian real estate in addition to its exclusive shipping rights into the island plus other assets. A lot of people estimated that this $5 stock (adjusted for splits) was worth much more. They tried to be patient, but nothing happened for several years. Then a Mr. Harry Weinberg showed up and bought 5 percent, then 9 percent, and finally 15 percent of the shares. That inspired other investors to buy shares because Mr. Weinberg was buying, and the stock hit a high of $32 before it was marked down to $16 in the October, 1987, sell-off. Seven months later it was back up to $30.

The same thing happened at Storer Broadcasting, and then at Disney. Disney was a sleepy company that didn't know its own worth until Mr. Steinberg came along to goad management into "enhancing shareholder values." The company was making progress anyway. It's done a brilliant job moving away from animated movies to appeal to a broader and more adult audience. It's been successful with the Disney channel and the Japanese theme park, and the upcoming European theme park is promising. With its irreplaceable film library and its Florida and California real estate, Disney is an asset play, a turnaround, and a growth company all at once.

No longer do you have to wait until your children have children for hidden assets to be discovered. It used to be that you could sit on an undervalued situation your entire adult life and the stock wouldn't budge a nickel. These days, the enhancement of shareholder values happens much quicker, thanks to the packs of well-heeled magnates roving around looking for every last example of an undervalued asset. (Boone Pickens came to our office a few years ago and told us exactly how a company such as Gulf Oil could hypothetically be taken over. I listened to his well-reasoned presentation, then promptly concluded that it couldn't be done. I was convinced that Gulf Oil was too big to be taken over—right up to the day that Chevron did it. Now I'm ready to believe that anything could be taken over, including the larger continents.)

With so many raiders around, it's harder for the amateur to find a good asset stock, but it's a cinch to know when to sell. You don't sell until the Bass brothers show up, and if it's not the Bass brothers, then it's certain to be Steinberg, Icahn, the Belzbergs, the Pritzkers, Irwin Jacobs, Sir James Goldsmith, Donald Trump, Boone Pickens, or maybe even Merv Griffin. After that, there could be a takeover, a bidding war, or a leveraged buyout to double, triple or quadruple the stock price.

Other sell signs:

• Although the shares sell at a discount to real market value, management has announced it will issue 10 percent more shares to help finance a diversification program.

• The division that was expected to be sold for $20 million only brings $12 million in the actual sale.

• The reduction in the corporate tax rate considerably reduces the value of the company's tax-loss carryforward.

• Institutional ownership has risen from 25 percent five years ago to 60 percent today—with several Boston fund groups being major purchasers.

18

The Twelve Silliest (and Most Dangerous) Things People Say About Stock Prices

I'm constantly amazed at popular explanations of why stocks behave the way they do, which are volunteered by amateurs and professionals alike. We've made great advances in eliminating ignorance and superstition in medicine and in weather reports, we laugh at our ancestors for blaming bad harvests on corn gods, and we wonder, "How could a smart man like Pythagoras think that evil spirits hide in rumpled bedsheets?" However, we're perfectly willing to believe that who wins the Super Bowl might have something to do with stock prices.

Moving back and forth from graduate school to my summer job at Fidelity, I first realized that even the most intelligent professors on the subject are as wrong about stocks as Pythagoras was about beds. Since then I've heard a continuous stream of theories, each as misguided as the last, which have filtered down to the general public. The myths and misconceptions are numerous, but I've written a few of them down: These are the Twelve Silliest Things People Say About Stock Prices, which I present in the hope that you can dismiss them from your mind. Some probably will sound familiar.

IF IT'S GONE DOWN THIS MUCH ALREADY, IT CAN'T GO MUCH LOWER

That's a good one. I'd bet the owners of Polaroid shares were repeating this very phrase just after the stock had fallen a third of the way along its long drop from a high of $143½. Polaroid had been a solid company with a blue-chip reputation, so when the earnings collapsed and the sales collapsed, as we've already reported, a lot of people didn't pay attention to how overpriced Polaroid really was. Instead they continued to reassure themselves that if "it's gone down this much already, it can't go much lower," and probably also threw in "good companies always come back," "you have to be patient in the stock market," and "there's no sense getting scared out of a good thing."

These phrases were no doubt heard again and again around investor households, and in the bank portfolio departments, as Polaroid stock sank to $100, then to $90, and then $80. As the stock broke below $75, the "can't go much lower" faction must have grown into a small mob, and at $50 you could have heard the phrase repeated by every other Polaroid owner who held on.

Newer owners were buying Polaroid all the way down on the theory that it couldn't go much lower, and many of them must have regretted that decision, because in fact Polaroid did go much lower. This great stock fell from $143½ to $14⅛ in less than a year, and only then did "it can't go much lower" turn out to be true. So much for the it-can't-go-lower theory.

There's simply no rule that tells you how low a stock can go in principle. I learned this lesson for myself in 1971, when I was an eager but somewhat inexperienced analyst at Fidelity. Kaiser Industries had already dropped from $25 to $13. On my recommendation Fidelity bought five million shares—one of the biggest blocks ever traded in the history of the American Stock Exchange—when the stock hit $11. I confidently asserted that there was no way the stock could go below $10.

When it reached $8, I called my mother and told her to go out and buy it, since it was absolutely inconceivable that Kaiser would drop below $7.50. Fortunately my mother didn't listen to me. I watched with horror as Kaiser faded from $7 to $6 to $4 in 1973—where it finally proved that it couldn't go much lower.

The portfolio managers at Fidelity held on to their five million shares, on the theory that if Kaiser had been a good buy at $11, it was undoubtedly a bargain at $4. Since I was the analyst who recommended it, I kept having to reassure them that it had a good balance sheet. In fact, it cheered us all up to discover that with only 25 million shares outstanding, at the $4 price the entire company was selling for $100 million. That same money would have bought you four Boeing 747s back then. Today, you'd get one plane with no engines.

The stock market had driven Kaiser so low that this powerful company, with its real estate, aluminum, steel, cement, shipbuilding, aggregates, fiberglass, engineering, and broadcasting businesses—not to mention jeeps—was selling for the price of four airplanes. The company had very little debt. Even if it were liquidated for the assets, we calculated that it was worth $40 a share. Nowadays a raider would have swooped in and taken it over.

Soon enough Kaiser Industries did rebound to $30 a share, but not before the drop to $4 had cured me of any further urge to announce, "It can't possibly go any lower than this."

YOU CAN ALWAYS TELL WHEN A STOCK'S HIT BOTTOM

Bottom fishing is a popular investor pastime, but it's usually the fisherman who gets hooked. Trying to catch the bottom on a falling stock is like trying to catch a falling knife. It's normally a good idea to wait until the knife hits the ground and sticks, then vibrates for a while and settles down before you try to grab it. Grabbing a rapidly falling stock results in painful surprises, because inevitably you grab it in the wrong place.

If you get interested in buying a turnaround, it ought to be for a more sensible reason than the stock's gone down so far it looks like up to you. Maybe you realize that business is picking up, and you check the balance sheet and you see that the company has $11 per share in cash and the stock is selling for $14.

But even so, you aren't going to be able to pick the bottom on the price. What usually happens is that a stock sort of vibrates itself out before it starts up again. Generally this process takes two or three years, but sometimes even longer.

IF IT'S GONE THIS HIGH ALREADY, HOW CAN IT POSSIBLY GO HIGHER?

Right you are, unless of course you are talking about a Philip Morris or a Subaru. That Philip Morris is one of the greatest stocks of all time is obvious from the chart on page 262. I've already mentioned how Subaru could have made us all millionaires, if we'd bought the stock instead of the car.

If you bought Philip Morris in the 1950s for the equivalent of 75 cents a share, then you might have been tempted to sell it for $2.50 a share in 1961, on the theory that this stock couldn't go much higher. Eleven years later, with the stock selling at seven times the 1961 price and 23 times the 1950s price, you might once again have concluded that Philip Morris couldn't go higher. But if you sold it then, you would have missed the next sevenbagger on top of the last 23-bagger.

Whoever managed to ride Philip Morris all the way would have seen their 75-cent shares blossom into $124.50 shares, and a $1,000 investment end up as a $166,000 result. And that doesn't even include the $23,000 in dividends you picked up along the way.

If I'd bothered to ask myself, "How can this stock possibly go higher," I would never have bought Subaru after it already had gone up twentyfold. But I checked the fundamentals, realized that Subaru was still cheap, bought the stock, and made sevenfold after that.

The point is, there's no arbitrary limit to how high a stock can go, and if the story is still good, the earnings continue to improve, and the fundamentals haven't changed, "can't go much higher" is a terrible reason to snub a stock. Shame on all those experts who advise clients to sell automatically after they double their money. You'll never get a ten-bagger doing that.

Stocks such as Philip Morris, Shoney's, Masco, McDonald's, and Stop & Shop have broken the "can't go much higher" barriers year after year.

Frankly, I've never been able to predict which stocks will go up ten-fold, or which will go up fivefold. I try to stick with them as long as the story's intact, hoping to be pleasantly surprised. The success of a company isn't the surprise, but what the shares bring often is. I remember buying Stop & Shop as a conservative, dividend-paying stock, and then the fundamentals kept improving and I realized I had a fast grower on my hands.

IT'S ONLY $3 A SHARE: WHAT CAN I LOSE?

How many times have you heard people say this? Maybe you've said it yourself. You come across some stock that sells for $3 a share, and already you're thinking, "It's a lot safer than buying a $50 stock."

I put in twenty years in the business before it finally dawned on me

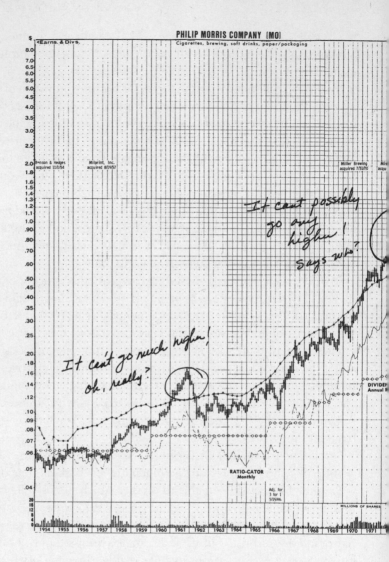

PHILIP MORRIS COMPANY (MO)
Cigarettes, brewing, soft drinks, paper/packaging

It cant possibly go any higher! says who?

It cant go much higher! oh, really?

that whether a stock costs $50 a share or $1 a share, if it goes to zero you still lose everything. If it goes to 50 cents a share, the results are slightly different. The investor who bought in at $50 a share loses 99 percent of his investment, and the investor who bought in at $3 loses 83 percent, but what's the consolation in that?

The point is that a lousy cheap stock is just as risky as a lousy expensive stock if it goes down. If you'd invested $1,000 in a $43 stock or a $3 stock and each fell to zero, you'd have lost exactly the same

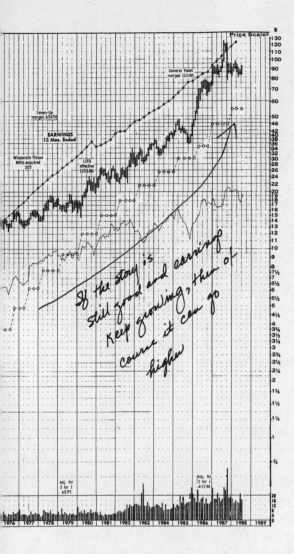

amount. No matter where you buy in, the ultimate downside of picking the wrong stock is always the identical 100 percent.

Yet I'm certain there are buyers who can't resist a bargain at $3 and say to themselves: "What can I lose?"

It's interesting to note that the professional short sellers, who profit on stocks that go down in price, usually take their positions nearer to the bottom than to the top. The short sellers like to wait until a company is so obviously foundering that bankruptcy is a certainty. It doesn't bother them to get involved at $8 or $6 a share instead of at $60, because if the stock goes to zilch, they'll make exactly the same profit in either instance.

And guess who they're selling to when the stock's at $8 or $6? All those hapless investors who are telling themselves, "How can I lose?"

EVENTUALLY THEY ALWAYS COME BACK

So will the Visigoths and the Picts, and Genghis Khan will ride again. People said RCA would come back, and after 65 years it never did. This was a world-famous successful company. Johns-Manville is another world-famous company that hasn't come back, and with all the asbestos lawsuits filed against it, the possibilities are too open-ended to measure. By printing hundreds of millions of new shares, the company has also diluted its earnings, just as Navistar did.

If I could only remember the names, I could give you a much longer list of smaller and lesser-known public companies whose blips have disappeared from the Quotrons forever. Perhaps you've invested in a few of these yourself—I wouldn't want to think I was the only one. When you consider the thousands of bankrupt companies, plus the solvent companies that never regain their former prosperity, plus the companies that get bought out at prices that are far below the all-time highs, you can begin to see the weakness in the "they always come back" argument.

Health Maintenance Organizations, floppy disks, double knits, digital watches, and mobile home stocks haven't come back so far.

IT'S ALWAYS DARKEST BEFORE THE DAWN

There's a very human tendency to believe that things that have gotten a little bad can't get any worse. In 1981 there were 4,520 active oil-drilling rigs in the U.S., and by 1984 the number had fallen to 2,200. At that point many people bought oil-service stocks, believing that the worst was over. But two years after that, there were only 686 active rigs, and today there are still fewer than 1,000.

People who invest on the basis of freight-car deliveries were amazed when business dropped from a peak of 95,650 units delivered in 1979, to a low of 44,800 in 1981. This was the lowest total in 17 years, and nobody imagined it could get much worse, until it dropped to 17,582 units in 1982, and then to 5,700 in 1983. This was a whopping 90 percent decline in a once-vibrant industry.

Sometimes it's always darkest before the dawn, but then again, other times it's always darkest before pitch black.

WHEN IT REBOUNDS TO $10, I'LL SELL

In my experience no downtrodden stock ever returns to the level at which you've decided you'd sell. In fact, the minute you say, "If it gets back to $10, I'll sell," you've probably doomed the stock to several years of teetering around just below $9.75 before it keels over to $4, on its way to falling flat on its face at $1. This whole painful process may take a decade, and all the while you're tolerating an investment you don't even like, and only because some inner voice tells you to get $10 for it.

Whenever I'm tempted to fall for this one, I remind myself that unless I'm confident enough in the company to buy more shares, I ought to be selling immediately.

WHAT ME WORRY? CONSERVATIVE STOCKS DON'T FLUCTUATE MUCH

Two generations of conservative investors grew up on the idea that you couldn't go wrong with utility stocks. You could just put these worry-free issues in the safety-deposit box and cash the dividend checks. Then suddenly there were nuclear problems and rate-base problems, and stocks such as Consolidated Edison lost 80 percent of their value. Then, just as suddenly, Con Edison gained back more than it had lost.

With the economic and regulatory troubles caused by expensive nuclear plants, the so-called stable utility sector has become just as volatile and treacherous as the savings-and-loan industry or the computer stocks. There are now electric companies that were or can be tenbaggers up and tenbaggers down. You can win big or lose big, depending on how lucky or careful you are at choosing the right utility.

Investors who didn't catch on to this new situation right away must have suffered terrible financial and psychological punishment. Their so-called prudent investments in Public Service of Indiana or Gulf States Utilities or Public Service of New Hampshire turned out to be as risky as if they'd taken fliers in unknown start-up biogenetic firms—or actually riskier since they weren't aware of the dangers.

Companies are dynamic, and prospects change. There simply isn't a stock you can own that you can afford to ignore.

IT'S TAKING TOO LONG FOR ANYTHING
TO EVER HAPPEN

Here's something else that's certain to occur: If you give up on a stock because you're tired of waiting for something wonderful to happen, then something wonderful will begin to happen the day after you get rid of it. I call this the postdivestiture flourish.

Merck tested everybody's patience (see chart). This stock went nowhere from 1972 to 1981, even though earnings grew steadily at an average of 14 percent a year. Then what happened? It shot up fourfold in the next five years. Who knows how many unhappy investors got out of Merck because they were tired of waiting, or because they yearned for more "action." If they had kept up to date on the story, they wouldn't have sold.

The stock of Angelica Corporation, manufacturers of career apparel, hardly budged a nickel from 1974 to 1979. American Greetings was dead for eight years; GAF Corporation for eleven; Brunswick for the entire 1970s; SmithKline (before Tagamet) for half the 1960s and half the 1970s; Harcourt Brace through Nixon, Carter, and the first Reagan administration; and Lukens didn't move for fourteen years.

I stuck with Merck because I'm accustomed to hanging around with a stock when the price is going nowhere. Most of the money I make is in the third or fourth year that I've owned something—only with Merck it took a little longer. If all's right with the company, and whatever attracted me in the first place hasn't changed, then I'm confident that sooner or later my patience will be rewarded.

This going nowhere for several years, which I call the "EKG of a rock," is actually a favorable omen. Whenever I see the EKG of a rock on the chart of a stock to which I'm already attracted, I take it as a strong hint that the next major move may be up.

It takes remarkable patience to hold on to a stock in a company that excites you, but which everybody else seems to ignore. You begin to think everybody else is right and you are wrong. But where the fundamentals are promising, patience is often rewarded—Lukens stock went up sixfold in the fifteenth year, American Greetings was a sixbagger in six years, Angelica a sevenbagger in four, Brunswick a sixbagger in five, and SmithKline a threebagger in two.

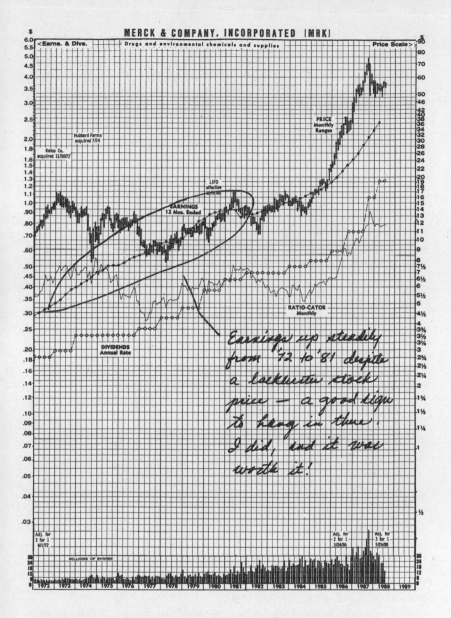

MERCK & COMPANY, INCORPORATED (MRK)

Drugs and environmental chemicals and supplies

Earnings up steadily from '72 to '81 despite a backwater stock price — a good sign to hang in there, I did, and it was worth it!

LOOK AT ALL THE MONEY I'VE LOST: I DIDN'T BUY IT!

We'd all be much richer today if we'd put all our money into Crown, Cork, and Seal at 50 cents a share (split-adjusted)! But now that you know this, open your wallet and check your latest bank statement. You'll notice the money's still there. In fact, you aren't a cent poorer than you were a second ago, when you found out about the great fortune you missed in Crown, Cork, and Seal.

This may sound like a ridiculous thing to mention, but I know that some of my fellow investors torture themselves every day by perusing the "ten biggest winners on the New York Stock Exchange" and imagining how much money they've lost by not having owned them. The same thing happens with baseball cards, jewelry, furniture, and houses.

Regarding somebody else's gains as your own personal losses is not a productive attitude for investing in the stock market. In fact, it can only lead to total madness. The more stocks you learn about, the more winners you realize that you've missed, and soon enough you're blaming yourself for losses in the billions and trillions. If you get out of stocks entirely and the market goes up 100 points in a day, you'll be waking up and muttering: "I've just suffered a $110 billion setback."

The worst part about this kind of thinking is that it leads people to try to play catch up by buying stocks they shouldn't buy, if only to protect themselves from losing more than they've already "lost." This usually results in real losses.

I Missed That One, I'll Catch the Next One

The trouble is, the "next" one rarely works, as we've already shown. If you missed Toys "R" Us, a great company that continued to go up, and then bought Greenman Brothers, a mediocre company that went down, then you've compounded your error. Actually you've taken a mistake that cost you nothing (remember, you didn't lose anything by not buying Toys "R" Us) and turned it into a mistake that cost you plenty.

If you failed to buy Home Depot at a low price, and then bought Scotty's, the "next Home Depot," then you probably made another mistake, because Home Depot is up twenty-five-fold since it came public, and Scotty's is up only 25–30 percent, underperforming the general market over the same period.

The same thing happened if you missed Piedmont and bought People Express, or you missed the Price Club and bought the Warehouse Club. In most cases it's better to buy the original good company at a high price than it is to jump on the "next one" at a bargain price.

THE STOCK'S GONE UP, SO I MUST BE RIGHT, OR . . .
THE STOCK'S GONE DOWN SO I MUST BE WRONG

If I had to choose a great single fallacy of investing, it's believing that when a stock's price goes up, then you've made a good investment. People often take comfort when their recent purchase of something at $5 a share goes up to $6, as if that proves the wisdom of the purchase. Nothing could be further from the truth. Of course, if you sell quickly at the higher price, then you've made a fine profit, but most people don't sell in these favorable circumstances. Instead they convince themselves that the higher price proves that the investment is worthwhile, and they hold on to the stock until the lower price convinces them the investment is no good. If it's a choice, they hold on to the stock that's risen from $10 to $12, and they get rid of the one that's dropped from $10 to $8, while telling themselves that they have "kept the winner and dumped the loser."

That's just what might have happened back in 1981, when Zapata, an oil stock at the height of the energy boom, must have seemed far more pleasant to own than Ethyl Corp., a so-called "dog that got run over" because of the EPA ban on its main product—lead additives for gasoline. However, the "better" stock of these two went from $35 to $2, and you couldn't have bailed that one out with the Big Dipper. Meanwhile Ethyl was getting great results from its specialty chemicals division, improved performance overseas, and rapid consistent growth from its insurance operation. Ethyl stock went from $2 to $32.

So when people say, "Look, in two months it's up 20 percent, so I really picked a winner," or "Terrible, in two months it's down 20 percent, so I really picked a loser," they're confusing prices with prospects. Unless they are short-term traders who are looking for 20-percent gains, the short-term fanfare means absolutely nothing.

A stock's going up or down after you buy it only tells you that there was somebody who was willing to pay more—or less—for the identical merchandise.

19

Options, Futures, and Shorts

Investment gimmicks have become so popular that the old motto "Buy a share in America" ought to be changed to "Buy an option on America." "Invest in the future of America" now means "take a flier at the New York Futures Exchange."

I've never bought a future nor an option in my entire investing career, and I can't imagine buying one now. It's hard enough to make money in regular stocks without getting distracted by these side bets, which I'm told are nearly impossible to win unless you're a professional trader.

That's not to say that futures don't serve a useful purpose in the commodity business, where a farmer can lock in a price for wheat or corn at harvest and know he can sell for that amount when the crops are delivered; and a buyer of wheat or corn can do the same. But stocks are not commodities, and there is no relationship between producer and consumer that makes such price insurance necessary to the functioning of a stock market.

Reports out of Chicago and New York, the twin capitals of futures and options, suggest that between 80 and 95 percent of the amateur players lose. Those odds are worse than the worst odds at the casino or at the racetrack, and yet the fiction persists that these are "sensible investment alternatives." If this is sensible investing, then the *Titanic* was a tight ship.

There's no point describing how futures and options really work, because (1) it requires long and tedious exposition, after which you'd still be confused, (2) knowing more about them might get you interested in buying some, and (3) I don't understand futures and options myself.

Actually I do know a few things about options. I know that the large potential return is attractive to many small investors who are dissatisfied with getting rich slow. Instead, they opt for getting poor quick. That's because an option is a contract that's only good for a month or two, and unlike most stocks, it regularly expires worthless—after which the options player must buy another option, only to lose 100 percent of his or her money once again. A string of these, and you're in deep kimchee.

And consider the situation when you're absolutely sure that something wonderful is about to happen to Sure Thing, Inc., and the good news will send the stock price higher. Maybe you've discovered a Tagamet, a cancer cure, a surge in earnings, or one of the many other positive fundamental signs you've learned to look for. You've found the perfect company, the nearest thing to a royal flush you'll ever encounter.

You check your assets, and there's only $3,000 in your savings account. The rest is invested in mutual funds that The Person Who Understands the Serious Business of Money won't let you touch. You comb the house looking for heirlooms to take to the pawn shop, but the mink coat is riddled with moth holes. The silver flatware is a possibility, but since you're having a dinner party over the weekend, the spouse is certain to notice it's missing. Perhaps you could sell the cat, but it doesn't have a pedigree. The wooden sloop leaks, and nobody would pay for rusty golf clubs with bad grips.

So the $3,000 is all you can come up with to invest in Sure Thing. It will only get you 150 shares at $20 a share. Just as you've resigned yourself to settling for that, you remember having heard about the remarkable leverage of options. You talk to your broker, who confirms that the April $20 call option in Sure Thing, now selling for $1, may be worth $15 if the stock goes to $35. A $3,000 investment here would give you a $45,000 payoff.

So you buy the options, and every day you open the paper, anxiously awaiting the moment the stock begins to rise. By mid-March there's still no movement, and the options you bought for $3,000 already have lost half their value. You're tempted to sell and get some of your money back, but you hold on because there's still a month to go before they expire worthless. A month later, that is exactly what happens.

Insult is added to injury when a few weeks after you've been out of the option, Sure Thing makes its move. Not only have you lost all your money, you've done it while being right about the stock. That's the biggest tragedy of all. You did your homework, and instead of being rewarded for it, you've been wiped out. It's an absolute waste of time, money, and talent when this happens.

Another nasty thing about options is that they are very expensive. They may not seem expensive, until you realize that you have to buy four or five sets of them to cover stock for a year. You're literally buying time here, and the more time you buy, the higher the premium you have to pay for it. There's a generous broker's commission attached to every purchase to boot. Options are the broker's gravy train. A broker with only a handful of active options clients can make a wonderful living.

The worst thing of all is that buying an option has nothing to do with owning a share of a company. When a company grows and prospers, all the shareholders benefit, but options are a zero-sum game. For every dollar that's won in the market there's a dollar that's lost, and a tiny minority does all the winning.

When you buy a share of stock, even a very risky stock, you are contributing something to the growth of the country. That's what stocks are for. In previous generations, when it was considered dangerous to speculate in stocks of small companies, at least the "speculators" were providing the capital to enable the IBMs and the McDonald'ses and the Wal-Marts to get started. In the multibillion-dollar futures and options market, not a bit of the money is put to any constructive use. It doesn't finance anything, except the cars, planes, and houses purchased by the brokers and the handful of winners. What we're witnessing here is a giant transfer payment from the unwary to the wary.

There's a lot of talk these days about the use of futures and options as portfolio insurance to protect our investments in stocks. Many of my fellow professionals have led the way down this slippery slope, as usual. Institutions have bought billions in portfolio insurance, to cover themselves in case of a crash. It turns out that they thought they were well-covered during the last crash, but the portfolio insurance worked against them. Part of the insurance program required them to automatically sell off stocks at the same time they were buying more futures, and the massive automatic selling drove the market lower, triggering more buying of futures and more selling. Among the plausible causes of the October collapse, portfolio insurance is a principal culprit, but many institutions are still buying the insurance.

Some individual investors have taken up this bad idea on their own. (Does it ever pay to imitate the experts?) They buy "put" options (which increase in value as the market goes down) to protect themselves in a decline. But "put" options, too, expire worthless, and you have to keep buying them if you want to be continually protected. You can waste 5–10 percent of your entire investment stake every year to protect yourself from a 5–10 percent decline.

Like the alcoholic enticed back into the gin bottle by the innocent tasting of beer, the stockpicker who invests in options as insurance often cannot help himself, and soon enough he's buying options for their own sake, and from there it's on to hedges, combinations, and straddles. He forgets that stocks ever interested him in the first place. Instead of researching companies, he spends all his waking hours reading market-timer digests and worrying about head-and-shoulder patterns or zigzag reversals. Worse, he loses all his money.

Warren Buffett thinks that stock futures and options ought to be outlawed, and I agree with him.

SHORTING A STOCK

You've no doubt heard of this ancient and strange practice, which enables you to profit from a stock that's going down. (Some people get interested in this idea by looking at their portfolios and realizing that if they'd been short instead of long all these years, they'd be rich.)

Shorting is the same thing as borrowing something from the neighbors (in this case, you don't know their names) and then selling the item and pocketing the money. Sooner or later you go out and buy the identical item and return it to the neighbors, and nobody is the wiser. It's not exactly stealing, but it's not exactly neighborly, either. It's more like borrowing with criminal intent.

What the shorter hopes to do is to sell the borrowed item at a very high price, but the replacement item at a very low price, and keep the difference. You could do it with lawn mowers and garden hoses, I suppose, but it works best with stocks—especially stocks that are inflated in price to begin with. For instance, if you figured out that Polaroid was overpriced at $140 a share, you could have shorted 1,000 shares for an immediate $140,000 credit to your account. Then you could have waited for the price to drop to $14, jumped in and bought back the same 1,000 shares for $14,000, and gone home $126,000 richer.

The person from whom you borrowed the shares originally will never have known the difference. These transactions are all done on paper and handled by stockbrokers. It's as easy to go short as it is to go long.

Before we get too excited about this, there are some serious drawbacks to going short. During all the time you borrow the shares, the rightful owner gets all the dividends and other benefits, so you're out some money there. Also, you can't actually spend the proceeds you get from shorting a stock until you've paid the shares back and closed out the transaction. In the Polaroid example, you couldn't simply take the $140,000 and run off to France for a long vacation. You are required to maintain a sufficient balance in your brokerage account to cover the value of the shorted stock. As the price of Polaroid dropped, you could have taken some of the money out, but what if the price of Polaroid had gone up? Then you would have had to add more money to cover your position.

The scary part about shorting stock is that even if you're convinced that the company's in lousy shape, other investors might not realize it and might even send the stock price higher. Though Polaroid had already reached a ridiculous plateau, what if it had doubled once more to an even more ridiculous $300 a share? If you were short then, you were very nervous. The prospect of spending $300,000 to replace a $140,000 item that you've borrowed can be disturbing. If you don't have the extra hundred thousand or so to put into your account to hold your position, you may be forced to liquidate at a huge loss.

None of us is immune to the panic that we feel when a normal stock drops in price, but that panic is restrained somewhat by our understanding that the normal stock cannot go lower than zero. If you've shorted something that's going up, you begin to realize that there's nothing to stop it from going to infinity, because there's no ceiling on a stock price. Infinity is where a shorted stock always appears to be heading.

Among all the folk tales of successful short sellers are the horror stories of shorters who watched helplessly as their favorite lousy stocks soared higher and higher, against all reason and logic, forcing them into the poorhouse. One such unfortunate was Robert Wilson, a smart man and a good investor, who a decade or so ago shorted Resorts International. He was right, eventually—most shorters are right, eventually—didn't John Maynard Keynes say in the long run "we all are dead"? In the meantime, however, the stock advanced from 70 cents to $70, a modest 100-bagger, leaving Mr. Wilson with a modest $20 or $30 million loss.

This tale is useful to remember if you're contemplating shorting something. Before you short a stock, you have to have more than a conviction that the company is falling apart. You have to have the patience, the courage, and the resources to hold on if the stock price doesn't go down—or worse, goes up. Stocks that are supposed to go down but don't remind me of the cartoon characters who walk off cliffs into thin air. As long as they don't recognize their predicament, they can just hang out there forever.

20

50,000 Frenchmen
Can Be Wrong

   Thinking back over my tenure as a stockpicker, I re-member several major news events and their effects on the prices of stocks, beginning with President Kennedy's election in 1960. Even at the tender age of sixteen, I'd heard that a Democratic presidency was always bad for stocks, so I was surprised that the day after the election, November 9, 1960, the market rose slightly.

   During the Cuban missile crisis and our naval blockade of the Russian ships—the one and only time America has faced the immediate prospect of nuclear war—I feared for myself, my family, and my country. Yet the stock market fell less than 3 percent that day. Seven months later, when President Kennedy berated U.S. Steel and forced the industry to roll back prices, I feared for nothing, yet the market had one of its largest declines in history—7 percent. I was mystified that the potential of nuclear holocaust was less terrifying to Wall Street than the president's meddling in business.

   On November 22, 1963, I was about to take an exam at Boston College when the news that President Kennedy had been shot spread across the campus. Along with my classmates I went to St. Mary's Hall to pray. The next day I saw in the newspaper that the stock market had fallen less than 3 percent, though trading was halted once the news of the assassination became official. Three days later the market recovered its losses of November 22, and then some.

In April, 1968, after President Johnson announced that he wouldn't seek a second term, that he would halt the bombing raids in Southeast Asia, and that he favored peace talks, the market rose 2½ percent.

Throughout the 1970s I was totally involved in stocks and dedicated to my job at Fidelity. During that period the great events, and the market reactions to them, were as follows: President Nixon imposes price controls (market up 3 percent); President Nixon resigns (market down 1 percent) (Nixon once remarked that if he weren't the president he'd be buying stocks, and a Wall Street wag retorted that if Nixon weren't president, he'd be buying stocks, too); President Ford's Whip Inflation Now buttons are introduced (market up 4.6 percent); IBM wins a big antitrust case (market up 3.3 percent), Yom Kippur War breaks out (market up slightly). The decade of the 1970s was the poorest for stocks of any of the five since the 1930s, and yet the major-percentage one-day changes were all up—on the days just mentioned.

The event of most lasting consequence was OPEC's oil embargo, October 19, 1973 (another lucky October 19!), which helped take the market down 16 percent in three months and 39 percent in twelve months. It's interesting to note that the market did not respond to the significance of the embargo, actually rising 4 points that day and climbing an additional 14 points in the five following sessions before starting its dramatic decline. ***This demonstrates that the market, like individual stocks, can move in the opposite direction of the fundamentals over the short term,*** which, in the case of the embargo, involved rising gasoline prices, long gas lines, escalating inflation, and sharply higher interest rates.

The 1980s has had more days of exceptional gains and losses than were seen in all the other decades combined. In the big picture, most of them are meaningless. I'd rank the 508-point drop in October, 1987, far below the meeting of economic ministers on September 22, 1985, for its importance to long-term investors. It was at this so-called G7 conference that the major industrial nations agreed to coordinate economic policy and to allow the value of the dollar to decline. After that decision was announced, the general market rose 38 percent over six months. It had a more dramatic impact on specific companies that benefited from the lower dollar, and whose stocks doubled and tripled in price in the following two years. As on October 19, 1987, I was in Europe at the time of both the Yom Kippur War and the G7 conference, but at least on those occasions I was out visiting companies instead of losing golf balls.

Trends and gradual changes stick in my mind. The period of conglomeration in the mid to late 1960s resulted in many major companies diworseifying, falling apart, and then not recovering for another fifteen years. Many have never come back, and others, such as Gulf and Western, ITT, and Ogden, have reemerged as turnarounds.

There was a great love affair with high-quality blue chips in the 1970s. These were known as the "nifty fifty" or "the one decision" stocks that you could buy and hold forever. This brief serendipity of overrated and overpriced issues was followed by the devastating market decline of 1973–74 (the Dow hit 1050 in 1973 and had regressed all the way back to 578 in December, 1974) with blue chips falling 50 to 90 percent.

The popular romance with small technology companies in mid-1982 to mid-1983 led to another collapse (60–98 percent) of the similarly beloved issues that could do no wrong. Small may be beautiful, but it's not necessarily profitable.

The rise of the Japanese market from 1966 to 1988 has taken the Nikkei Dow Jones up seventeenfold as our Dow Jones has only doubled. The total market value of all Japanese stocks actually passed that of U.S. stocks in April, 1987, and the gap has widened since. The Japanese have their own way of thinking about stocks, and I don't understand it yet. Every time I go over there to study the situation, I conclude that all the stocks are grossly overpriced, but they keep going higher, anyway.

Nowadays the change in trading hours makes it harder to pay attention to fundamentals and keep your eye off the Quotron. For eighty years until 1952 the New York Stock Exchange opened at 10 A.M. and closed at 3 P.M., giving the newspapers time to print up the results for the afternoon editions so investors could check their stocks on the ride home. In 1952, Saturday trading was eliminated, but the daily closing hour was advanced to 3:30, and in 1985, the opening hour was moved to 9:30, and now the market closes at 4:00. Personally, I'd prefer a much shorter market. It would give us all more time to devote to analyzing companies, or even to visiting museums, both of which are more useful than watching stock prices go up and down.

Institutions have emerged from their minor role in the 1960s to dominate the stock market in the 1980s.

The legal status of major brokerage firms has changed from partnerships, where the individuals' personal wealth was on the line, to corporations, where the individual liability is limited. Theoretically this was supposed to strengthen the brokerage firms, since as corporations they could raise capital by selling stock to the public. I'm convinced it has been a net negative.

The rise of the over-the-counter exchange has brought thousands of secondary issues that were once traded by the obscure "pink sheet" method—where you never knew if you were getting a fair price—into a reliable and efficient computerized marketplace.

The nation is preoccupied with up-to-the-minute financial news, which twenty years ago was scarcely mentioned on television. The incredible success of *Wall $treet Week, with Louis Rukeyser,* from its debut on November 20, 1970, has proven that a financial news show can actually be popular. It was Rukeyser's achievement that inspired the regular networks to expand their financial coverage, and that in turn led to the establishment of the Financial News Network, which has brought the ticker tape into millions of American homes. Amateur investors can now check their holdings all day. All that separates Houndstooth from the professional trader is a 15-minute tape delay.

The boom and then bust in tax shelters: farm land, oil wells, oil rigs, barges, low-rent housing syndicates, graveyards, movie productions, shopping centers, sports teams, computer leasing, and almost anything else that can be bought, financed, or rented.

The emergence of merger and acquisition groups, and other buyout groups, that are willing and able to finance $20-billion purchases. Between the domestic buyout groups (Kohlberg, Kravis, and Roberts; Kelso; Coniston Partners; Odyssey Partners; and Wesray), the European firms and buyout groups (Hanson Trust, Imperial Chemical, Electrolux, Unilever, Nestlé, etc.), and the individual corporate raiders with sizable bankrolls (David Murdock, Donald Trump, Sam Hyman, Paul Bilzerian, the Bass brothers, the Reichmanns, the Hafts, Rupert Murdoch, Boone Pickens, Carl Icahn, Asher Edelman, et al.) any company, large or small, is up for grabs.

The popularity of the leveraged buyout, or LBO, through which entire companies or divisions are "taken private"—purchased by outsiders or by current management with money that's borrowed from banks or raised via junk bonds.

The phenomenal popularity of these junk bonds, as first invented by Drexel Burnham Lambert and now copied everywhere.

The advent of futures and options trading, especially of the stock indexes, enabling "program traders" to buy or sell bushels of stocks in the regular stock markets and then reverse their positions in the so-called futures markets, throwing around billions of dollars for tiny incremental profits.

And throughout all this tumult, SS Kresge, a moribund five-and-dime company, develops the K mart formula and the stock goes up fortyfold in ten years; Masco develops its one-handle faucet and goes up 1,000-fold, becoming the greatest stock in forty years—and who would have guessed it from a faucet company? The successful fast growers turn into tenbaggers, the whisper stocks go bankrupt, and investors receive their "Baby Bell" shares from the breakup of ATT and double their money in four years.

If you ask me what's been the most important development in the stock market, the breakup of ATT ranks near the top (this affected 2.96 million shareholders), and the Wobble of October probably wouldn't rank in my top three.

Some things I've been hearing lately:

I've been hearing that the small investor has no chance in this dangerous environment and ought to get out. "Would you build your house over an earthquake?" one cautious advisor asks. But the earthquake isn't under the house, it's under the real estate office.

Small investors are capable of handling all sorts of markets, as long as they own good merchandise. If anyone should worry, it's some of the oxymorons. After all, the losses of last October were only losses to people who took the losses. That wasn't the long-term investor. It was the margin player, the risk arbitrageur, the options player, and the portfolio manager whose computer signaled "sell" who took the losses. Like a cat who sees himself in a mirror, the sellers spooked themselves.

I've been hearing that the era of professional management has brought new sophistication, prudence, and intelligence to the stock market. There are 50,000 stockpickers who dominate the show, and like the 50,000 Frenchmen, they can't possibly be wrong.

From where I sit, I'd say that the 50,000 stockpickers are usually right, but only for the last 20 percent of a typical stock move. It's that last 20 percent that Wall Street studies for, clamors for, and then lines up for—all the while with a sharp eye on the exits. The idea is to make a quick gain and then stampede out the door.

Small investors don't have to fight this mob. They can calmly walk in the entrance when there's a crowd at the exit, and walk out the exit when there's a crowd at the entrance. Here's a short list of stocks that were the favorites of large institutions in mid-1987 but sold at sharply lower prices ten months later, in spite of higher earnings, exciting prospects, and good cash flows. The companies hadn't changed, but the institutions had lost interest: Automatic Data Processing, Coca-Cola, Dunkin' Donuts, General Electric, Genuine Parts, Philip Morris, Primerica, Rite Aid, Squibb, and Waste Management.

I've been hearing that the 200-million share day is a great improvement over the 100-million share day, and there's great advantage in a liquid market.

But not if you're drowning in it—and we are. Last year 87 percent of all the shares listed on the NYSE changed owners at least once. In the early 1960s a six- to seven-million-share trading day was normal, and the turnover rate in stocks was 12 percent a year. In the 1970s a forty- to sixty-million-share day was normal, and in the 1980s it became 100–120 million shares. Now if we don't have 150-million-share days, people think something is wrong. I know I do my part to contribute to the cause, because I buy and sell every day. But my biggest winners continue to be stocks I've held for three and even four years.

The rapid and wholesale turnover has been accelerated by the popular index funds, which buy and sell billions of shares without regard to the individual characteristics of the companies involved, and also by the "switch funds," which enable investors to pull out of stocks and into cash, or out of cash and into stocks, without delay or penalty.

Soon enough we'll have a 100 percent annual turnover in stocks. If it's Tuesday, then I must own General Motors! How do these poor companies keep up with where to send the annual reports? A new book called *What's Wrong with Wall Street* reports that we spend $25 to $30 billion annually to maintain the various exchanges and pay the commissions and fees for trading stocks, futures, and options. That means we spend as much money on passing old shares back and forth as we raise for new issues. After all, the raising of money for new ventures is the reason we have stocks in the first place. And when the trading is finished, come every December, the big portfolios of 50,000 stockpickers look about the same as they did the previous January.

The large investors who've caught this trading habit are fast becoming the short-term churning suckers that neighborhood brokers used to love. Some have called it the "rent-a-stock market." Now it's the amateurs who are prudent and the professionals who are flighty. The public is the comforting and stabilizing factor.

The flightiness of trust departments, the Wall Street establishment, and the Boston financial district may be an opportunity for you. You can wait for out-of-favor stocks to hit the crazy low prices, then buy them.

I've been hearing that the October 19th drop, which happened on a Monday, was only one of several historic declines that have taken place on Mondays, and researchers have spent entire careers studying the Monday effect. They were even talking about the Monday effect back when I went to Wharton.

After looking this up, I've discovered that there seems to be something to it: from 1953 through 1984 the stock market gained 919.6 points overall, but lost 1,565 points on Mondays. In 1973 the market was ahead 169 points overall, but down 149 on Mondays; in 1974, down 235 overall and 149 on Mondays; in 1984, ahead 149 overall and down 47 on Mondays; in 1987, down 483 on Mondays and up 42 overall.

If there is a Monday effect, I think I know why. Investors can't talk to companies for two days over the weekend. All of the usual sources of fundamental news are shut down, giving people sixty hours to worry about the yen sell-off, the yen bid-up, the flooding in the Nile River, the damage to the Brazilian coffee crop, the progress of the killer bees, or other horrors and cataclysms reported in the Sunday papers. The weekend is also when people have time to read the gloomy long-term forecasts of economists who write guest columns on the op-ed pages.

Unless you're careful to sleep late and ignore the general business news, so many fears and suspicions can build up on weekends that by Monday morning you're ready to sell all your stocks. That, it seems to me, is the principal cause of the Monday effect. (By late Monday you've had a chance to call a company or two and find out that they haven't gone out of business, which is why stocks rebound the rest of the week.)

I've been hearing that the 1987–88 market is a rerun of the 1929–30 market and we're about to enter another great depression. So far, the 1987–88 market has behaved quite similarly to the 1929–30 market, but so what? If we have another depression, it won't be because the stock market crashed, any more than the earlier depression happened because the stock market crashed. In those days, only one percent of Americans owned stocks.

The earlier depression was caused by an economic slowdown in a country in which 66 percent of the work force was in manufacturing, 22 percent was in farming, and there was no social security, unemployment compensation, pension plans, welfare and medicare payments, guaranteed student loans, or government-insured bank accounts. Today, manufacturing represents only 27 percent of the work force, agriculture accounts for a mere 3 percent, and the service sector, which was 12 percent in 1930, has grown steadily through recession and boom and now accounts for 70 percent of the U.S. work force. Unlike the thirties, today a large percentage of people own their own homes; many own them free and clear or have watched their equity grow substantially as property values have soared. Today, the average household has two wage earners instead of one, and that provides an economic cushion that didn't exist sixty years ago. If we have a depression, it won't be like the last one!

On weekends and weekdays I've been hearing that the country is falling apart. Our money used to be as good as gold, and now it's as cheap as dirt. We can't win wars anymore. We can't even win gold medals in ice dashes. Our brains are being drained abroad. We're losing jobs to the Koreans. We're losing cars to the Japanese. We're losing basketball to the Russians. We're losing oil to the Saudis. We're losing face to Iran.

I hear every day that major companies are going out of business. Certainly some of them are. But what about the thousands of smaller companies that are coming into business and providing millions of new jobs? As I make my usual rounds of various headquarters, I'm amazed to discover that many companies are still going strong. Some are actually earning money. If we've lost all sense of enterprise and will to work, then who are those people who seem to be stuck in rush hour?

I've even seen evidence that hundreds of these same companies have cut costs and learned to make things more efficiently. It appears to me that many of them are better off than they were in the late 1960s, when investors were more optimistic. CEOs are brighter and more heavily pressured to perform. Managers and workers understand that they have to compete.

I hear every day that AIDS will do us in, the drought will do us in, inflation will do us in, recession will do us in, the budget deficit will do us in, the trade deficit will do us in, and the weak dollar will do us in. Whoops. Make that the strong dollar will do us in. They tell me real estate prices are going to collapse. Last month people started worrying about that. This month they're worrying about the ozone layer. If you believe the old investment adage that the stock market climbs a "wall of worry," take note that the worry wall is fairly good-sized now and growing every day.

I'd developed a whole counterargument to the common argument that the trade deficit will do us in. It turns out that England had a big trade deficit for seventy years, and England was thriving around it. But there's no point bringing this up. By the time I thought of it, people had forgotten about the trade deficit and had started to worry about the next trade surplus.

Why does the emperor of Wall Street always have to have no clothes? We're so anxious to catch that act that every time he parades around in full regalia we think we're seeing a nude.

I've been hearing that investors ought to be delighted when companies in which they've invested are bought out by corporate raiders, or taken private by management, sometimes doubling the stock price overnight.

When a raider comes in to buy out a solid and prosperous enterprise, it's the shareholders who get robbed. Maybe it looks like a good deal to the shareholders today, but they're giving away their stake in the future growth. Investors were only too happy to tender their shares in Taco Bell when Pepsi-Cola bought in the shares for $40 apiece. But this fast grower continued to grow fast, and on the strength of the earnings an independent Taco Bell might be worth $150 a share by now. Let's say a depressed company is on its way back up from $10, and some deep pocket offers to take it private for $20. It seems terrific when it happens. But the rest of the rise to $100 is cut off to all but the private entrepreneur.

More than a few potential tenbaggers have been taken out of play by recent mergers and acquisitions.

I've been hearing that we're rapidly becoming a nation of useless debt-mongering, cappuccino-drinking, vacation-taking, croissant-eaters.

Sadly, it's true that America has one of the lowest savings rates in the developed world. Part of the blame goes to the government, which continues to punish savings by taxing capital gains and dividends, while rewarding debt with tax deductions on interest payments. The Individual Retirement Account was one of the most beneficial inventions of the last decade—finally Americans were encouraged to save something free of tax—so what does the government do? It cancels the deduction for all but the modest wage earner.

Frequent follies notwithstanding, I continue to be optimistic about America, Americans, and investing in general. When you invest in stocks, you have to have a basic faith in human nature, in capitalism, in the country at large, and in future prosperity in general. So far, nothing's been strong enough to shake me out of it.

I'm told that the Japanese started out making little party favors and paper umbrellas to decorate Hawaiian cocktails, while we started out making cars and TVs; and now they make the cars and the TVs, and we make the party favors and the little umbrellas to decorate Hawaiian cocktails. If so, there's got to be a fast-growing company that makes party favors somewhere in the U.S. that ought to be looked into. It could be the next Stop & Shop.

If you take anything with you at all from this last section, I hope you'll remember the following:

- Sometime in the next month, year, or three years, the market will decline sharply.
- Market declines are great opportunities to buy stocks in companies you like. Corrections—Wall Street's definition of going down a lot—push outstanding companies to bargain prices.
- Trying to predict the direction of the market over one year, or even two years, is impossible.
- To come out ahead you don't have to be right all the time, or even a majority of the time.
- The biggest winners are surprises to me, and takeovers are even more surprising. It takes years, not months, to produce big results.
- Different categories of stocks have different risks and rewards.
- You can make serious money by compounding a series of 20–30 percent gains in stalwarts.
- Stock prices often move in opposite directions from the fundamentals but long term, the direction and sustainability of profits will prevail.

- Just because a company is doing poorly doesn't mean it can't do worse.
- Just because the price goes up doesn't mean you're right.
- Just because the price goes down doesn't mean you're wrong.
- Stalwarts with heavy institutional ownership and lots of Wall Street coverage that have outperformed the market and are overpriced are due for a rest or a decline.
- Buying a company with mediocre prospects just because the stock is cheap is a losing technique.
- Selling an outstanding fast grower because its stock seems slightly overpriced is a losing technique.
- Companies don't grow for no reason, nor do fast growers stay that way forever.
- You don't lose anything by not owning a successful stock, even if it's a tenbagger.
- A stock does not know that you own it.
- Don't become so attached to a winner that complacency sets in and you stop monitoring the story.
- If a stock goes to zero, you lose just as much money whether you bought it at $50, $25, $5, or $2—everything you invested.
- By careful pruning and rotation based on fundamentals, you can improve your results. When stocks are out of line with reality and better alternatives exist, sell them and switch into something else.
- When favorable cards turn up, add to your bet, and vice versa.
- You won't improve results by pulling out the flowers and watering the weeds.
- If you don't think you can beat the market, then buy a mutual fund and save yourself a lot of extra work and money.
- There is always something to worry about.
- Keep an open mind to new ideas.
- You don't have to "kiss all the girls." I've missed my share of tenbaggers and it hasn't kept me from beating the market.

Epilogue:
Caught with My Pants Up

I started this book with a vacation story, so maybe I should end it with one. It's August, 1982. Carolyn and I and the children have piled into the car. We're driving to Maryland to attend the wedding of Carolyn's sister, Madalin Cowhill. I've got eight or nine stops to make between Boston and the wedding. They're all publicly traded companies within a hundred-mile radius of the direct route.

Carolyn and I have recently signed a contract to buy a new house. August 17th is the last day we can get out of the deal without forfeiting the ten percent we've put down. I remind myself that this represents my combined salary from my first three years at Fidelity.

The house purchase requires substantial faith in the future of my own income, which in turn is heavily dependent on the future of corporate America.

Lately the mood has been downbeat. Interest rates have risen into the double digits, causing some people to fear we'll soon be as bad off as Brazil, while others are satisfied that we'll soon be as bad off as the 1930s. Sensible bureaucrats are wondering if they should learn to fish, hunt, and gather berries, to get a head start on the millions of other jobless souls who will soon be heading for the woods. The Dow Jones industrial average is in the 700s, while a decade earlier it had been in the 900s. Most people expect that things will get worse.

If the summer of 1987 was optimistic, the summer of 1982 was the exact reverse. We grit our teeth and decide not to cancel the house deal. Somewhere in Connecticut we realize the new house is ours. The hard part is how we're going to pay for it, long term.

Ignoring all this, I stop in to visit Insilco, in Meriden, Connecticut. Carolyn and the kids spend three hours at a video arcade, researching Atari. When I finish my meeting, I call the office. They tell me that the market is up 38.8 points. Starting from a level of 776, that's the equivalent of a 120-point day in the summer of '88. Suddenly people are excited. They are even more excited on August 20th, when the market is up another 30.7 points.

Almost overnight everything has changed. People who had reserved their campsites in the woods have rushed back to buy every stock they can get their hands on. They are stumbling all over each other to jump back on the bull. There's a mad rush to invest in all sorts of prosperous enterprises that a week earlier were given up for dead.

There's nothing for me to do, except business as usual. I'm fully invested—before and after this extraordinary rebound. I'm always fully invested. It's a great feeling to be caught with your pants up. Besides, I can't rush back to buy more stocks. I've got to visit Uniroyal in Middlebury, Connecticut, and then Armstrong Rubber in New Haven. The next day I've got to stop in at Long Island Lighting in Mineola, New York, and Hazeltine in Commack. The day after that it's Philadelphia Electric and Fidelcor in Philadelphia. If I ask enough questions, maybe I'll learn something I didn't know. And I can't miss my sister-in-law's wedding. You have to keep your priorities straight, if you plan to do well in stocks.

Acknowledgments

Several individuals and organizations deserve recog-nition for their gracious and adept assistance in preparing this updated version of *One Up on Wall Street:* for general support—Doe Coover, literary agent; Paula Caputo, marketing director, Fidelity Capital; and Ellen Hoffman, Devonshire Publishing; for gathering and checking data—Ned Davis Research; FactSet; Dow Jones; Scott Machovina from Fidelity Market Research; and the Fidelity Technical Group, especially Patricia Mulderry, Denise Russell, Shawn Bastian, and Krista Wilshusen; for editorial assistance—Airié Dekidjiev and Doris Cooper at Simon & Schuster.

Since the 1960s I have had the wonderful fortune to be a member of a special family, Fidelity Management and Research, affectionately known as Fido. Fido is a corny, old-fashioned sort of place, appropriately located in an ancient nine-story building complex in Boston, where people get along in spite of their differences, where debates over stocks do not escalate into cubicle wars, and where birthdays are still celebrated with parties and cakes.

So many individuals have inspired me that it would take an entire chapter to list all their names. Below I've named a few, and I apologize sincerely to people I've omitted.

Over the past fifteen to twenty years, and in some cases back to 1966, I would like to thank: the late Mike Allara, Sam Bodman, Donald Burton, Bill Byrnes, the late Warren Casey, Sandy Cushman, Leo Dworsky,

Dorsey Gardner, Joe Grause, Allan Gray, Barry Greenfield, Dick Haberman, Bill Hayes, Bob Hill, the late Mr. Johnson II, Ned Johnson, Bruce Johnstone, Caleb Loring, Malcolm MacNaught, Jack O'Brien, Patsy Ostrander, the late Frank Parrish, Bill Pike, Dick Reilly, Dick Smith, Cathy Stephenson, the late D. George Sullivan, John Thies, and George Vanderheiden.

I've been helped immeasurably by another group of dedicated Fidelity money managers, including: the late Jeff Barmeyer, Gary Burkhead, William Danoff, George Domolky, Bettina Doulton, Bill Ebsworth, Rich Fentin, Karie Firestone, Bob Haber, Steve Kaye, Alan Leifer, Brad Lewis, Steve Peterson, Ken Richardson, Bob Stansky, Beth Terrana, and the late Ernest Wiggins.

I have also been helped by an outstanding group of securities traders who buy and sell stocks for the Magellan Fund, and I would especially like to thank those who made the smooth transition from a small fund to a multibillion-dollar enterprise: Robert Burns, Carlene De Luca O'Brien, and Barry Lyden.

Outside Fidelity, and in spite of everything I've said about the foibles of Wall Street professionals, I've been aided by friends and colleagues from two groups: industry analysts from the brokerage community and managers of other funds. Again I mention just a few, and I apologize to many more I'll think of later.

Analyst List
John Adams, *Adams, Harkness & Hill*
Mike Armellino, *Goldman, Sachs & Co.*
Steve Berman
Allan Bortel
Jon Burke
Norm Caris, *Gruntal & Co.*
Tom Clephane, *Morgan Stanley & Co.*
Art Davis
Don DeScenza (deceased), *Nomura Securities*
David Eisenberg, *Sanford Bernstein*
Jerry Epperson
Joe Frazzano
Dick Fredericks
Jonathan Gelles
Jane Gilday, *McKinley Allsopp*
Maggie Gilliam
Tom Hanley
Herb Hardt, *Monness, Crespi, Hardt & Co., Inc.*
Brian Harra, *Brean Murray, Foster Securities*
Ira Hirsch, *The Fourteen Research Corp.*
Ed Hyman
Sam Isaly

Lee Isgur
Robert Johnson
Joe Jolson
Paul Keleher
John Kellenyi
Dan Lee
Bob Maloney, *Wood Gundy Corp.*
Peter Marcus
Jay Meltzer, *Goldman Sachs & Co.*
Tom Petrie
Larry Rader
Tom Richter, *Robinson Humphrey*
Bill Ritger, *Dillon Reed & Co.*
Elliot Schlang
Elliot Schneider, *Gruntal & Co.*
Rick Schneider
Don Sinsabaugh, *Swergold, Chefitz & Sinsabaugh*
Stein Soelberg, *Baird, Patrick & Co.*
Oakes Spalding
Stewart Spector
Joseph Stechler, *Stechler & Co.*
Jack Sullivan (deceased), *Van Kasper & Co.*
David Walsh
Skip Wells, *Adams, Harkness & Hill*

Fund Manager List

James Roger Bacon, *Putnam Management*
George Boltres, *Tiedman, Karlin, Boltres*
Tom Cashman, *Massachusetts Financial Services*
Ken Cassidy, *Cassidy Investments*
Tony Cope
Richard Corneliuson
Gerald Curtis, *Webster Management*
Peter deRoetth, *Account Management*
Tom Duncan, *Frontier Capital Management*
Charles Flather, *Middlegreen Associates*
Richard Frucci, *Putnam Management*
Mario Gabelli, *Gabelli & Company*
Bob Gintel, *Gintel & Company*
Dick Goldstein, *Richard Goldstein Investments*
Jon Gruber, *Gruber Capital Management*
Paul Haagensen, *Putnam Management*
Bill Harris (retired), *Massachusetts Financial Services*
Ken Heebner, *Capital Growth Management*
Philip Hempleman, *Ardsley Partners*
Ed Huebner (deceased), *Hellman, Jordan Management*

Richard Jodka
H. Alden Johnson, Jr. (deceased), *Massachusetts Financial Services*
Donald Keller, *Rollert & Sullivan*
David Knight, *Knight, Bain, Seath & Holbrook*
Kathy Magrath, *Valuequest*
Terry Magrath, *Valuequest*
Ed Mathias, *The Carlyle Group*
Joe McNay, *Essex Investment Management*
Bill Miller, *Legg Mason*
Neal Miller, *Fidelity*
David Mills
Ernest Monrad, *Northeast Investors*
John Neff (retired), *Wellington Management*
Michael Price, *MFP Investors, LLC*
Jimmy Rogers
Binkley Shorts, *Wellington Management*
Rick Spillane, *Eaton Vance (now Fidelity)*
Richard Strong, *Strong Corneliuson*
Eyk Van Otterloo, *Grantham, Mayo, Van Otterloo*
Ernst H. von Metzch, *Wellington Management*
Wally Wadman, *Constitution Research & Management Inc.*
Matt Weatherbie, *M.A. Weatherbie & Co., Inc.*

I owe special gratitude to an outstanding man who has been a friend of my family for over forty years: Father John J. Collins, S.J., of Boston College. As chairman of the finance department when I attended the school, he taught me many useful things. Later he baptized all three of our children and has been a constant source of support to me and to hundreds of other B.C. students and graduates.

This book would never have been written without the hard work and persistence of Peggy Malaspina of Malaspina Communications. Thanks, also, to Jane Lajoie, and author Derrick Niederman who spent months researching and checking facts for this book. Many thanks to Cathy Davis and Jack Cahill, the Fidelity Research Library, Robert Hill of the Fidelity Technical Department, several individuals from the Fidelity Equity Research Department and other fund managers, Bettina Doulton for her special help, my four secretaries who so graciously contributed long and late extra hours, Paula Sullivan, Evelyn Flynn, Natalie Trakas, and Karen Cuneo.

Special thanks to Bob Bender, senior editor, Simon & Schuster, and Doe Coover of the Doe Coover Agency for their assistance on this project from beginning to end.

Finally I must pay the greatest tribute to John Rothchild for making this book possible. His attitude, talent, flexibility, and extraordinary hard work have been invaluable to me over the last year.

Index